THE ABUSE
OF POWER

THE ABUSE
OF POWER

Confronting injustice in public life

THERESA MAY

HEADLINE

First published in 2023 by
HEADLINE PUBLISHING GROUP

1

Cataloguing in Publication Data is available from the British Library

Hardback ISBN: 978 1 0354 0988 4
Trade paperback ISBN: 978 1 0354 1046 0

Designed and typeset by EM&EN
Printed and bound in Great Britain by Clays Ltd, Elcograf S.p.A.

Headline's policy is to use papers that are natural, renewable and recyclable
products and made from wood grown in well-managed forests and other
controlled sources. The logging and manufacturing processes are expected
to conform to the environmental regulations of the country of origin.

HEADLINE PUBLISHING GROUP
An Hachette UK Company
Carmelite House
50 Victoria Embankment
London EC4Y 0DZ

www.headline.co.uk
www.hachette.co.uk

To my parents,

Hubert and Zaidee Brasier,

who taught me the meaning of service.

Contents

Introduction

Stepping down as Prime Minister brought with it many changes in my life. There were the obvious ones: no longer being in No. 10, not having a large support team running day-to-day operations and advising me on every issue. It meant having more time to spend with my husband and with friends. Perhaps the thing I noticed most of all – something former Prime Minister David Cameron said to me when I spoke to him after I had agreed to stand down – is that I was no longer spending all my time making decisions.

It also meant I had more time to think. At first, there was a process of letting go, of life calming down and of significantly reduced stress levels. But then I started to spend more time thinking about all I had done in my time in government. This wasn't just about reflecting on what went well and what didn't. Having more time to think about my experience enabled me to consider the themes that underpinned the issues I had encountered. Because, although in some sense every problem or opportunity I dealt with was different, over time I started to understand the similarities between them and to recognise more clearly what had driven behaviours and hence outcomes.

Introduction

I love walking in the Swiss Alps, as does my husband – we go every year in the summer. The atmosphere there encourages relaxation and contemplation. It was on holiday in Zermatt, some time after I had stepped down, that I first had the idea for this book. While reflecting on my time in the Home Office and No. 10, I realised what had been in the back of my mind for quite a while: namely that there was a thread running through many of the issues I had dealt with.

That thread is the abuse of power exhibited so often in the way the institutions of the state, and those who work within them, put themselves first and the people they are there to serve second. It was a thread which had first become apparent to me when I met Margaret Aspinall and Trevor Hicks of the Hillsborough Families Support Group, and a thread which reappeared in so many issues I addressed in government.

I started to write – in longhand in an exercise book – and over time, I realised more and more that fundamental change is needed in the attitude of the institutions of government. I wanted to write about the impact this attitude has had on so many lives and about what we need to do to change. I thought I might have enough to form a book. Over the following months, I continued to write about what I had seen and heard, and about what had been reported in one official review after another. In the end, I had enough to bring together to show the world how the abuse of power can be hidden for so long, and even defended by those who should have known better.

This is that book.

It is a book about power. Or rather, it is about the abuse of power and the injustices that can occur when the

Introduction

powerful abuse their position. It shines a light on a number of issues which came across my desk during my nine years first as Home Secretary (2010–16) and then as Prime Minister (2016–19). Many of these issues hit the national headlines, such as the Grenfell Tower tragedy or the child sexual abuse in Rotherham. Each of these stories is different and would normally be considered in isolation. Yet all of them have a common theme. At their hearts, they portray people who chose not to use their power in the interests of the powerless, but rather to serve themselves or to protect the institution to which they belonged.

While shining a light on those whose selfish use of power has impacted negatively on the lives of others, the book also recognises and pays tribute to those who have spoken out, those who have made their voices heard to expose such abuses and those who have put others before themselves.

A number of the examples I describe led to official inquiries, and I am grateful to all those who led and participated in them. These inquiries were able to explore the circumstances of each case and identify what went wrong, often in considerable detail. I do not go into such detail in this book, but I do set out the key aspects of each case so that the reader can see why I have described it as evidence of an abuse of power. I hope the authors of those inquiry reports feel I have done justice to the issues they explored.

While the various circumstances I describe add up to a deeply worrying register of abuse of power, this is not a complete list of all the examples I came across in government. But even one of the sets of events I describe should be sufficient to make us think again about how we approach the relationship between the powerful and the powerless.

Introduction

On the day I became Prime Minister – 13 July 2016 – I stood on the steps of 10 Downing Street and pledged to fight against the burning injustices in our country. I vowed that my government would work for those who were just managing:

> We will do everything we can to give you more control over your lives. When we take the big calls, we'll think not of the powerful, but you. When we pass new laws, we'll listen not to the mighty, but to you. When it comes to taxes, we'll prioritise not the wealthy, but you. When it comes to opportunity, we won't entrench the advantages of the fortunate few. We will do everything we can to help anybody, whatever your background, to go as far as your talents will take you.

The mission was to make Britain a country that works for everyone. This book describes many examples of injustice against ordinary people perpetrated by the powerful and mighty. It shows how deeply we need to reconsider who we are as a country and the urgent need for those in authority to ensure that in all they do, they are putting the country and the people first.

Shortly before I left 10 Downing Street in July 2019, I gave an interview to a long-standing and respected political journalist, Simon Walters, during which I said that too many politicians today see being Prime Minister as a position of power when in fact it is a position of service. The immediate response was that surely it was a position of power, because as PM you have the power not just to get things done but to do anything you want.

Setting aside the fact that the PM is *primus inter pares* (that is, first among equals in a Cabinet of ministers), the problem with this view is that it can lead to a sense of being able to take decisions in one's own personal or political interests rather than in the interests of others.

If you see being PM as a position of service, then every decision should be taken in the collective or national interest. Sometimes, of course, personal interests and collective interests coincide, but the danger is that without a sense of service it becomes too easy to put personal interests above doing what you believe to be right for the country; too easy to persuade yourself that what is good for you is always good for the country.

By personal interest, I don't mean personal financial interest. This is much wider than that. It is about seeking to further your own interests, protecting your position, ensuring you can't be blamed, making yourself look good, protecting your power and in so doing keeping yourself in power.

Thus seeing the role of PM as a position of power could all too easily lead to abuse of that power. To a sense that you are set apart, above the rules. That there is one rule for you and another for everyone else. This attitude is not unique to politicians. It is seen elsewhere in the public sector and in the private sector too. It has led to a world where all too often people have taken certain decisions or undertaken certain actions simply because they could.

Sadly, this is often combined with a desire to protect not only the individual taking the decision but the organisation of which they are a part. There is often a sense that protection of the institution is more important than fairness, justice or seeking the truth.

Throughout my political career – at the time of writing, over twenty-five years in front-line politics – I have seen too many examples of this abuse of power, from Hillsborough to Brexit.

I see it too in today's world politics. It could be said that geopolitics is by definition the exercise of power solely and absolutely in one's own country's interests. But that has not always been the case. In the past, countries have been willing to give up some of their own interests for the wider good. That is why countries have been willing to join together in multilateral organisations like NATO that often involve ceding an element of sovereignty. Unfortunately, in today's world, some leaders believe that their individual interests are at best aligned with, and at worst more important than, their country's interests. All too often that leads to deeply entrenched positions and an unwillingness to compromise.

In this book, I give examples of where the failure to recognise the importance of the collective good led to devastating results for individuals and, in most cases, significantly damaged the reputation of, and trust in, key parts of the public sector and of our democracy. What the cases can also show, however, is individuals putting aside their own lives to campaign for a greater good.

I give a frank and direct account of three types of abuse of power which I have witnessed at first hand. The first is close to home and involves Parliament and the exercise of power by MPs, both in their personal behaviour and in their approach to particular issues. Some will find it hard to accept my description of the handling of Brexit as an abuse of power, but to my mind that is exactly what it was – with people acting in their own interests rather than for the greater good. The second type of abuse of power is exemplified in issues of social injustice, such as what

Introduction

happened at Hillsborough and institutional child sexual abuse. The third lies in the world of international politics, and much of what I say focuses on the various abuses of power by Russia, not least on the streets of Salisbury.

The examples here mostly reflect issues that I was personally involved in during my time in office as either Home Secretary or Prime Minister, but also include some I have commented on from the backbenches. There will be other examples that those reading this will be aware of or may have been involved in. The cases I cite relate to the public sector and politics, but there will be many from the private sector too.

The cases I describe all reflect the sense of personal interest or institutional interest being more important than the interests of the public. In that way, they represent what has been bad in our politics. In the concluding chapters, I look further into how this situation arose and what we can do about it.

This book is not an attempt to justify certain decisions I made in office or to provide a detailed retelling of historical events. Rather, it sets out a series of shocking examples of abuses of power and tries to identify what lies behind them, and how actions and attitudes need to change. It is about how lives have been damaged and sometimes destroyed by others simply because they had the power to do so.

1

My Perspective

The musty silence of a parish church, the genteel atmosphere of a country vicarage and the carefree days in a village school may not seem like the ideal preparation for the raucous, aggressive political battleground that is Prime Minister's Questions. Yet it was this very background that led to my interest in politics and ultimately to me occupying 10 Downing Street.

Perhaps the background of growing up as a vicar's daughter is not so far removed from the requirements of being a senior politician as it might at first seem. As a child of the vicarage, you are not just yourself, and you are not just seen as representing your parents (although when your father is the local vicar, that is more significant than it is for most children). Like it or not, you are also a representative of a wider body – the Church.

Thus at a young age, it was incumbent on me to consider how my words and actions reflected not just on me but on others. This has stayed with me throughout my life and political career. There were times when I stopped myself from making a funny aside or what I thought was a humorous quip because it could have been taken out of context. And so, while I consider it has stood me in good stead, in today's world of social media, rolling TV news and personality politics, it has meant that I have been seen as being too careful with my words, not sufficiently willing to open up, robotic and uninteresting.

Despite being portrayed as having these characteristics, I still try to be very careful with what I say today. Old habits die hard, but more than that, being careless in speech can cause deep trouble for others. This natural inclination to hold my tongue served me well when I was Home Secretary and when I was PM. But it takes personal restraint. I remember one occasion when I was Home Secretary when I had a conversation with another senior colleague. There was a counter-terrorism story in the papers, and we were being asked a certain question about the individuals concerned. We knew the answer but for security reasons could not divulge it. My colleague wanted to do so, or at least to give an answer that gave a strong hint. When I said no, he could not do so his response was that not doing so would make him look stupid. I'm not sorry to say that my answer was, 'So look stupid then.'

Caring about the impact on others of what you do and say should be the abiding mantra of any politician. If you think that sounds holier than thou, this desire to be ultra-careful was honed in the years when I was a parliamentary candidate. At the end of John Major's premiership, the Opposition and the media were constantly looking for the slightest differences in tone, nuance or words used by Conservative politicians, particularly government ministers. Any difference, even the slightest variation in emphasis, was leapt on as a gaffe or a split in the party or the government. So careful speech has a political importance too.

My Perspective

This was not the only way in which that country-vicarage background shaped my thinking. As an only child, I was in some ways treated as an adult. Certainly, I was urged to take an interest in what was going on beyond our home in the country and the world, and I was encouraged to argue and debate with my parents, particularly my father. But don't get the wrong idea. This wasn't all about world affairs. There were hard-fought arguments about many topics – perhaps especially about cricket, above all about who was England's best opening batsman. My father, being a Surrey supporter, was adamant that it was John Edrich. I couldn't agree, and argued the case vociferously for Geoffrey Boycott. My father cited Edrich's strokeplay. I argued for Boycott's dogged determination and capacity to occupy the crease thanks to his ability to play with a straight bat. Later in life, I was to cite these characteristics not just as the reason for valuing Geoffrey Boycott's approach to cricket, but also as being useful for a politician.

So argument and debate were a regular part of my upbringing. My mother sometimes worried that this happened too much, but my father was always very willing to debate with me. In fact, I used to get rather loud when I was putting my case, and time after time my father would say, 'No need to shout. You are not addressing a public meeting.' Little did he know!

It is a great sadness to me that neither of my parents lived to see me elected to Parliament, let alone occupying the highest elected office in the land. Indeed, they didn't even see me elected to Merton Council, which included Wimbledon, where my paternal great-grandfather had been an alderman.

My Perspective

Careful speech, argument and debate – these were all parts of my upbringing. But there were other aspects that perhaps fitted me for a career in politics. My father was always speaking in public through his sermons. I learnt a lot from him about that, but I also took a lesson from my mother. If his sermon went beyond ten minutes, there would be questions asked at lunch in the vicarage. I can't claim to only ever speak for ten minutes, but it does remind me of the importance of knowing the message you want to give, keeping your remarks short and your audience engaged.

This background served me well, and from an early age I was interested in becoming an MP. But I always point out that, unlike William Hague, I didn't read Hansard under the bedclothes. I was more likely to have the radio tuned to *Test Match Special* from some overseas tour. Indeed, that was how I heard of John Snow's 7 for 49 against the West Indies. A major moment for clergy children.[*]

Although my interest in getting into Parliament was sparked early in life – at about the age of twelve – I always thought that it was sensible to do something else first. Bringing wider experience into the House of Commons is important. It means you have a better understanding of the issues that affect people day to day. And if you work in the private sector, you have a greater understanding of what drives the economy. Moreover, if you have been in a position which involved managing people, budgets and projects, that is good experience for being a government minister.

---

[*] John Snow, the Sussex and England bowler, missed the first test in the West Indies in 1968, then took 7 for 49 as the West Indies were bowled out for 143 in the second test in Jamaica. His father was the vicar of Bognor Regis.

While argument, debate and being brought up watching my father speaking in public were important aspects of my upbringing that helped to shape my future, they were not as important as the sense of duty and public service that were instilled in me by my parents.

Being a priest is a vocation, not just a job. Serving God is fundamental in that role, but part of that is serving people – being there for them when they need support and advice, comforting them in their hour of need, as well as encouraging them in their faith. For my father, public service wasn't just about supporting people who came to him. It was about reaching out to people as well. He would go out and about in his parish visiting people, sometimes unannounced, occasionally – as he well knew – not always welcome. I now see echoes of this in my work as an MP, going out and knocking on doors in my constituency. This is something I have done regularly over the years, including when I was Prime Minister.

As well as the public service, and indeed duty, shown by my father, we should never forget the commitment required from a vicar's wife or partner. Many a time, my mother would have to do something or attend an event simply because she was the vicar's wife. That sense of duty is seen in the partners and other halves of MPs today when they attend functions, wait at home because there is a late vote, or see their personal lives disrupted. Disruption can come in many forms, be it constituency events which mean key family moments like birthday celebrations are missed, or major events which may lead to Parliament being recalled to sit during what should be a parliamentary recess, requiring a family holiday to be cut short. In 2011, for example, two days into my fortnight's summer holiday, I had to return to the UK to deal with the riots taking place in London and elsewhere.

My father also instilled in me an understanding of the importance of every individual – that we are all equal. For him, every parishioner counted. It didn't matter what their background was or whether they came to church or not. His mission was to everyone and all were equal in the sight of God. Thus he also cared about fairness and justice – again linked to his faith.

This sense of the equality of everyone, regardless of gender, ethnicity or background, was another feature of my upbringing that has always stayed with me. Not just that: my parents were positive that there was no limit to what I could achieve, no limit imposed purely because I was female. This wasn't a mantra that was drummed into me along the lines of 'You're a girl, you can do anything,' but it was the unspoken theme of the encouragement I received from them both when I was at school and at university. What I did was very much up to me. They had hopes and aspirations for me – of different types, because I'm pretty sure at one stage my mother wanted me to become a nun – but the decision was mine. What they expected was that in all things, I would do my best.

That belief – that what people make of themselves is up to them, their talents and their hard work – has underpinned my politics and my view that education and opportunity are critical in the development of an individual. We should never assume that someone will turn out a particular way, either as a success or as a failure in life, because of their background. People from all sorts of backgrounds achieve great things – it's about them and their hard work.

My Perspective

Perhaps I feel this particularly because of my experience all those years ago in that country vicarage. Time and time again, I felt the interests of the parish or of individual parishioners taking priority. Against that background, I came to see public service very much in terms of putting other people first and yourself second. Too often others have adopted the opposite approach, as we can see quite clearly in the behaviour of parliamentarians set out in the chapters that follow.

Part One

Power and Politics

Throughout this book, the episodes of abuse of power which I set out all involve politicians or politics in some way. For example, in the case of the tragedy at the Hillsborough Stadium, the story embraces not just the people responsible on the day, but the then-government's response. In instances of social injustice like this, the prime abuse of power is not generally committed by politicians themselves; rather, they are cases where the underlying politics or the protection of the political establishment played a large part in that particular abuse.

In the next few chapters, I look at cases of the abuse of power which involve politicians very directly. I started this book by saying that too many people think being Prime Minister is a position of power when actually it is a position of service. That is no less true, for some people, of the role of a Member of Parliament. For that reason, I recount significant events where I believe politicians have clearly acted in their own personal interest rather than in the overall national interest. Indeed, I believe it goes further than that and has an international dimension in the sense that anything that diminishes Parliament or our democracy reduces the UK's standing in the world.

As you read this, the cynical among you may feel that these chapters are superfluous. Sadly, too many people these days see politicians as only ever acting in their own interest rather than for the greater good. My experience during over a quarter of a century in Parliament is that most MPs actively want to make life better for others, and particularly want to make life better for those who are less fortunate than themselves. We may disagree about priorities and about how we achieve our aims, but most people come into politics to improve the country and life within it.

This was perhaps best expressed by the late Jo Cox MP, who said, 'We are far more united and have far more in common than that which divides us.'

The line is crossed when those in authority fail to recognise that power can be corrosive and corrupting, and allow it to shape their thinking and behaviour. It is also crossed when leaders become so bound up in their own role in events and so intent on their own vision winning through that they become incapable of standing back and seeing the wider picture, and are unable or unwilling to ask whether there is another way that will better serve the greater good.

I have also included a focus on Parliament, because I believe it is important to think about the role that politicians play in the development of our society, its culture and its attitudes. Although people today have less respect for positions of authority, MPs included, being a Member of Parliament is nonetheless still a position of leadership. How an MP behaves matters. Those of us who are in active politics should set an example.

I was in Parliament when the MPs' expenses scandal broke in 2009. It was a difficult time. Even those MPs who were not identified as having done anything wrong found it hard to speak to constituents on the doorsteps. The widespread anger was fierce, for many reasons. Of course, the main one was the belief that this simply showed how deeply MPs had their snouts in the trough when their constituents were finding life difficult. It exemplified what many had always thought about MPs being in it for themselves.

Another source of anger was the perception that somehow MPs were able to get away with breaking the sort of rules which they would expect everyone else to follow. This was to have another manifestation under Boris Johnson's premiership, when those in 10 Downing Street and elsewhere in Whitehall were found to have broken Covid pandemic lockdown rules. The idea that there has been one rule for the public and another for MPs provokes public cynicism and leads increasingly to the charge of hypocrisy. In other words, why should we do what you say when you don't do it yourself?

Above all, it shatters any sense that MPs are leaders in society. Yet I still believe we have a responsibility to try to show such leadership. It may be harder in today's world, but that doesn't mean we shouldn't try.

All the cases I describe are ones in which I was involved or had an interest, and that had a major impact on the UK's future – such as Brexit. In some of them, people knowingly exercised their power in their own interests. In others, no one actively set out to abuse power, but the way they used their power came to the same thing in the end.

2

Parliamentary Abuse

It is shocking, but right, to start with the abuse of power at the heart of our democracy in Parliament. In a democracy, those who have been elected exercise power over people's lives. This should be reflected in the atmosphere in Parliament, where the serious nature of the decisions being taken and the impact they have on the day-to-day lives of the people should lead those involved to adopt a careful and considered approach to exercising their power.

All elected individuals should be wary of the power they hold and should only be willing to use it for the common good. The 1995 report of the Nolan Committee* explained the need to restate the principles of public life – selflessness, integrity, objectivity, accountability, openness, honesty and leadership. It also declared that not only is it necessary for MPs to maintain the highest standards of conduct, but 'it is essential for public confidence that they should be seen to do so'.

If this approach is to be expected in the way individuals exercise their power over the lives of the public, they

---

* *Standards in Public Life: First Report of the Committee on Standards in Public Life*, May 1995, Cm 2850–1.

should behave in the same way in their relationships with colleagues and staff. After all, if you exercise power carelessly in one aspect of your life, the chances are that you will do the same in other areas.

Sadly, the evidence of recent years has been that the exercise of power by MPs in their dealings with their own staff and with the staff of the House of Commons, and indeed among the staff themselves, has been the opposite of careful. It has shown the abuse of power at its worst. In some of these cases, this has been in pursuit of sexual gratification. And usually the behaviour has been gender related, often a male exercising power over a female.

This is not a recent development. Arguably, these abuses had been evident for decades, but in previous eras, when women were pressurised to keep quiet and to see unwelcome advances or bullying from their boss as something to be endured, there was no impetus to come forward and report the abuse. This all came to a head during my time as Prime Minister, largely as the result of the exposure of sexual abuse in the film industry and through the #MeToo campaign.

The term 'MeToo' had been adopted in 2006 on social media by the American activist Tarana Burke, who wanted to empower women by means of empathy, to let women who had been sexually abused and had suffered sexual violence know they were not alone and should not feel ashamed. The comfort generated by someone saying 'I have been through that too' would help those who were feeling that somehow they were responsible for the abuse or who just felt too ashamed to speak out. Since then, the #MeToo movement has spread to cover other issues of marginalisation.

Parliamentary Abuse

The term was then adopted separately in 2017 in the film industry by those exposing allegations against the producer Harvey Weinstein. Here again, the abuse of actresses was nothing new – the adage that 'she got the role because of her performance on the casting couch' was a very old one. In that year, however, those who had suffered at Weinstein's hands started to come forward and share their experiences with a wide audience.

This led to a flurry of examples of abuse, primarily of women, in various areas of life. What the exposures in the film industry did was to make it acceptable for women to admit to having been abused. It also showed them that they were not alone, just as Tarana Burke had envisaged. This is critical in encouraging victims to come forward and talk about what has happened to them, and to identify their abusers.

It was against this background that people in the political world started to come forward to talk about abuse in their workplaces, both in Parliament and in constituencies. The victims were both male and female. In many cases, the abuse was at the hands of an MP, but sometimes it was a staff member against another staff member. Some of the allegations were of sexual abuse, others of bullying and harassment.

In the face of these reports, the government and the House of Commons took action to try to remedy the situation or at least put in place procedures that would make it easier for victims to report their experiences. It was hoped that in due course, this would lead to a reduction in abuse. In November 2017, as Prime Minister, I convened a cross-party working group to develop an independent grievance procedure. The group went on to be chaired by the then-Leader of the House of Commons, Andrea Leadsom MP, who put considerable thought and effort into trying to resolve the problems.

As part of its inquiry, the Working Group commissioned a survey which was opened up to responses from a wide range of people working in, or working with, Parliament. The survey, taken together with others conducted among MPs' and peers' staff, showed that the scale of the problem was significant and the group concluded, shockingly, that 'bullying, harassment and sexual harassment have been a feature in the lives of many who work in or with Parliament'.

This Working Group reported on 8 February,* and set out a number of recommendations, notably the establishment of a Parliament-wide behaviour code and independent complaints and grievance schemes to both respond to and manage complaints of either sexual harassment or bullying and harassment. These recommendations were endorsed in a vote in the House, and the House of Commons Commission was asked to authorise officials to do the necessary work to implement the recommendations of the Working Group. (The Commission is the body that administers the Commons. Chaired by the Speaker, it includes MPs and lay members.)

As the revelations and allegations mounted, Dame Laura Cox was commissioned by the House of Commons in April 2018 to look into these issues and report.

The Cox report† was delivered in October 2018 and it made depressing reading. The issue was summed up in

---

* *Report of the Working Group on an Independent Complaints and Grievance Policy.*

† *The Bullying and Harassment of House of Commons Staff: Independent Inquiry Report*, October 2018.

a quotation from a member of the Commons staff with which Dame Laura opened her report:

> We are proud to work in the House of Commons, but when we are abused those who lead us should support us, not abandon us to our fate and cover up the traces. And those who abuse us should be held accountable. Establishing a new complaints and grievance process won't come close to solving the problems in this place. We need a seismic shift. But the institution is worth fighting for.

The quotation exposes the various elements of the problem. First there is the abuse itself. Then there is the attempt to cover it up. Then the failure to bring those responsible to account for their actions. Finally, there is the recognition that this is about more than just a handful of 'bad apples', as some have claimed. It is about a culture in Parliament that enabled this behaviour by encouraging the view that somehow MPs were different from everyone else.

As Dame Laura said, 'Abusive conduct of this kind is pervasive and no workplace is immune, but the culture in which it has been able to take hold in the House of Commons and the ineffective mechanisms for dealing with it make this a particularly serious case.' Reflecting on the instances of sexual harassment, she said that 'Sexual harassment is frequently more about power than it is about sex. And it is an abuse of power of the most insidious kind.' There we have it clearly spelt out. Those MPs and staff members guilty of sexual harassment were clearly exercising an abuse of power.

In the course of her report, Dame Laura also highlighted the fact that a number of people had felt unable to come forward to report their experiences of abuse either because the memory was too painful or because they were worried that they would lose their job (although everyone was assured that any contributions would be confidential).

The extent of the problem was clear from the report and was vividly summed up as follows:

> The unhappy fact is that the overwhelming major-ity of contributions, from staff working across the House, reveal widespread, enduring and profound disaffection with a culture that is as embedded as it is shocking. They indicate that bullying, harassment and sexual harassment of members of staff, both by other members of staff and by some MPs, has been known about and tolerated for far too long, despite efforts by some, including recognised trade unions, to persuade the senior administration to take it seriously . . . such misconduct has been able to thrive over many years, and to become entrenched as part of an excessively hierarchical, 'command and control' and deferential culture, which has no place in any organisation in the 21st century.

This was a damning indictment of the culture of the House of Commons. The report identified many of the fea-tures that are seen in the cases of abuse of power identified in later chapters, including the unwillingness of those in positions of authority to listen to complaints or to do anything to stop the abusive behaviour.

One of the contributors expressed it like this:

> In relation to bullying and harassment, the culture of the senior administration is generally to bury their

heads in the sand, to hope that the problem goes away, to seek to ensure that there is the minimum of disruption to the business of the House, to cover backs, to cover up and to conceal problem behaviour, as necessary, to protect the reputation of the House rather than the safety of the individual, and to move the problem on elsewhere rather than tackle it head on. Gradually and inexorably more and more members of staff become disaffected. And because they are unsupported, bullying and harassment becomes normalised. A bubble of anger and discontent builds and then eventually bursts.

In themselves, these revelations would be shocking in any workplace. That they related to what has been popularly known as the mother of parliaments, the heart of our democracy, made them all the worse. But this was not even the whole picture of what was happening behind those world-famous walls.

Broadly speaking, there are two groups of staff in the House of Commons. The first are the staff who work for the House itself. The second are the staff who work in MPs' offices. The Cox inquiry was set up to consider behaviour relating to the former. The House of Commons Commission set Dame Laura a remit that did not cover the behaviour of MPs towards the staff in their own offices. This may have been for two reasons. First, House of Commons staff are formally appointed by the Commission, so it has responsibility for and to them. Secondly, the origin of the Cox report lay in allegations made in March 2018 of bullying and sexual harassment of members of the Commons staff by some male MPs. The fact that the alleged perpetrators were MPs should have given a warning sign about the behaviours of MPs generally. Not allowing Dame Laura to look into their behaviour towards their own staff proved to be a critical omission, as became clear the following year with the report of Gemma White QC. This review was commissioned by Parliament, while the Cox inquiry was ongoing, to look into allegations of bullying and harassment which were not within the scope of that inquiry. It was a recognition of the fact that not everybody working in Parliament was covered by the Cox inquiry, and critically it looked into the experience of staff working for MPs.

The White report[*] stated, 'Many contributors to this inquiry, particularly those working in constituency offices, have emphasised how isolated from the rest of the parliamentary community they feel and have said that this is the first time they feel anyone has been prepared to listen to them and take account of their views.'

Gemma White went on to outline the sort of incidents reported to her:

> By far the most common form of offending behaviour described to me was MPs who shout at, demean, belittle and humiliate their staff on a regular basis, often in public. The constant 'drip, drip', as more than one contributor put it, eats away at the employee's self-confidence until they become anxious, exhausted and ill, incapable of performing their job and (often following a period of sick leave) resign or are dismissed . . . Sexual harassment is also a problem, with

---

[*] *Bullying and Harassment of MPs' Parliamentary Staff: Independent Inquiry Report*, July 2019, HC 2206.

staff being subject to unwanted sexual advances, often accompanied by touching, sometimes forceful. There is an unacceptable level of sexual 'banter' and unwelcome discussion of intimate sexual details . . . In the words of one contributor, there has been a 'general disregard for the dignity, wellbeing and employment rights of MPs' staff'.

The outcome of all of this work was the Independent Complaints and Grievance Scheme (ICGS), which consists of the Behaviour Code, the Bullying and Harassment Policy and the Sexual Misconduct Policy. There have been various developments since, notably the decision of the House of Commons in June 2020 to set up an Independent Panel of Experts to determine cases under the Complaints and Grievance Scheme and decide on sanctions in those cases which related to MPs.

It is perhaps telling that in July 2018, in accepting that the Behaviour Code should be incorporated in the Code of Conduct, the House of Commons agreed to include a new rule that 'a Member must treat their staff and all those visiting or working for or with Parliament with dignity, courtesy and respect'. One might have thought that should have gone without saying, that every MP should automatically have acted in that way. But the evidence was to the contrary as far as some MPs were concerned, and so it had to be spelt out for all. A further critical decision was taken by Parliament in 2019 when it agreed to include historic cases in the Complaints and Grievance Scheme.

Despite all these efforts, in the years since there have been further allegations of this sort of misbehaviour by MPs. Indeed, in early 2022 it was reported that since 2018, there had been fifty-six allegations against MPs, including some against Cabinet ministers.

While all these issues were being brought to the surface, reports written, policies revised and new structures established, the person who more than any other is there to ensure good behaviour in the way the Commons conducts its business – the Speaker, John Bercow – was himself subjecting staff to appalling bullying.

This was the ultimate example of an abuse of power which had not come to light because of concerns about the impact of complaining among those who were on the receiving end of the abuse. I suspect there was also a sense among his victims that there was little point in trying to complain because they didn't really have anyone to complain to other than the perpetrator himself. As Dame Laura Cox had said in her report in relation to Parliament generally, some staff expressed regret for being unwilling to come forward with their experiences because they were afraid of losing their jobs, despite the assurance given of confidentiality. There may also have been some who were concerned about what revealing their problem would mean for the reputation of Parliament. They may have put the reputation of the House above justice for themselves.

For some time, there were stories circulating in the House about the Speaker's behaviour, but no formal complaint was made. It is worth just considering briefly those who did finally come forward in relation to John Bercow's conduct towards them. These were not junior staff unable to deal with a senior figure. They were not shrinking violets. They were senior staff who had given years of service to Parliament and were well able to deal with difficult MPs. Two were employed as Secretary to the Speaker, one of whom was a former naval captain. The third was the Clerk of the House – the Corporate Officer of the House and its principal constitutional adviser.

The nature of John Bercow's behaviour is best set out in the words of the report of the Independent Panel of Experts* who looked at the Standards Commissioner's determination in relation to complaints made against him:

> Overall, we concluded that: the ICGS Bullying and Harassment Policy was breached repeatedly and extensively by the most senior Member of the House of Commons. In all, 21 separate allegations were proved and have been upheld. The House may feel that his conduct brought the high office of Speaker into disrepute. This was behaviour which had no place in any workplace. Members of staff should not be expected to have to tolerate it as part of every-day life. No person at work, however senior, indeed particularly such a senior figure, should behave in this way. This was an abuse of power.

The Panel's Chairman went on to say:

> It is for historians to judge whether the respondent was a successful reforming Speaker of the House of Com-mons. However, there was no need to act as a bully in order to achieve that aim. A great office can be filled forcefully and effectively without descending to such behaviour. The findings of the Parliamentary Com-missioner for Standards, which we have upheld, show that the respondent has been a serial bully. Like many

---

* *The Conduct of Mr John Bercow*, March 2022, HC 1189.

bullies, he had those whom he favoured and those whom he made victims. These three complainants were victims. His evidence in the investigations, the findings of the Commissioner, and his submissions to us, show also that the respondent has been a serial liar. His behaviour fell very far below that which the public has a right to expect from any Member of Parliament. The respondent's behaviour was so serious that, had he still been a Member of Parliament, we would have determined that he should be expelled by resolution of the House. As it is we recommend that he should never be permitted a pass to the Parliamentary estate.

There we have it. The charge sheet for John Bercow was that he was not just a bully but also a serial liar. We have a right to expect better from the House of Commons, although arguably he was not the only MP to whom that description could be applied.

This behaviour by the Speaker was significant not just because of the behaviour itself. It is always difficult to bring about real reform in any organisation if its head is a perpetrator of the behaviour in question. John Bercow left Parliament at the 2019 general election. In a sense, that made it easier to ensure that the procedures put in place by the House of Commons to address abuses of power by MPs and staff were followed effectively. Perhaps more important was the fact that the procedures allowed the extent and nature of his own behaviour to be revealed.

The findings of the Commissioner and the Independent Expert Panel show that it is possible to have a system that enables the victims of abuse to come forward and see their case considered and, where appropriate, upheld. It is important for the future of Parliament that those working there do feel able to report abuse, confident that they will not be prevented from doing so by the conviction that their abuser holds all the power. I hope that examples like this will give greater strength to victims, encouraging them to come forward, and that they will also make perpetrators think twice. It is sad to be suggesting that the threat of being caught could be what makes potential parliamentary perpetrators desist. Much better that they should desist because they recognise that this is not behaviour that belongs in any workplace, and certainly not at the heart of our democracy where we are making the laws that others are expected to follow.

So why is it that we see these abuses of power taking place? The answer is also depressing. It is that too many in Parliament feel that they are special, different from mere mortals doing a job in any other workplace. I remember having an argument in the Members' Tea Room years ago with a long-standing MP who had heard me refer to being an MP as a job. It wasn't a job, he said, because we had been elected.

Being an MP *is* a job, and Parliament, impressive a building though it is and important though it is for the work done within its walls, is a workplace. It may be a workplace like no other. The process by which MPs get their jobs may be different from the way most people get theirs. But contrary to the views of many, being elected doesn't make MPs a breed apart to whom the normal rules of human behaviour in the workplace do not apply. We expect others to behave in a certain way in their places of work. Indeed, we sometimes legislate for that. We should not think that those rules do not apply to us.

MPs are not a breed apart. They do not gain elevated status by being elected. Being the choice of your constituents is a huge honour, but it is also a huge responsibility and it brings with it certain duties. Among those duties is the duty to set an example to the public, and key to that is putting them first and yourself second. Of course, MPs are human beings, and as such they will make mistakes, get annoyed and angry at times, and suffer frustrations. But those frustrations should not be taken out on others and certainly not on staff.

Election gives an MP the benefit of power, but that power must be exercised in the interests of others and in the common good, not to satisfy the desires or appease the frustrations of the MP. As if that were not enough to temper behaviour, MPs also have to remember that they are on show in their constituency and in Parliament.

The phrase 'one rule for them and another for us' has been used many times in recent history in relation to MPs. It may seem trite, but it reflects the opinion of members of the public who do expect their MPs and ministers to at least follow the rules the public are expected to follow, and at best to be role models. Some politicians may say that is unfair, but before they do so, I would ask them to reflect on the fact that people put their trust in us through their votes. They bestow on us the power to take decisions which can change their lives.

This probably sounds holier than thou or even utopian, but it is not intended to be. If people are to trust their politicians, they have a right to expect certain standards of personal behaviour driven by a recognition of the significance of the job we do. I am not saying that MPs must lead saintly and blameless lives. As with any group of people,

MPs in the House of Commons are a mixed bag. But being an MP requires us to think more carefully than others about our actions. We are public servants. We are in the service of the public. We serve at their behest. It is perhaps little wonder that there is a lack of trust in politics and politicians if MPs' own behaviour is shown to be so lacking.

One of the arguments sometimes put forward to excuse MPs' misbehaviour is that the stresses of the job are such that errors should be forgiven. Certainly the stresses of some jobs are great, and those stresses increase in ministerial office, particularly when you are Prime Minister. But not all MPs are Prime Minister, and not all have to bear the stresses which that role brings. Yes, the life is different. There is a stress in being separated from partners and families, although the stress is often felt more by those left at home who have to cope with the vicissitudes of life without their partner's support.

Being an MP is not the only job that requires separation for periods of time from family – think of those serving in the armed forces. What's more, being an MP is not the only job which carries stress – think of the strain of working as a doctor. So while there may be times when an individual MP finds it hard to deal with the pressures of parliamentary life, that does not give them carte blanche to behave in unacceptable ways towards staff and others.

There is simply no excuse for the sort of behaviour that has been seen from some MPs. It would not be accepted in other workplaces and should not have been accepted in Parliament for so long. The work that has been done to establish better codes of conduct and guidance, support for victims, channels for reporting bad behaviour and action against offenders is all necessary and welcome. It should help to change the environment in which staff are working in Parliament. Unfortunately, it will not on its own be sufficient to ensure that change is embedded and that in future people coming to work in Parliament can look forward to the normal standards of behaviour expected in a workplace.

Ultimately, the situation will only be rectified by a change in culture of the organisation, though such a change is the hardest thing to achieve. It requires all concerned first to recognise the need to change, then to identify how to change, and finally to put that change into practice. Although there are many MPs who recognise the need for change, I fear that for a number, the sense of entitlement that comes from being elected will remain for some time to come.

While the House authorities take responsibility for the arrangements relating to the employment of House staff, and the Independent Parliamentary Standards Authority (IPSA) does so for MPs' staff, and while the House authorities have established codes of conduct and grievance mechanisms, responsibility for the culture of MPs also rests with political parties. It is the parties that choose the candidates and, although the electorate will determine which candidate wins in any one seat, the responsibility for determining the character of the people standing for election as candidates rests with the parties.

Over the years, I have been involved at different times in changing the selection procedures for the Conservative Party, not least as party Chairman in 2001–2, when I worked with others to introduce a system that removed unconscious bias against women. One of the key elements of the selection procedure at that time was to give a tub-thumping speech to the assembled party members. There was no element that tested listening skills or the ability to interact with constituents. By and large, the rousing speech was more likely to be given by a man and the better listening skills were more likely to be possessed by a woman. So we changed the process to ensure that there was less reliance on the first and more identification of the second. The driving force for that was the recognition of the need to get a more diverse group of candidates. The emphasis at first was on getting more women to stand for election, but we were also keen to enlist people from ethnic minorities and people from a greater diversity of backgrounds generally.

As you might imagine, parties will give consideration to ensuring that their potential candidates are genuinely supportive of the principles and policies of the party. In the past in the Conservative Party, candidates were also asked if there were any skeletons in their cupboard – that is to say, if there was anything in their past that would cause the party embarrassment if revealed later on. Today, someone's background is as likely to be revealed by looking at their social media history. Given the issues of poor behaviour that we have seen in Parliament, I think it is time for parties to look more carefully at the character of their candidates and at their approach to the job of being an MP.

It is not enough to be an ardent supporter of a party on a particular issue. Indeed, it is politically dangerous for parties – which will, by definition, be a broad church of views underpinned by a set of values – to set too much store by whether an individual candidate has a particular viewpoint on a specific issue. In the Conservative Party, this latter tendency has been seen most recently in relation to Brexit. The danger is that in looking for a specific stance on one issue, the wider questions about character and integrity get overlooked.

I remember in my early days on the candidates' list having a conversation with someone who, like me, later entered Parliament. Talking about constituency selection meetings, he said that on some subjects you had to be careful not to give an opinion until you had got a sense of what the majority of the audience thought. Then you could say that was your view. How cynical, but also how likely to lead to future problems. People don't want to see someone who tailors their views according to how the wind blows. What people want to see is honesty and authenticity.

Looking at the behaviour of some MPs – and, indeed, of some staff members – leads inexorably to the view that they believed themselves to be special simply by virtue of being elected or simply because they worked in Parliament. They abused others because they could.

3

Brexit

I may as well step right into the most controversial issue. When I am asked what I want the legacy of my time in government to be, I say I would like it to be the legislation for net zero emissions by 2050, or the Modern Slavery Act. When I say that, I know in my heart of hearts that the political reality is that my premiership will always be seen in the context of Brexit and my failure to get a deal through the House of Commons.

Brexit took up a significant amount of my time at No. 10, but that is not why I have included it in this book. I dare say some readers will think it is odd to include a chapter on Brexit in a book about power and in particular about the abuse of power. Brexit was not an example of social injustice of the sort I describe in later chapters. The failure to get the deal my government struck with the EU through the House of Commons, however, was due in large part to the misuse of power – too often, it was used to satisfy personal interests rather than the overall national interest.

Aha! I hear you exclaim – she's trying to blame others for her own mistakes. I am not. What I want to do is to show how the power plays in Parliament contributed to the stalemate that ensued until it was broken by the general election of 2019. I could have made some different decisions that might have helped my cause. I also should have realised that just because some Conservative MPs had campaigned for many years to leave the EU, it didn't mean they would accept a deal to leave that was different from their favoured option. Perhaps I should also have appreciated that it didn't mean they would accept a deal negotiated by, and presented to them by, someone who had voted to remain.

At its heart, the problem was that both sides of the argument – the Brexiteers and the Remainers – felt they had the power to achieve their desired outcome regardless of its impact on the country. Despite what individual MPs might now claim, it became a battle of the tribes rather than a battle for the best interests of the United Kingdom.

Before I explore that in detail, however, I must talk about what I believe was the greatest abuse of power during this whole process. An abuse of power that came from what should have been the most unlikely source – the very person above all others who should be absolutely neutral in their work, the Speaker of the House of Commons.

I have now served under four Speakers, each with their own characteristics and each with their own way of dealing with the House. There have been times in the past when I and others will have felt we were being hard done by. There were other times when we have counted ourselves fortunate not to come under greater challenge from the Chair. Until John Bercow took office, I had never seen someone so blatantly abuse the power they held as Speaker to promote a particular view, not just in a single debate, but time after time throughout the whole process of Brexit.

Brexit

In retrospect, I should not have been surprised. I had already experienced what I believed was Bercow's willingness to work with the Opposition against the government when, as Home Secretary, I was putting through the arrangements necessary to readopt a number of European Union justice and home affairs measures. This was about whether or not we should opt back into certain EU regulations, including the European Arrest Warrant, which made it much easier for the UK to extradite criminals from other EU member states to face justice here.

I won't go into all the details of the debate, which became one of those House of Commons events that leave most people cold. If you are interested, look at Hansard for 10 November 2014. Suffice to say that, following a move by the Labour Opposition to exploit an unexpected and in many ways esoteric piece of parliamentary practice, we found ourselves debating not the issue in hand but the proposal 'that the question be not now put'. It took some time for many Members to understand the implications of this. It meant that if the motion was passed, the government's business for that day would fail.[*] I therefore found myself having to continue speaking in the debate in order to allow time for the Prime Minister and others who were not in Parliament to come back to vote. David Cameron and some other ministers and MPs were at the Lord Mayor's banquet and, as they were wearing white tie and in the middle of a good dinner, they were not best pleased at being called back to Parliament.

---

[*] Government business refers to the subjects the government wants to timetable for debate. This is usually legislation it wants to bring in. On most days in the House of Commons, the items for debate will have been decided by the government.

43

We won the vote. But it seemed clear to me that the Labour Party had been able to make use of a rarely invoked parliamentary procedure to force an unexpected vote only because the Speaker had permitted it. When intending to use such a procedure, it would not be unusual to discuss this with the Speaker first, so it was my belief that before the Labour Party launched their challenge, they were almost certain to have raised it with him. The role of the Speaker is such that they would not be expected to advise – and certainly not to encourage – the Labour Party to use this mechanism to stop the government's business from going through. The use of this procedure took the government benches completely by surprise. I could not recall it being used before and could not help but wonder about the extent of the discussions that had taken place beforehand. Mind you, on that occasion, this was not our only problem. Jacob Rees-Mogg, Conservative Member of Parliament and later a Cabinet minister, appeared to be conniving with the Labour Party to oppose the Conservative government, as shown in Michael Cockerell's BBC documentary *Inside the Commons*. Indeed, he voted with the Labour Party on this occasion.

Over and over again, but particularly in the latter days of my administration, it seemed clear to me that John Bercow was trying to thwart the delivery of Brexit. He seemed so clearly to be following his personal agenda, and the impression was that he was working with those who favoured a second referendum and against the policy of the government.

This was manifested in different ways. He reinterpreted Standing Orders. He ruled that amendments could not be laid when the rules should have allowed them to be put down. He overrode the long-standing convention that the government determined the business of the House. Crucially, just when the Democratic Unionist Party had indicated privately that they would vote with the government, thus enabling the deal to be agreed by the House of Commons, the Speaker ruled that he could not accept another vote on the deal. As a result, the debate was not allowed and no vote took place at that time. At that point, I am certain that he scuppered the Brexit deal.

As a result, the carefully crafted Withdrawal Agreement unwound and was to be no more. Had the debate been held, and had the vote been taken with the DUP voting with the government, there was every prospect that we would have delivered an earlier exit from the EU, maintained better relations with our European partners and, above all, delivered an agreement which would have been more beneficial for Northern Ireland and hence for the future integrity of the UK than the one that Boris Johnson signed.

John Bercow accepted the Opposition's tactic of using their Opposition Day debates to put down motions for a Humble Address to be sent to Her Majesty the Queen on topic after topic designed only to thwart the government. A Humble Address is a communication from the House to the monarch. Its most frequent use is after the debate on the monarch's speech at the opening session of Parliament, when a Humble Address is sent to the monarch thanking them for their speech. During my premiership, the Opposition used this procedure on a number of occasions to petition the Queen to require the government to take certain action. It meant bringing the Queen into political matters. And when the government chose not to play ball with these motions, the Speaker threatened to hold ministers in contempt of Parliament.

This use of the Humble Address was not just an affront to parliamentary procedure, it also involved Her Majesty in ongoing political debates in a way which rode roughshod over the accepted lines between the role of the elected House and the constitutional monarch. In my view, this was completely unacceptable. Regrettably, it is a mechanism that has come to be an accepted part of the Opposition's armoury.

Arguably, this set a precedent which was later reflected in the decision by Boris Johnson's government to prorogue Parliament in August 2019, a move which required the monarch's acceptance. That prorogation, designed to stop all parliamentary business, was of course later found to be unlawful by the Supreme Court.

This was not the first time Brexiteers had suggested prorogation. As noted earlier, apart from a limited number of items, such as business determined by the Backbench Business Committee, business of the House of Commons each day is decided by the government. Following the 2017 election, although the Conservatives had more MPs than any other party, I did not have an overall majority. I was able to form a government because of an agreement with the members of the Democratic Unionist Party in Parliament. This meant that obtaining a majority in the Commons on any vote was difficult. These difficult numbers emboldened Remainers who wanted to bring forward motions and indeed legislation that would enable them to require the government to take a particular position in the Brexit negotiations. They were desperately keen to use Parliament to stop a no-deal Brexit. This was, of course, opposed by the Brexiteers, and so earlier in 2019, Jacob Rees-Mogg, a leading Brexiteer, suggested to me that the way through this was to ask Her Majesty to prorogue Parliament, thus removing the opportunity for such business to be brought forward. I refused.

It was also suggested to me by the same source that, if the Remainers did pass a bill that the Brexiteers didn't like, I should ask Her Majesty not to give it Royal Assent. Again, I refused. I resisted both of these proposals, not just because of the implications for the role of Parliament, but mainly because of my firm belief that it would have been unthinkable to bring the monarch into these matters.

By sanctioning the idea of prorogation, the hard-line Brexiteers were taking a sledgehammer to the British constitution.

Perhaps what I find most shocking about John Bercow's approach is that the Speaker's role is to uphold democracy. Yet here was a Speaker who, it seemed to me, was deliberately using his power in a way that favoured those who wanted to try to overturn the democratic will of the people. There is no doubt that for many people, any faith they had in Parliament was being shattered by the attempts by MPs to overturn the result of the referendum. Throughout the Brexit debate, there were too many parliamentarians, holding their positions through the democratic will of the people, who worked tirelessly to try to overturn the will of the people, and I believe that John Bercow was key among them.

Of course, he would probably say in his defence that the outcome of the 2017 election meant that the Conservative Party did not have a working majority on its own, and he was merely balancing things out.

I absolutely accept that the result of the 2017 general election made the position in Parliament far more difficult.

The expectation when we went to the polls had been that Labour voters who had supported Brexit would vote Conservative to ensure Brexit took place. That did not happen then, although it did two years later in the 2019 general election. At that point, two years on, after Jeremy Corbyn and the Labour Party had consistently refused to back my deal, Labour Leave voters recognised that Labour would not deliver Brexit. That is when they put their desire to leave the EU above their allegiance to party, and gave Boris Johnson his landslide majority.

The result of the 2017 general election meant that both Remainers and Brexiteers felt they had the power to press for the outcome they wanted, and with the numbers in Parliament, they were both right. What united them in their approach was that they were both pursuing the outcome that was in line with the cause they had espoused during the 2016 referendum. For the hard-line Remainers, the fact that 48 per cent had voted to stay in the EU made them call for a second referendum. For the hard-line Brexiteers, the fact that 52 per cent had voted Leave meant not just that we should leave but that we should leave with the hardest possible deal.

Instead, they should both have accepted that the close vote – the country was virtually equally divided in the referendum – meant that they should have been considering what the best outcome would be that would meet the need to leave the EU while taking into account the concerns of those who wanted to stay. Of course, both sides dressed up their position as being what was right for the country, but the hardest-line Brexiteers never thought about the 48 per cent who had voted to remain, and the hardest-line Remainers didn't think about the 52 per cent who had voted to leave.

Neither did the hard-line Remainers think about the impact of their position on the state of our democracy. One of the spurs to the Brexit vote, I am sure, was the feeling for many that they were being left behind and that politicians were not listening to them. How much stronger would that feeling of alienation have been if Parliament had voted for a second referendum, had patted people on the head and said, 'That was the wrong result. You need to try again and get it right this time'? And what would have been the consequences for our democracy?

I should emphasise that there were plenty of my colleagues on both sides of the argument who just wanted to get Brexit done and move on. I was personally very grateful to those who didn't play tricky parliamentary games and just supported what the government was trying to achieve, even when it didn't accord with their ideal outcome. But unfortunately, through the long debates, the positions of the hard-liners on both sides became entrenched and more extreme. So some Brexiteers who had said previously that it would be acceptable to stay in the customs union or the single market came to see these as steps on the road to perdition. And some Remainers who had once pledged to respect the result of the referendum came to champion a second referendum as a means of overturning the original result and staying in the EU.

Needless to say, I thought – and still think – that both were wrong. Neither side was willing to cast aside the prejudices of the past and look to a new future. Hence they argued about how much of the past relationship to keep or throw away. The real question was about what the best future relationship should be. This was one of the most frustrating aspects of the whole debate. It still frustrates me when I see commentators describing my deal as a hard-line deal because it did not include membership of the EU's customs union and single market. That is to look at the future through the eyes of the past. What I wanted to do was to get a deal that retained the advantages of the single market and the customs union without the full obligations of membership. In other words a new relationship – and we were close to doing it. Rather than arguing over the entrails of EU membership, we should have been arguing over the shape of a new partnership on trade, security and much else. But the hard-liners on both sides couldn't get over their rigid adherence to the ideas of the past.

You might still be wondering why this constituted an abuse of power. Let me put it like this. Without a majority in Parliament, both sides could continue to pursue their own interests and stymie the process. Rather than ask whether the proposals would meet the majority of aspirations of both sides, albeit not 100 per cent of the views of either, and thereby give the country some hope of unity, they chose to go for broke and scupper the deal – because they could.

At this point, I should put my hands up and say mea culpa, because what lay behind these moves on both sides was the result of the 2017 general election, which gave power to those who wanted to disrupt the proceedings in the House of Commons. 'Serves you right,' I hear you say, and yes, I must take responsibility for calling the election and for mistakes that were made.

At the point in 2017 when I decided to call the general election, I wanted it to be a very quick, snap election, but the Fixed-term Parliaments Act didn't, in practice, allow for that. The Johnson government was absolutely right to abolish this Act in 2021–2. It had been necessary to bring it in back in 2010 to give a degree of certainty that the Conservative–Liberal Democrat coalition would continue in office and would not rapidly collapse. This was important for the sake of our economy. But the Act is not needed in normal circumstances. Indeed, it disrupted the traditional functioning of our constitution.

I accept that I made mistakes in the campaign. I should have done the TV debates. I had always thought that preparing for those debates took up too much campaign time and did not add much to the overall arguments. I now realise that they have come to be an accepted part of campaigns that may not change the view of many voters but do shape the media's approach to the party leaders.

I also allowed myself to be presented with a personal campaign plan that did not play to my strengths and was a style much more suited to my predecessor, David Cameron. I am not at my best delivering prepared and crafted texts to small groups in order to get media coverage. I am much happier walking the streets and knocking on doors – maybe that has shades of John Major's 'soapbox' election campaign in 1992.

The most obvious, and arguably the defining, mistake was the press conference after the revision of our social care policy where I said nothing had changed. Obviously something had changed. I knew what I meant – that the fundamental policy had not changed – but it was a fatal error on my part.

The upshot was that I lost my majority, and that made getting Brexit done even harder because it gave both sides the opportunity to exercise their power in order to achieve what became increasingly entrenched aims. This was the abuse of power. Neither of their approaches reflected the close nature of the referendum result.

I describe this as an abuse of power because it was a very good example of how power could have been used to achieve a result that would have brought the country together. This was what was needed after the referendum, but it required a degree of compromise from both sides. Instead, both sides, over time, changed their positions to take a more hard-line view. In doing so, they were using their power to promote their own views of the world rather than serving the overall national interest. This is not unknown in politics, but it is frustrating when it leads to greater division rather than greater unity.

A clear example of an unwillingness to prioritise the national interest came in the arguments about the border between Northern Ireland and the Republic of Ireland. What was missing from the calculation of both sides was an acknowledgement of the interests of the people of Northern Ireland. There was no real understanding of how to ensure continued peace in Northern Ireland and uphold the Good Friday Agreement of 1998. What was needed to meet these commitments was dismissed as not being a 'proper Brexit' and therefore unacceptable.

As an example, I remember one Brexiteer saying to me that there had to be a change in people's experience of crossing the border between Northern Ireland and the Republic so that they knew they really had left the EU. To this Brexiteer and many like him, not only peace in Northern Ireland but also the future of Northern Ireland as part of the UK took second place to the need to deliver a fixed view of Brexit.

Brexit

Of course in politics, as in life, there are times when it is right to stick rigidly to a particular position or view. One example is the way that Margaret Thatcher and her government held fast to their view of the importance of breaking the overbearing power of the trade unions which had done so much damage to the UK economy. Even so, in putting that into practice, Mrs Thatcher showed great caution and was not afraid to postpone action until the point where she was confident of winning through.

Brexit was not one of the times when absolute rigidity was required, beyond accepting that people had voted to leave and we should do so. At stake was the continued existence of the United Kingdom of Great Britain and Northern Ireland. That was far more important than delivering a particular model of Brexit. It was possible to maintain peace in Northern Ireland, ensure the future of the Union and deliver Brexit – but the deal that would deliver just that was rejected by those exercising their power in Parliament.

This included representatives of the Northern Irish electorate who took their seats at Westminster. After the 2017 election, these were almost solely from the Democratic Unionist Party, since Sinn Féin do not take their seats in the House. The one exception to this was Sylvia Hermon, who sat as an Independent and did a valiant job in trying to alert the House to the wider views of people in Northern Ireland. It was a pity that there were no SDLP or Alliance members in the House at this time. This would have helped to deliver a more balanced view from Northern Ireland because, after a deal had been thwarted by the Speaker, the DUP appeared to choose to follow the lead of the hardest-line Brexiteer among their members. From my experience, this was most notably Sammy Wilson, the MP for East Antrim, although others might wish to claim that mantle.

The insistence of the DUP that they voted as a bloc meant that their position could be swayed by a single MP, regardless of the view of the leadership. In this case, it meant that they rejected a deal which would have ensured not only a seamless border with the Republic of Ireland but also a seamless border with the rest of the UK.

At the heart of the argument was what came to be known as the backstop. This was an agreement that would have come into operation if the overall deal with the EU had failed to provide a seamless border with the Republic of Ireland. In essence, it meant Northern Ireland operating under EU rules for agricultural products and goods so that they could be traded across the border with the Republic – that is, across the border with the EU into the EU's single market – without checks. I considered this to be essential to meeting the aims of the Good Friday Agreement which had underpinned the return to peace in Northern Ireland.

The corollary of this, however, was that there would have to be checks for goods going from Great Britain to Northern Ireland. But remember, this was a contingency arrangement which would come into play only if we failed to agree a good overall trade deal with the EU; and I considered it highly unlikely that the backstop would be put in place and continue. As the then-Attorney General, Geoffrey Cox, said at the time, it would have put Northern Ireland in a very advantageous economic position. To deal with the issue of goods going from GB to NI, I was willing to commit that if this backstop were to come into force, then Great Britain would operate to the same rules in key areas, thus allowing seamless borders all round for Northern Ireland.

This reflected my fundamental view that in the interests of the Union, there could not be a border down the Irish Sea. Indeed, I said that a deal which created such a border was one to which no British Prime Minister could agree. Little did I know at the time that the Prime Minister who succeeded me – Boris Johnson – would do just that and declare it a great victory.

Indeed, having argued against the backstop, when he came to be Prime Minister Boris effectively accepted it as part of the deal he signed with the EU. More than that, in my deal it was a backstop to act as a contingency, whereas in his, it was the frontstop and came into operation when we left the EU. He did not have to do this, and the fact that he did strongly suggests to me that he put his personal interest in getting a deal before the national interest in getting a deal that worked for the whole of the UK.

The deal I had negotiated was welcomed by many businesses in Northern Ireland which considered it gave them a great economic opportunity – seamless access to both the EU and GB markets. But the DUP were not willing to embrace this opportunity. They didn't want to risk the possibility of the backstop. I committed to introducing legislation to ensure no border checks between GB and NI, but they complained that this would only be domestic legislation, whereas the Withdrawal Agreement was an international treaty. They also used to say that, no matter what I promised to do, they couldn't trust whoever might succeed me. How true those words were.

As a result, they ended up with a deal which effectively

made the backstop operational from 1 January 2020 – in the form of the Northern Ireland Protocol.

When the EU had first proposed this solution, I rejected it. The deal that was finally agreed by Boris Johnson meant he had caved in and accepted the EU's preferred position, effectively placing a border down the Irish Sea between Great Britain and Northern Ireland. This was not the result of EU intransigence. It was the deal the UK government chose to sign. The DUP rejected this deal as well, but they had already misplayed their hand. They could have supported a result that would have been of maximum benefit to Northern Ireland rather than one that has caused problems for people in Northern Ireland and for British businesses.

Following Rishi Sunak's appointment as Prime Minister, he set about renegotiating the Northern Ireland Protocol and delivered the Windsor Framework. This introduced a form of dual recognition which enables goods travelling from GB to NI which are destined only for NI to be free of 'third country processes'. Instead, there are new data-sharing arrangements based on ordinary commercial information with physical checks used only when there is a specific risk or intelligence basis for them, such as to prevent smuggling or other forms of criminality.

The Framework also introduces the concept of the 'Stormont brake'. This would be operated when the Northern Ireland Assembly objects to changes to EU laws that apply in Northern Ireland. (Of course, to be effective, the Assembly – Stormont – needs to be in place and functioning, which at the time of writing it was not, due to the unwillingness of the DUP to go back into government after the election which gave Sinn Féin the position of First Minister.) The UK would then notify the EU, at which point the rule changes would not apply. If the EU and UK then agreed that the changes should apply to Northern Ireland, that would, in general, need cross-community consent. There is arbitration available in the event that the EU and the UK disagreed on the application of the brake. This is similar to what was effectively a Westminster brake, which formed part of my deal. As was the case then, those who object complain that there would be consequences if the changes were not applied. Of course there would be, and these could include a reimposition of certain checks at the border between GB and NI. It would be up to Stormont and the UK to decide whether to tolerate those consequences or assent to the changes in EU law. In other words, they would have to decide whether the benefits of rejecting the changes would outweigh the disadvantages of increased border friction.

Power is a privilege. It must be exercised judiciously for the greater good, not thoughtlessly to deliver personal preferences. Regrettably, in the whole debate about Northern Ireland and Brexit, those involved often failed to consider what was in the best interests of the people of Northern Ireland. When I was negotiating with the EU, I had a number of meetings with businesses and others in Northern Ireland who were in no doubt about the benefits of freedom across both their borders – with the Republic of Ireland and with GB. But too many politicians were not willing to sacrifice their personal views of what Brexit meant and put the people first.

So far, I have not expanded on the actions of the Labour Party in this parliamentary battle. Her Majesty's Official Opposition had the power, because of the numbers in the Commons, to deliver Brexit by supporting the government's position or even by abstaining on key votes. They chose to abuse their power by putting party politics first and the interests of the country second. At every stage, they chose to frustrate Brexit and, as a result, they paid the price at the ballot box. There were some Labour MPs who spoke up to support Brexit, but they too paid the price at the election.

One of the most vocal was Caroline Flint, who consistently and bravely challenged her front bench and at times voted with the government. But arguing that the result of the referendum should be respected didn't prevent her from being caught up in the move by Leave-supporting Labour voters to insist on Brexit through the ballot box, and she was carried away by the tide that swept out so many Labour MPs. There were others who made their views known, such as John Mann and Ian Austin, and some who spoke privately about their belief that this was the deal that should be accepted.

There was an opportunity for Labour to work with the government and show the country that politicians could put aside their party-political labels for the greater good. For decades, Jeremy Corbyn had argued against EU imperialism, and Labour had promised in the 2017 general election to respect the outcome of the referendum. But in the end, Labour were caught between Jeremy Corbyn, who couldn't bear to do a deal with the Conservatives, and Keir Starmer, who was playing to those in the Labour Party who wanted a second referendum. I leave it to the reader to decide whether the latter took that stance purely through conviction or with an eye on his own leadership ambitions. When push came to shove, I was willing to compromise in order to deliver Brexit. Jeremy Corbyn and the Labour Party were not.

Once again, the Labour Party had the power to make the difference. If they had been willing to compromise, Parliament could have agreed the deal. Instead, it appears they abused their power by putting their internal party agendas first and the country second. As a result, they ended up with a deal that gave them less of what they wanted and a general election that decimated their traditional seats. High on the power they could wield in a hung Parliament, they ended up with a Conservative majority in the Commons of eighty seats. Again, some might say 'serves them right', but the real loser in all this was the UK.

The public should be able to expect their elected representatives to respect their democratic decisions and to do so in a way that works for as many people across the country as possible – not just for the privileged few or for the true believers, but for the many. These abuses of power simply let the public down.

The final player in all this, of course, was the European Union. They had already had an opportunity to work with the UK to ensure it was able to stay in the Union. Their intransigence in negotiations with David Cameron and their unwillingness to give him more on the free movement of people meant that the revised relationship with the EU which he put to the British people in the referendum did not resolve voters' main concern about membership. This made losing the referendum more likely.

As regards my own negotiations, I know that many of the British public and indeed a good number in my own party will say the problem was not MPs but was entirely the European Union. Undoubtedly, decisions taken by the EU made the process more difficult, but negotiations take two sides and it would be wrong to place the blame all on one side or the other. A deal was negotiated, but Parliament rejected it. Indeed, one of the reasons the EU did not move further towards the UK's requests on the backstop was precisely because they could see the problems in Parliament and didn't want to give anything more away when they didn't think I could get a deal through. This was clear from the way I was repeatedly questioned by them on what was happening and on the numbers in Parliament.

It was a vicious circle. The EU wouldn't give me anything more in negotiations because they thought I couldn't get a deal through the Commons, and I couldn't get a deal through the House of Commons because they wouldn't give me anything more. In the end, because of their recalcitrance and the parliamentary arithmetic, the EU were able to impose the terms they had always wanted. Own goal, UK!

Where the EU did abuse their power unhelpfully was in the way they structured the negotiations. I think some EU leaders would themselves accept that insisting on negotiating the Withdrawal Agreement first and the future partnership second was a mistake, because it made getting the overall deal more difficult. There were those in Parliament who didn't want to agree the withdrawal arrangement without knowing what the end deal would be. Thus from the very beginning, the EU had skewed the negotiations against getting an agreement through Parliament. They had the power to do this, but it was not in the overall interests of getting a good deal for both sides, nor did it help to preserve a fruitful relationship between the UK and the EU.

In the event, we were able to get the outline of a future relationship in place in the political declaration alongside the Withdrawal Agreement. Indeed, there was more in the political declaration than many in the EU had initially wanted to give us. It was not enough for those who wanted the whole package and crucially, it gave some the opportunity to reject the deal, at least partly on the basis that the future wasn't tied down.

The Brexit debate and the final deal did not work for everyone. I still consider that the deal I and my government negotiated was a better deal for the whole country than the one that Boris signed, and indeed would have been preferable to the deal under the Windsor Framework. But, against what I considered to be the best interests of the country, the abuses of power I have identified led to people scuppering that deal.

4

Social Media

While Brexit marked a significant change in the UK's relationship with the EU, it is not the only change that has markedly affected our politics in recent decades. One of the biggest changes has been the increasing role of social media over the last twenty years or so. We all enjoy the benefits of social media and it really came into its own during the Covid pandemic. It can also be abused, with sometimes devastating effects.

Social media is a key part, and for some an essential part, of everyday life. People are in constant communication with each other. Politicians are no different. Just as we use social media in our personal lives, so we use it in our work too. Added to which, politicians often feel the need to be constantly showing themselves and justifying themselves on social media.

To my mind, this can be taken to unnecessary lengths. I don't know of anyone who actively wants to know what an MP had for breakfast or what sort of cup they drink their coffee from. Neither do I think that the constant posting of photos of where politicians are does much to enhance the life of the country.

Posts like this don't make for better government decisions; indeed, too much focus on social media can have the opposite effect. It can give the impression of activity without delivery. It may heighten the perception of being in touch, but doesn't always enable politicians to really understand what is driving the views of the public. Throughout my political career, I have believed that you don't understand what is important to people through opinion polls or, latterly, through tweets. Focus groups can provide a better understanding of people's views, but to find out what really matters to people, go and knock on their doors and speak to them.

At its most basic, social media is just another way of communicating with people. More instant and more flexible than other means of communication, it is an extra platform on which to put out views or let electors know what their MP is doing on key issues. In that sense, it can be a benefit. There are other aspects of the use of social media, however, that give rise to greater concern in relation to our politics and our democracy. Social media gives both the users and the corporate providers of the platforms power that can be abused in their own interests.

First, the users. While I have no doubt that social media platforms are used nowadays as a valuable source of news, they can also be seen to validate extreme views. I have always described it like this: social media enables the man who used to sit on the end of the bar in his local pub, muttering into his beer and being generally ignored, to mutter his views to the world. Often, his views were ignored because they were extreme or did not have any basis in reality. Now, through social media, all the other people muttering at the end of bars and being ignored respond to him. Suddenly, it looks like his view is the world's view. This gives him and the others who agree with him the confidence to produce more extreme views, in some cases hatred, and gradually others who don't really agree with them tailor their views because otherwise it looks like they are out of touch. So the world's view shifts. What started as one person's unacceptable view can become the accepted norm.

Social media is indeed a powerful tool – but some might say it is a weapon. Indeed, hostile states use it as a weapon to disseminate propaganda, spread lies, misinform the public and disrupt social and political life in the countries they are attacking.

The use or misuse of social media can also create societal problems. Through this extended medium, the unkind playground quip, which while hurtful could be dismissed, can become a group 'hate' that eats away at the mental health of the victim. No one can persuade me that social media has not contributed to increasing mental health problems for young people.

So social media can be a power for good, but when that power is abused, it can become downright dangerous. We see this in the use of social media to bully, harass and threaten. All too often, the victims are female, though anyone can be the victim. It has an impact on people up and down the country, of all ages and all backgrounds. It leaves behind a trail of frightened individuals whose lives have all too often been destroyed. But it goes beyond the impact on individuals.

We should all be worried about the chilling effect it can have on our democratic politics. There are those who use social media to harass, bully and sometimes threaten politicians. Anonymity can encourage the feeling that it doesn't matter what you say because no one knows who you are. Social media gives people the power and they abuse it. It can shut down proper and necessary debate. It can lead to fewer women being willing to enter the political fray. And it has led to a coarser level of discourse and a greater aggression in debate.

A study by the Inter-Parliamentary Union on violence against women MPs back in 2016* showed that 27.3 per cent of those surveyed said that images or highly disrespectful comments with sexual connotations about them had been shared by traditional media. But that rose to 41.8 per cent when they were asked about extremely humiliating or sexually charged images disseminated through social media.

For those who use social media in this way, there is no room for reasonable debate, no views but their own are valid, no one else is ever right. This has increased the move towards absolutism in our politics in the sense of all-or-nothing thinking. I am sorry to say that the Brexit debate after the referendum and during the negotiations to leave was a victim of this approach. In the social media world, you had to be a strong advocate of one side or the other. There was little room for those who wanted to deliver a deal with something for both sides.

Another area is the 'woke' agenda and culture wars. I suspect that many people who decry the idea of being woke couldn't actually define it. Indeed, can those who claim to be woke? The *Oxford English Dictionary* definition is: 'Originally: well-informed, up-to-date. Now chiefly: alert to racial or social discrimination and injustice.' On that basis,

---

* Inter-Parliamentary Union, *Sexism, harassment and violence against women parliamentarians*, October 2016.

who would not want to be woke? Sadly, the word has been interpreted as indicating a particular view on other issues, such as sexual orientation, and indeed for some is taken to be a sign of political affiliation. Now it is being used as a war cry by left and right in politics, with social media being a key tool with which to enter and prolong this battle.

Some using social media are using the power it gives them not to enhance our political life but, through their threats and abuse, to severely damage our politics. They have the power. They do it because they can. The full consequences have yet to be seen, but it has already had an impact and our democracy is the poorer for it.

The second theme is the role of the providers. Throughout my time in government, I dealt with the social media companies, particularly when I was Home Secretary. The key issues were the exploitation of their platforms by child abusers and paedophiles and by extremists and terrorists. These people use the platforms because they can. But the real problem comes when the companies providing the platforms do so little to stop the activities of these individuals, even if they don't go as far as promoting them.

There are a number of reasons for their inactivity, but they all come down to commercial interests. Each provider will be concerned that if they act to remove material or stop material reaching their sites, their customers will go elsewhere. This is not just about users who may be using the platform for inappropriate material; there is also a concern that, as the whole point of the internet and of social media is their freedom, any attempt to clamp down will lead to the loss of users. Finally there is the concern about getting sued. This was often raised in conversations I had with the service providers, who would complain that any action to deal with extremist material could lead to legal action against them. In all of these cases, the companies were putting their commercial interests before those of the public – in other words, they were abusing their power.

To be fair to the industry, there has been some success in getting the companies to act on child-abuse images, but less success in relation to extremism and terrorism. In 1996, the industry set up a worldwide organisation called the Internet Watch Foundation, which established a hotline for the public and IT professionals to report potentially criminal online content falling within their remit. This was to cover images and videos of child sexual abuse. The Foundation was the 'notice and take down' body for this sort of content. Under the E-Commerce Regulations (liability of intermediary service providers), once notified, the host or internet service provider (ISP) was duty-bound to quickly remove or disable access to the relevant material.

The E-Commerce Regulations no longer apply to the UK as the UK has left the EU and the wider European Economic Area, and the transition period is over. However, the government maintained a 'notice and take down' regime in relation to illegal content, recognising the importance of upholding the liability protections. The government is also introducing the Online Safety Bill, which addresses the responsibilities of providers in relation to material on their platforms.

Despite the excellent work of the Internet Watch Foundation, it was felt that more needed to be done on the question of child-abuse images and content. So in November 2013, David Cameron hosted an internet safety summit and warned that action had to be taken to stop illegal content or the government would legislate.

This was followed by the #WePROTECT Children Online summit in London in December 2014. #WePROTECT was a global alliance of ninety-eight governments, fifty-three companies and sixty-one civil organisations which brought experts together to protect children from sexual exploitation and abuse online. In 2016, it merged with the Global Alliance Against Child Sexual Abuse Online.

At the 2014 summit, the government announced a series of measures and technical innovations designed to tackle those who were using the internet to view and share illegal images. These measures included a new law to make it illegal for an adult to send a sexual communication to a child and the establishment of a joint team formed by the National Crime Agency and GCHQ (Government Communications Headquarters, whose responsibilities include cyber security), which would use all the techniques and expertise they employ to track down terrorists to track down paedophiles on the 'dark net'. Also critical was the creation of a single secure database of indecent images of children – the Child Abuse Image Database or CAID – which would help law enforcement to improve and speed up their investigations.

This work on child sexual exploitation and abuse continued. CAID was launched in December 2014 and there were changes to the law the following year. In January 2017, the Home Office established the Centre of Expertise on Child Sexual Abuse, and in December 2020, the government published its interim code of practice on online child sexual exploitation and abuse.

Despite all this activity, the problem has not been solved, and children continue to be exploited and images shared on the internet with devastating consequences.

Social Media

While the Internet Watch Foundation worked well and has been regarded as a model for action in other areas, it has proved harder to get agreement on action on issues like extremism. People generally recognise what a child sexual abuse image is and how abhorrent the activity is that has led to that image. It is therefore easier to reach agreement on action. The issue of extremism is open to more debate, because what one person may describe as extremism another may argue is free speech.

Moreover, the link between extremist material and terrorist activity is not always accepted. At some point, a terrorist has almost certainly been exposed to material – written, visual or oral – that is extremist and that has led them down the path to terrorist activity, but not everyone who views extremist material then goes on to commit an act of terrorism.

Although action on extremist material developed later than that on child abuse, there have been a number of efforts to encourage the internet companies to recognise their wider social responsibilities in this area. In December 2015, the EU Internet Forum was launched, bringing technology companies together with Europol and EU governments. This was in the aftermath of the appalling terrorist attacks in Paris in November 2015 which left 130 dead, including 90 people who died in the attack at the Bataclan theatre. The aim of the work was to counter terrorist content and hate speech online. The move was a welcome one, but progress was slow.

The need for action was reinforced by further terrorist attacks. The 2017 G7 meeting, which was hosted by Prime Minister Paolo Gentiloni of Italy in Taormina in Sicily, came just four days after the horrific terrorist attack in the Manchester Arena. Twenty-two people died and 1,017 were injured. The attacker also died. This was a particularly callous attack, targeting as it did young people and children out to enjoy themselves at an Ariana Grande concert.

Shortly after the attack, I visited some of the survivors in hospital, and also met members of the emergency services called to the scene and the police team conducting the criminal investigation. The stories told by those who had been there were horrific. The impact of having not only to deal with their injuries, but also to come to terms with what they had seen, and in most cases with the loss of loved ones and friends, was incredibly traumatic.

Reaching international agreement is never easy. It requires dedicated hard work, but as I sat around that summit table as Prime Minister in 2017, I realised that the fact that the terrorist had targeted children and young people had had a powerful impact on the leaders of the G7. You could not fail to be moved by the stories from the survivors and from those who came forward to help the victims.

I was clear that we needed to put out a strong statement against the terrorists and argued for just that. For most of us sitting around the G7 table, there was no doubt that that was important, nor was there any question that we needed to support and encourage the industry to do more. A separate statement on the Manchester attack was agreed,* and included within it was a passage about social media:

> We encourage industry to act urgently in developing and sharing new technology and tools to improve the

---

* 'G7 Taormina Statement on the Fight Against Terrorism and Violent Extremism', 26 May 2017.

automatic detection of content promoting incitement to violence, and we commit to supporting industry efforts in this vein including the proposed industry-led forum for combating online extremism.

The next month, June 2017, after the general election, I visited President Macron in Paris and we agreed a joint British–French action plan for preventing the internet from being used as a safe space for terrorists and criminals. There were four priority points:

1. to improve methods to remove illegal content from the internet
2. to support the efforts of civil society organisations to promote alternative and counter-narratives
3. to work together to ensure access to each other's data for investigative purposes
4. to improve access to digital evidence across borders

That was also the month when the Global Internet Forum to Counter Terrorism, led by Facebook, YouTube, Twitter and Microsoft, was established, with UK government support. The Forum had been created in the aftermath of the Westminster terror attack, which had taken place in London in March of that year. In this attack, a terrorist drove a van into pedestrians on Westminster Bridge, killing four and injuring fifty, before running through the gates of Parliament and stabbing and killing a police officer on duty, PC Keith Palmer. The terrorist was himself then shot dead by an armed police officer.

Since it was set up, the Forum has been expanded to include over a dozen platforms committed to countering the spread of terrorist and violent extremist content online.

It created a Global Research Network and has also over-seen the expansion of sharing digital fingerprints, including the development of a Content Incident Protocol. This has helped to disrupt the distribution of terrorist content. It has also encouraged investment in research to understand the spread of this material.

This was all well and good, but I wanted to ensure we held the companies' feet to the fire to ensure they meant what they said about working with governments to deal with terrorist content online. That meant raising the pro-file of the issue and their commitment to tackling it more widely on the international scene.

September is always the month for the UN General Assembly meeting. This gives countries an opportunity not only to make a major speech to the Assembly, but also to arrange and to attend separate meetings bringing interested parties together on key issues. I decided that this was a great opportunity to raise the profile of the issue of extremist and terrorist content online.

President Macron and Prime Minister Gentiloni agreed to co-host an event with me, and Kent Walker from Google agreed to represent the Global Forum. This was the first time that world leaders and the tech industry had come together to speak on this issue at the United Nations. The work done by the industry was acknowledged, but we had to keep pressing and encourage them to reduce the time it took to remove terrorist content online, and also to increase efforts to stop it being uploaded in the first place.

I have set all of this out to show the extent of efforts made by governments – often led by the UK – to per-suade the internet companies to act. And this list is not comprehensive.

In 2019, the world saw yet another awful reminder of the need to keep pressing. On 15 March that year, Brenton Tarrant killed fifty-one people at two mosques in Christchurch, New Zealand. He didn't just carry out the attacks. He live-streamed them to Facebook. Copies could still be found on YouTube as long as eight hours after the streaming was first posted, and Facebook had to remove 1.5 million copies. This was another stark reminder of the need to do much more to stop material going online in the first place, and if it was uploaded, to remove it much more quickly.

After the attack, the New Zealand Prime Minister, Jacinda Ardern, and President Macron convened another group of government leaders and representatives of technology companies at an Online Extremist Summit in Paris. The UK was a founding supporter of the Christchurch Call to Action to Eliminate Terrorist and Violent Extremist Content Online which was announced at the summit.

The Call to Action was signed by Amazon, Facebook, Google, Microsoft and Twitter, which published nine steps that they planned to take to deal with this issue. The steps included updating their terms of use, establishing methods for user reporting, enhancing technology, identifying checks on livestreaming, publishing data on the removal of content, sharing technological developments, creating a crisis protocol, educating the public about violent content online and working collaboratively to tackle the root causes of hate and extremism online.

This was a major change in approach by the companies. Back in 2013, Facebook had refused to remove a clip of someone being beheaded, reportedly saying people had a right to depict the 'world in which we live'. After a backlash, they did remove the video, saying they were evaluating their policy and their approach to that type of content.

Initially, seventeen countries signed up to the Christchurch Call and a further thirty-one signed later that year. It was all the more disappointing, therefore, that social media played a role in the attack where a teacher was beheaded in France in October 2020.

The frustration of all of this is that these are companies that are at the forefront of technology. If anyone can develop technological solutions and find ways to identify and remove content quickly, surely they can. Indeed, in June 2018, on the issue of child abuse and the internet, Will Kerr, Head of Vulnerabilities at the National Crime Agency, said:

> We know that there are thousands of children being unnecessarily exploited and abused in the United Kingdom while actually industry has the technological ability now to stop that at source . . . There is the technological means now to pre-screen images before they are put on to hosting platforms, so why do we have, when we can technologically stop it, indecent images of children . . . on any of these platforms at all that are then shared hundreds if not thousands of times, [so] that children are revictimised again and again . . .*

That attitudes were changing was clear from evidence given to the House of Commons Home Affairs Select Committee in January 2021.† This was days after the

---

* Reported in the *Guardian*, 21 June 2018.
† House of Commons Home Affairs Select Committee Oral Evidence, Online Harms, 20 January 2021, HC 342.

storming of the Capitol in Washington, DC. Nick Pickles from Twitter said, 'I think it is impossible for anyone who works in the technology sector to look at those events and not ask "Did we play a part in this?" I think the answer has to be yes. The link between offline harm and online content is demonstrably real. Four years ago you may have heard a different answer to that question.'

At the #WePROTECT summit in 2014, which I attended as Home Secretary, I said that giving law enforcement agencies access to communications data was vital in disrupting networks of paedophiles. It is also vital in identifying terrorists and preventing terrorist attacks. Over the years, we have seen the job of the intelligence agencies and law enforcement in identifying and dealing with actual or potential terrorists made more difficult by the use of strong encryption. Why did the companies do it? Because they could. But also, of course, because it gave them a commercial advantage and customers like it.

In developing this additional feature for customers, the companies gave, and in some cases continue to give, little thought to the impact on society of their actions. They have the power. They use it to hamper governments in their job of keeping people safe. Many would say that was an abuse of power.

On the other hand, there are those who promote the benefit of the freedoms offered by social media and the importance of free speech, and object to government attempts to regulate social media in any way. So they, in turn, would say government action was an abuse of power.

I have long thought that we need to find a way to cut through the argument from the companies that they are not publishers, so should not be subject to rules regarding publications, but are simply platforms. The answer is they are neither. We need to find a third category and establish laws for that third category. The UK government has been considering the right approach to these problems for some time. My colleague Jeremy Wright in particular focused on this when he was Secretary of State for Digital, Culture, Media and Sport during my premiership. This work was carried forward under my successors in the shape of the Online Safety Bill, which is a valiant effort to find a way through this minefield.

The Bill follows an *Online Harms* white paper which was published by my government in April 2019 and set out our proposed approach for tackling harmful content. This content could be something that harmed an individual or acted as a threat to our way of life in the UK. The white paper explained:

> Online services can be used to spread terrorist propaganda and child abuse content, they can be a tool for abuse and bullying, and they can be used to undermine civil discourse. Despite the many benefits of the internet, more than one in four adult users in the UK have experienced some form of harm related either to content or interactions online . . .
>
> The most appalling and horrifying illegal content and activity remains prevalent on an unacceptable scale. Existing efforts to tackle this activity have not delivered the necessary improvements, creating an urgent need for government to intervene to drive online services to step up their response.

The white paper proposed a single regulatory framework to tackle the range of harms. The key element was to be a duty of care imposed on the internet companies, including social media platforms. Compliance with the requirements would be overseen and enforced by an independent regulator.

The proposals were subject to a consultation, a full response to which was published in December 2020. This confirmed that there would be a duty of care introduced and that the regulator would be Ofcom. The Bill was included in the Queen's Speech in May 2021. This meant it would be part of the government's legislative programme, and the draft Bill was published that month. The Bill had its second reading in the House of Commons on 19 April 2022, and at the time of writing it is still being considered in the House of Lords.

The duty of care would be imposed on providers of online content-sharing platforms and search services. Originally, the intention had been that providers would need to act on content that was lawful but still harmful, but following concerns expressed in Parliament about this aspect, the government chose to remove the provision from the Bill. In enforcing compliance, Ofcom would be able to fine companies. It would also be able to block access to sites. During debate in the Commons, the government agreed to introduce an amendment to make senior managers criminally liable for breaches of the Bill's child safety duties. This would apply to those who have consented to or connived in ignoring enforceable requirements, risking serious harm to children.

In addition, companies would be required to report child sexual exploitation and abuse content identified on their services. This provision is included to ensure that they provide law enforcement with the high-quality information they need to safeguard victims and investigate offenders.

The debate on this issue is not easy, as the length of time it has taken to get the Bill this far shows. Some continue to argue that the framework in the Bill threatens freedom of expression and privacy. Concerns have also been raised that the Bill doesn't go far enough, because it is only the largest and most popular platforms that would be required to act on content that was legal but harmful to adults. Others worry about the definition of harm, being concerned that it is too narrow because it may fail to address issues such as non-state intervention in elections, racist abuse and content that can contribute to self-harm and negative body image.

The argument about the impact on freedom is perhaps not surprising. The internet was set up with freedom at its heart. Free speech is one of our core values and underpins our democracy. Curtailing that freedom requires fine judgements. We must not follow the path of dictatorship in trying to stop access to the internet; on the other hand, we do not want to see it being used freely by those who would do us harm or wish to undermine our democracy.

As Alistair Cooke, the British-American writer who broadcast his weekly *Letter from America* for fifty-eight years, said, 'Liberty is the luxury of self-discipline.' At least some of the problems with social media would be mitigated, if not resolved, if more people using it exercised that self-discipline, and if the companies providing the platforms accepted more social responsibility. Users are abusing their power by showing a total disregard for the impact of their comments on individuals and on society more generally. And the companies providing the platforms are abusing their power by putting their commercial interests first and the interests of the public second. Companies need to recognise that their position of power should be used to provide service. In other words, we need individuals and companies to think of the impact of their actions, and not simply to act because they can.

Part Two

Social Injustice

I was first prompted to think about the issue of abuse of power by various cases I dealt with in government which showed public sector bodies acting to defend themselves, to cover up the truth, in ways which caused real harm or suffering to groups of citizens. These were real-life examples of the powerful acting to deny the powerless their voices and, critically, to deny them justice. They were and remain examples of social injustice, but social injustice caused by bodies whose driving force should be social justice.

In this part of the book I recount those cases, describing not just what I learnt from my discussions with those involved, but also the often devastating findings of public inquiries set up to uncover the truth. It should not take lengthy inquiries costing millions of taxpayers' pounds to get to the truth. If the public bodies concerned had been more willing to accept their mistakes and less keen on protecting themselves, then not only would the victims and survivors have benefited, but so too would the public overall.

There is a moral argument for ensuring that when a public disaster occurs, every effort is made to get to the truth and provide justice for the victims and their families, but it also makes sense for the taxpayer. Finding out at an early stage what happened and who or what was at fault makes it easier to rectify any issues that need to be addressed, rendering it less likely that others will suffer in the same way. But it also costs the state – in other words, the taxpayer – less in the long run.

You would think this would be obvious, but in the examples that follow, it was not obvious to the public bodies responsible, which chose instead to hunker down in defence regardless of the impact on those affected. The powerful were using their power to deny justice to the powerless – clear examples of the abuse of power.

5

Hillsborough

When considering the tragedy at Sheffield's Hillsborough Stadium, I feel I should make a confession right up front. Back in 1989 when I heard about what had happened at that fateful football match, I too believed the propaganda being put out by the media, police and politicians that it was the fault of the Liverpool fans. That was what we were all led to believe back then. It fitted the general view about hooliganism in football, and because of that it was an easy position for those looking on from afar to take.

When I became Home Secretary in May 2010, however, I had to make a decision on the continuation of the Hillsborough Independent Panel. This had been set up following representations made to the then-Home Secretary, Alan Johnson, in July 2009 by the Hillsborough Family Support Group and a group of Merseyside MPs. With increasing public awareness that there were issues surrounding the Hillsborough disaster and questions about the various inquiries and investigations that had followed, they presented a case for disclosure. The Home Secretary met the Hillsborough Family Support Group, and in January 2010 the Independent Panel was set up, chaired by the Anglican Bishop of Liverpool, James Jones.

It was only at the point where I had to decide whether the Panel's work should continue that I looked more carefully at the events of 15 April 1989 and heard the testimony of those who had been fighting for justice for over twenty years. Ninety-five people died that day at Hillsborough following a crush on one of the terraces. Tony Bland died four years later of injuries sustained at Hillsborough. Then in July 2021, Andrew Devine, a further victim who had suffered brain damage that day, died – bringing the total number of deaths as a result of Hillsborough to ninety-seven. This is a stark reminder that the damage of Hillsborough lives on and is felt by families to this day.

What shone through to me all those years later was the burning sense of injustice felt by the families who had held fast to the memories of those who died and had kept the flame of hope alive for so long. My first meeting with representatives of the Hillsborough families – Margaret Aspinall and Trevor and Jenni Hicks, together with Charles Falconer, the former Lord Chancellor – was affecting. Margaret had lost her son James at Hillsborough, and Trevor and Jenni's daughters Sarah and Vicki had also died there. There was a desperate desire to clear the names of their loved ones from the slur which had been laid on them by the police, and to ensure that the country learnt the truth of the events of that tragic day.

I was also struck by the case put to me by Bishop James Jones, whose care and compassion shone through. As the Bishop of Liverpool at the time he chaired the Panel, he understood the level of hurt felt by the families and how strongly felt the issue was across Liverpool. He also understood their deep suspicion of the authorities, who had so often let them down. So many politicians had failed to deliver for the families, yet those families had kept the fight for justice alive – and of course, delivery was in the hands of the politicians.

I was clear after those meetings that the Panel should be allowed to continue its work. But it was not just for me to mandate that. While the Home Office was the lead department, there were three other departments sharing the cost – Justice, Health, and Culture, Media and Sport. This was because these departments or their predecessors had been responsible for elements of what happened that day and the response to it. The Home Office covered the police, the Department of Health covered the ambulance service, which had attended the tragedy, the Department for Culture, Media and Sport was now responsible for sports events and sports grounds, and the Ministry of Justice's interest lay in the coronial process – the inquests which had proved to be so problematic for the families.

Not all the other senior ministers agreed with me about the need to continue with the Panel's work. Indeed, one of them – who shall remain nameless – was reputed to have hidden in a cupboard rather than meet the families. Another thought it was all so long ago that it was best to let sleeping dogs lie. But I was in no doubt about what needed to be done if there was to be any hope of justice for the victims. So I persevered and the work went ahead.

The Panel consulted with the families and worked to pull together all the documentation relating to the events of that fateful day, and in doing so also consulted with around eighty different organisations. These ranged from government departments such as the Cabinet Office and Attorney General's Office through the South Yorkshire and West Midlands police forces to other emergency services and local authorities. This may sound relatively straight-forward. In fact, it was anything but. Not everyone wanted to disclose everything they had and, even if they were willing to do so, finding all related documents was sometimes difficult.

For example, there were many South Yorkshire police officers' notebooks that were held not by that police force but by the officers themselves – many of whom were no longer working in the force. Moreover, even government departments sometimes found that despite their best efforts, documents existed which hadn't been identified in initial searches because, for example, they had been filed under a non-related title. When such documents finally came to light, I can understand that the families might have been concerned that this was part of a conspiracy of silence. In fact, in the cases I was aware of, it was administrative error.

Having brought the documents together, the Panel's key task was to see what their understanding of the events of 15 April 1989 was and the extent to which it differed from the 'public narrative' of the day. This was the critical part of their work – and they delivered. They did indeed find something different from the then-still accepted under-standing of the events of the day. In fact, their findings were the polar opposite of the accepted understanding. They found that the fans were not the cause of the disaster.*

The report of the Panel in itself justified my decision to let their work continue. The importance of that decision was further underlined by the verdict in the second coroner's inquests. The first inquests had delivered a verdict

---

* *Hillsborough: The Report of the Hillsborough Independent Panel*, September 2012, HC 581.

of accidental death. Following the Panel's report and an application by the Attorney General, Dominic Grieve, the High Court quashed the verdicts in the original inquests and ordered fresh inquests to take place. The verdict of the jury hearing all these cases together was very different. They found that the Liverpool fans had been unlawfully killed due to grossly negligent failures by the police and the ambulance service to fulfil their duty of care.

Given that the events of 1989 occurred under a Conservative government, as did the first inquiry into the events that day – which led to the Taylor report* and also the first coroner's inquests – it was not an obvious call for a new Conservative government to take a decision which questioned the actions of previous Conservative ministers. Nevertheless, getting to the truth was paramount and, as the Panel's report and the new inquests showed, the truth had been deliberately hidden, covered up for years.

The verdict of the second coroner's jury was devastating news. That the victims had been unlawfully killed was what the families had felt all along. It completely changed the public perception of the events of that day, and it revealed an absolutely shocking tale of deliberate lies, misinformation and cover-up.

It was entirely right for the Prime Minister, David Cameron, to stand up in the House of Commons and give a fulsome apology to the families of the victims.

There were various attempts over the years to bring to justice people involved in what happened at Hillsborough,

---

* On 17 April 1989, the Home Secretary, the Rt Hon Douglas Hurd MP, appointed Lord Justice Taylor to look into what had happened at Hillsborough and to make recommendations on crowd control and safety at sports grounds.

culminating in a final court case which was dismissed in 2021. Some felt that the handling and failure of that case reflected the injustice that had been felt by the families over the years since the event. The only successful case up to this point had been a health and safety charge. The last case had been brought against two police officers and a solicitor for South Yorkshire Police. The charge was perversion of the course of justice due to the alteration of evidence to the Taylor inquiry. The case was dismissed because the inquiry was not part of the justice system but was carrying out an administrative function for the Home Office. Therefore, although it was acknowledged that the evidence had been altered, it did not count as perversion of the course of justice. This means that, tragically for the families, it is still the case that no one has been successfully prosecuted for their role in what the coroner's jury had identified as unlawful killings.

But the findings of the Panel and of the second inquests are clear. No blame rests with the Liverpool fans. Instead, the terrible loss of life and the ordeal faced by the Liverpool fans were the result of gross negligence by the very organs of the state – the police and the ambulance service – which were expected to protect people and minister to them in their hour of need.

At this point, it may be helpful to recap what happened on 15 April 1989. It was a sunny day, and an important game in the English football season – an FA Cup semi-final between Liverpool and Nottingham Forest – was to be held at the neutral ground of the Hillsborough Stadium in Sheffield, in South Yorkshire. Fans of both clubs travelled to the stadium, which had a mixture of areas of seating and standing terraces. As was common practice at the time, the fans would be separated into different parts of the ground. No doubt they were excited, pleased to have tickets for the match, expecting a good game and eager to cheer on their teams.

As the match started, however, it soon became evident that there was a problem at the Leppings Lane end, where pens in the stand had been allocated to the Liverpool fans. The pens were separated by fences, and there was also a fence between the pens and the pitch. There were small gates at the front of each pen, but these were locked.

The terrace had been overcrowded even before the match started, but soon after kick-off it could be seen that the Liverpool fans were in considerable difficulty. Quite simply, fans were being crushed to death. Some collapsed underfoot and were trampled to death; others desperately struggled to find ways out, including trying to climb over the high fence on to the pitch. But the fence was too high and the crush behind them pushed them up against the fence. Fans were struggling to breathe. Life was literally being crushed out of them.

Watching the TV footage of what happened is distressing enough. What is more distressing is seeing, as I did all those years later, the videos from behind the pens looking out on to the pitch. The desperation of the fans is all too evident. They were struggling for life, some trying to help others, all caught up in a horrifying trap where every second counted and there was no way out.

It should have been obvious to anyone involved in ground control seeing these images or in the police control centre that there was a problem. Police officers on the ground patrolling the perimeter of the field must have seen the tragedy unfold before their eyes. But this was happening in an atmosphere where the expectation was that the fans would only ever create trouble. The police officers in particular had had it instilled into them that their priority was to deal with issues of public order rather than public safety. That meant it took too long before anyone understood how bad the situation was and did anything to help.

Eventually, after five minutes and thirty seconds, the match was stopped and the small gates on to the pitch were opened to allow fans through. Advertising boards were torn down by fans to carry the dead and the dying. It became all too evident that this was no public order issue, but a major human tragedy.

What had happened was that shortly before kick-off, in order to try to ease overcrowding outside the entrance turnstiles, the police match commander, Chief Superintendent David Duckenfield, had ordered that an exit gate should be opened, which led to an influx of even more supporters into the pens. Chief Superintendent Duckenfield had limited experience of policing Hillsborough. Indeed, he had been appointed as match commander only twenty-one days before the game, replacing an experienced match commander, Chief Superintendent Brian Mole. The Panel found no explanation for this change of personnel.

The police officers inside the ground were not given any instructions for managing the flow of fans coming through or to direct them to particular areas. What happened was that those entering the pens from the back were pushing people at the front up against the fence. How were they to know? The police had opened the gate to let them in. Keen to see the match, they poured through the gate. They didn't know what was happening ahead of them.

This decision to let more fans into the pens led to the tragedy of the highest death toll in British sporting history. In addition, thousands of people who were there and witnessed the tragedy first-hand were traumatised. There are people who were there on that day who still find it hard to talk about it, having witnessed fans having the breath of life squeezed out of them.

It was estimated by the Panel that up to forty-one of the fans who died could have survived had the reactions and coordination of the emergency services been better. I cannot begin to imagine the distress felt by families who had to cope first with the outrage of false accusations against their loved ones who'd died, and then with the knowledge for some that had the emergency services responded in a different way, their loved ones might have lived.

There were ambulance staff on the ground, but like the police, they assumed that fans trying to save themselves by climbing over the fence were trying to invade the pitch. The attitude that the action of fans was all about public disorder was paramount – with fatal consequences.

In the decades that followed before the inquest finding of unlawful killing, there were a number of reports and investigations into the events of that day. One of the things that was revealed at an early stage was that problems with the Hillsborough Stadium had previously been identified. Indeed, at an FA Cup semi-final between Tottenham Hotspur and Wolverhampton Wanderers in 1981, there had also been serious congestion at the turnstiles at the Leppings Lane end and crushing on the restricted outer concourse. Not only that, but this led to problems in the Leppings Lane terrace and injuries to fans. Again, fans were crushed, but as the terraces had not been divided into pens at the time, it was possible for people to move along the length of the terrace, thus helping to relieve the problem. Moreover, the Panel report showed that the police acted to divert fans to side access points, which relieved pressure at the centre. A rather different picture from the actions of the police in 1989.

What followed that earlier incident was a dispute about responsibility between South Yorkshire Police and Sheffield Wednesday Football Club, whose ground was Hillsborough Stadium. It was after a recommendation from the police that the lateral fences were introduced to create the pens. But a recommendation to channel fans from specified turnstiles into particular pens was not put into practice. Had it been, it would have been possible to monitor how many fans were going into each pen.

There were other safety concerns about the stadium. The Fire Brigade questioned the emergency evacuation of the terraces, in particular the width of the perimeter fence gates, which was below the standard recommended in the official *Guide to Safety at Sports Grounds*. There was also an issue about the gradient of the tunnel leading on to the terrace, which again was in breach of the recommendations.

Moreover, the problems of access to the turnstiles and congestion at those turnstiles were not resolved. The question of the maximum capacity for the Leppings Lane terrace and safety concerns were repeatedly raised. The club did not change the capacity figure.

So there were many issues arising from the use of the Hillsborough Stadium and concerns around safety before that fateful day in April 1989. For me, as Home Secretary at the time of the Independent Panel's report, however, the most shocking findings related to the actions of South Yorkshire Police. Not only did senior officers take the initial decision which led to the crush among the fans that caused death and injury, but after the event, there was a concerted effort to put the blame on the fans and blacken their name. That is bad enough, but even more concerning are some of the tactics used by the police.

The Panel found that 164 witness statements had been altered. Of these, 116 were amended to remove or change negative comments about South Yorkshire Police. This willingness by the police to alter witness statements – that is to say, to alter evidence – supports those who believe that the culture at the time was one where it was accepted that the end justified the means. This issue of the end and the means is a philosophical question at the best of times and can lead to lengthy debate when the end in question is identifying the truth. But here, the end that was being justified was not the search for truth. It was the defence of the police.

The public look to the police to protect them and to search out and act against criminality. They expect the police to be honest in what they say and do, to act within the law and to act without fear or favour. If you or a member of your family were accused of something by the police, you would expect the evidence to be truthful. You would not expect the police to deliberately change the evidence to suit their case. What is more, you would not expect a concerted effort by the police to doctor the evidence against you. Yet that was what happened to the Liverpool fans and their families.

At Hillsborough, the abuse of power by the state and

others went further because there was a consistent effort by police, the media and some politicians to smear the names of the Liverpool fans.

The families had to endure claims of drunkenness as reported by South Yorkshire Police. This led to the Sheffield coroner taking the exceptional decision to test the blood alcohol levels of the victims, including that of a child aged ten. These showed that the fans were not drunk.

It was reported by South Yorkshire Police and then by the press that the fans had conspired to arrive late in order to get into the ground without a ticket. The Panel found no evidence of this. Added to this, there were allegations of violence, including the claim that fans had seriously burnt a police horse – a claim made by a police officer and a farrier who happened to be a friend of his. In 2017, the Crown Prosecution Service announced that they would not prosecute the police officer. Although there was evidence that he had given an untrue account, it was not enough to prove to a criminal standard that his statements were made up. They found enough evidence to charge the farrier with intending to pervert the course of justice, but decided that it was not in the public interest to do so, citing as one reason that he was acting out of misplaced loyalty to the police officer rather than being part of a systemic attempt to tarnish the names of fans. These are just some examples of the allegations made against the fans.

This effort to paint the fans in the worst possible light was not confined to the police. The most obvious public example was the notorious headline in the *Sun* newspaper, which, on 18 April 1989, claimed to be printing 'The Truth'. It included allegations that the fans had been drunk, had forced the gates open because they didn't have tickets, had stolen from corpses lying on the ground, had assaulted police and other emergency services personnel, had stolen cameras and equipment from press photographers and had urinated on police officers who were helping the victims. The initial shock to the families of their loss just three days earlier was compounded by the impact of the lies published in the paper, which made it much harder to cope with what had happened.

The Panel's conclusion was that these false claims came from a local press agency and were based on information from police officers, and on interviews with the Conservative MP Irvine Patnick and the South Yorkshire Police Federation Secretary Paul Middup. In 2012, Irvine Patnick apologised, saying that he now accepted that the information he had received from some police officers at the time was 'wholly inaccurate, misleading and plain wrong'.* However welcome a late apology might have been, it could not undo the hurt of the previous twenty-three years.

This is what the families had to endure until the truth came out in the Panel's report. The question is, why did they have to go through this? Why was there not more effort at the time to get to the truth?

I fear that the answer lies in the corrosive, defensive culture of so many parts of the public sector, but that flaw is not confined to the public sector. It is the culture that allows institutions to be seen as more important than the people they serve. As a result, protecting the institution takes priority over delivering justice.

---

* Statement by Sir Irvine Patnick issued through the Conservative Party, 13 September 2012.

What happened at Hillsborough was a gross and blatant abuse of power – captured in more eloquent language in the title of a report I commissioned from Bishop James Jones, published in 2017 – *The patronising disposition of unaccountable power.*[*]

Being in a position of power led people to think they could exercise their power in the way they saw fit, in what they considered to be the overwhelming priority – in this case, protection of the institutions of the state. For this, of course, we can also read protection of themselves.

A concept of service within those institutions would surely have led to an inherent understanding that power is there to be used in the service of others, that therefore the people came first and that everything should be done to reveal the truth. Instead of exercising their power to deliver for the people they were there to serve, South Yorkshire Police and others exercised their power to deliver for themselves.

We should also reflect on why the politicians at the time didn't recognise what had happened or see the need to look into the event more closely. Despite all the reports over the years, I believe it wasn't until the reaction of the crowd at the event in 2009 to mark the twentieth anniversary of Hillsborough that the need to delve more deeply into what had happened was fully accepted at a senior political level. Andy Burnham, a Greater Manchester MP who was Culture Secretary in the government at the time, went on the pitch to speak at that event, but was booed by the

---

[*] *The patronising disposition of unaccountable power: A report to ensure the pain and suffering of the Hillsborough families is not repeated*, November 2017, HC 511.

crowd, and gradually a chant grew among those present: 'Justice for the 96'. Burnham himself said later that at that moment, he fell out of love with Westminster politics.

Following that event, the Hillsborough Family Support Group presented their case for disclosure of the truth to the Home Secretary, Alan Johnson, which led to the appointment of the Hillsborough Independent Panel in January 2010. In May 2010, the coalition government came to power, and that is where I came in as the new Home Secretary.

There had been plenty of opportunity for both Conservative and Labour governments to do more up to this point. And it was not as if there had not been activity – there was the review and report by Lord Justice Taylor in January 1990, a review by West Midlands Police, civil litigation, criminal and disciplinary investigations, inquests into the deaths, judicial reviews, judicial scrutiny of new evidence undertaken by Lord Justice Stuart-Smith, and the private prosecution of the two most senior police officers in command that day. Not all of these, of course, were instigated by government. Yet the truth had still not come out.

It is instructive to look at the approach taken by the government back in 1989 when the Hillsborough disaster happened. This was the government of Margaret Thatcher, which had been in power for a decade. Among the issues it was dealing with, football hooliganism was undoubtedly one. There was certainly public concern about trouble at football matches. All too often, the weekend news would report at best skirmishes between fans and at worst violent exchanges.

I was a councillor in the London Borough of Merton at the time, and my ward included Plough Lane, the then-home of Wimbledon Football Club. When there was a big match, away fans were marched down Durnsford Road by police from Wimbledon Park tube station, which was also in my ward. The Council regularly had discussions with local commanders about the policing of the matches, as did I. The abiding concern was always the risk of hooliganism and disruptive behaviour by the fans with resulting risks to local people. The local police commander had a simple rule of thumb when referring to the football fans. If his gang was bigger than their gang, everything would be okay. If their gang was bigger than his gang, there would be trouble.

At the time of Hillsborough, the behaviour of fans had become a matter of political controversy. The Conservative government pledged their determination to do something about it and introduced the Football Spectators Bill, which among other things introduced the concept of a national membership scheme. This would require each club to issue membership cards to its fans which would have to be shown for entry to a match involving that club with a view to stopping 'football hooligans' from accessing grounds. This scheme was opposed by Labour, who doubted it would work, and in response they were accused by the government of not wanting to do anything about hooliganism.

The result was that the government showed every sign of seeing everything football-related through the lens of fans' behaviour. When Home Secretary Douglas Hurd gave a statement in the House of Commons on 17 April 1989 about the Hillsborough disaster, he announced the Taylor inquiry, which would be asked 'to inquire into the events at Sheffield Wednesday football ground on 15 April 1989 and to make recommendations about *the needs of crowd* *control* and safety at sports grounds' (my emphasis).* In responding to the Shadow Home Secretary, who had raised the dangers of perimeter fencing, Douglas Hurd said, 'The purpose of the barriers and in particular the perimeter fences is to increase security and improve protection from one type of threat – *that of violence*' (my emphasis again).†

Indeed, this approach was reflected some four weeks after the tragedy when Margaret Thatcher met the families of those who had died following a memorial service in Liverpool's Anglican Cathedral. Margaret Aspinall told me that she had felt unable to shake Mrs Thatcher's hand, and when asked by the Prime Minister, 'Why ever not, my dear?', she had explained that she would only feel able to do so when she found out why her son was in his grave. After Mrs Thatcher had made a reference to the police on duty that day, Margaret Aspinall had asked what they were all doing, to which the reply came: 'Their job, my dear.' This sense that the police were in the right pervades the government's statements about Hillsborough.

Given that, it is easy to forget that the interim report by Lord Justice Taylor published on 1 August 1989‡ concluded that 'policing on 15 April broke down' and that, although there were other issues that contributed to the events that unfolded that day, 'the main reason for the disaster was the failure of police control'. Parliament was not sitting when this report came out, so there was no statement to the

---

* Statement by The Rt Hon. Douglas Hurd MP, Hansard, 17 April 1989, HC Deb., vol. 151, col. 19.
† Ibid., col. 21.
‡ *The Hillsborough Stadium Disaster, 15 April 1989: Inquiry by the Rt Hon. Lord Justice Taylor, Interim Report*, August 1989, Cm. 765.

House of Commons. One was made, however, in response to the final Taylor report published in January 1990.*

That final report focused on recommendations relating to football stadia – perimeter fences, tunnels, turnstiles and so forth – and one of the main outcomes was the requirement for all-seater stadia. The theory was that if everyone was sitting down, there would be less trouble. Despite this focus, the statement made in Parliament could have been an opportunity to recognise the role the police had played, and the recommendations made by Taylor in relation to issues like police training. Yet when he gave that statement, the Home Secretary David Waddington made no reference to the role of the police in the events of that day, other than to state that the final report acknowledged the crucial role of the police in crowd control.

Indeed, the Home Secretary went on to thank the police in general for their work in policing football matches. He did add that the report 'recognises the advances made in the last couple of years in the effectiveness of the policing of football, particularly inside grounds, and to the major impact of closed-circuit television *on the hooligan problem*' (my emphasis).† There it is again. Reference to the hooligan problem.

Governments have to juggle many different topics, and it can be difficult to ensure that priority is given to the right issues. Yet we have to ask why the politicians at the time appear to have paid no attention to the role of the police in the events that led to the death of nearly one hundred

---

* *The Hillsborough Stadium Disaster, 15 April 1989: Inquiry by the Rt Hon. Lord Justice Taylor, Final Report*, January 1990, Cm. 962.
† Statement by the Rt Hon. David Waddington MP, Hansard, 29 January 1990, HC Deb., vol. 166, col. 19.

Liverpool fans. A decade into the Thatcher government, one might have thought that they could take a more considered approach to issues and not be swept along in response to public opinion. But of course, this was near the end of Margaret Thatcher's time as Prime Minister. At such moments, it can be harder to challenge accepted thinking.

Certainly, the government seems to have been most focused on getting its proposals in the Football Spectators Bill through Parliament, although following the negative comments about the idea of a national membership scheme in the Taylor report, they had to row back on that.

It does seem that the government was blinkered by previous experience. At a time when the weekend news had so often been dominated by crowd problems at football matches, they were unable to look beyond the issue of the behaviour of fans. Undoubtedly, this was a matter of public concern at the time, but the country had just witnessed the biggest sporting disaster in its history. Surely this called for a more dispassionate assessment of what had happened. Moreover, an inquiry had identified not only that the main reason for the disaster was the failure of police control, but also that senior officers had been 'defensive and evasive witnesses' who had refused to accept any responsibility for error.

Did nobody think to look beyond the stereotype of fans' behaviour and ask why Lord Justice Taylor's work had laid the main blame on the police? Or was it that a Conservative Party in government with its narrative on law and order and support for the police was simply not willing to recognise when the police got it wrong?

I suspect this was a significant element in the thinking at the time. Later, as Home Secretary, I commissioned

Sir Tom Winsor to undertake a review into police officer and staff remuneration and conditions, and I discovered that as a Conservative, I was expected simply to accept the police as they were and not ask too many questions. I give an example of this attitude as it relates to Home Secretaries later when I discuss the case of Daniel Morgan in Chapter 11.

Yet one has to say that whatever the expectations, the search for truth should come first. South Yorkshire Police created a web of obfuscation and lies to lay the blame on fans. The media fuelled that story and stoked it up. It fitted the government's political narrative. They had the power, and so they all ignored the need for justice – because they could.

I couldn't write about Hillsborough without exploring further the impact that it had on the families and what it represented in relation to the approach of organs of the state. There can be no doubt that the example of Anne Williams, who so often seemed to be acting alone in the fight for the truth of what had happened to her son Kevin, is an inspiring story, and it was told movingly in the ITV drama series *Anne*, shown in January 2022. But I never met Anne Williams. When I was considering whether to maintain the Hillsborough Independent Panel, I met and discussed it with the Panel's Chairman, Bishop James Jones, who suggested that I should meet some of the families. That led to the meeting I referred to earlier with representatives of the Hillsborough Family Support Group. I also met other family representatives from the Hillsborough Justice Campaign, but it was that initial conversation with Margaret, Trevor and Jenni that inspired me to continue with the work of the Panel. The searing pain of their losses came through clearly in our conversation, as did their thirst for justice, and it was evident that they had sacrificed a great deal, and suffered many setbacks, to get to where they were.

Talking to Margaret, the extent of that sacrifice is all too obvious. She and the families have been fighting since 1989, and are still fighting today, to bring about change so that no other families have to suffer in the way that they have. It is easy to forget the toll endless campaigning has on people. As Margaret said to me, she lost her son James, and then she missed her other children growing up because she was putting so much effort into the campaign for justice for James and the other ninety-six. Perhaps this sacrifice is best understood through the story she told me of working in the office one day when a phone call came through for her. The caller said, 'Can I have an appointment to see my nana please?' This request from her granddaughter reflected the amount of time Margaret was having to spend working on the campaign for justice. It isn't just the individuals themselves who pay a toll, but their families and friends too.

At heart for the campaigners was their single-minded determination to prove that the state had done wrong and had spent the decades since the tragedy covering up that wrong. Theirs was a sacrifice for their families but also a service to others. The families hadn't always agreed on everything. It had taken diplomatic skills and good legal support to hold them together. But their determination reflects the strength of the Liverpool community. They kept the flame of desire for justice burning bright.

What characterised their fight was the way that the state put obstacle after obstacle in their way. The story about Hillsborough had been written by those with power who abused that power to peddle lies.

I pay tribute to all those involved in the campaign for justice for the ninety-seven. Without them, the truth would never have been revealed. Distressingly, apart from the minor case relating to health and safety legislation already discussed, no one has been successfully prosecuted for their part in what led to the unlawful killing of so many innocent Liverpool fans. But the truth is now out there, and the Liverpool fans have been exonerated.

6

Primodos

While Hillsborough was a tragedy of which I had been aware the day it happened, Primodos was a different matter. This was something which I had not come across until I entered Parliament, and to be honest I was not really focused on it until many years after I became an MP. Even when I first became aware of it, I did not get involved. Later, when I was PM, I saw MPs raising it in the House of Commons with great passion, and it was then that I took a direct interest in the issue.

Arguably, I should have turned my attention to it at an earlier stage, because it was a women's health issue. More than that, it was an horrendous scandal. My only explanation for being remiss in this way is that I had never had a departmental responsibility for health matters and had been focused on my many other responsibilities. It was only later when it became clear that the Primodos campaigners were constantly beating their heads against the brick wall of government intransigence that I felt the need to act.

The scandal of Primodos was ably explained by Baroness Cumberlege in her Independent Medicines and Medical

Devices Safety Review.[*] The review also considered issues relating to the use of pelvic mesh and sodium valproate in pregnancy, but it was questions about the use of Primodos that led to my involvement. In a nutshell, over a number of years, despite warnings about the impact of the use of Primodos, it continued to be given to women to test whether they were pregnant, with some heart-wrenching effects on babies. This is an example not only of the abuse of power, but also of the patronising attitude towards women which was characteristic of so many in positions of power for too long – and is still evident today. It was as if the powerful men involved were patting them on the head and saying, 'There, there, dear, you're just imagining it, you don't really know what you're talking about.'

Far from imagining it, these women were convinced that the problems they and their children had experienced were due to them using Primodos for a pregnancy test. The problems included still births and children born with various abnormalities or birth defects, including blindness, damage to internal organs and limb defects.

To make matters worse, campaigners had to wait many years for their case to be given a full hearing and be in any way accepted by government. This issue has been a matter of argument and debate since the 1960s, and, despite the Independent Review's report in 2020, continues to be so today. The company that now owns the manufacturers of Primodos has not accepted that their drugs caused the sort of problems referenced above, and in May 2023, the case taken by more than a hundred UK families seeking

---

[*] *First Do No Harm: The Report of the Independent Medicines and Medical Devices Safety Review*, July 2020.

compensation was struck out by the High Court. Mrs Justice Yip ruled that in the absence of sufficient new evidence, the claimants had no reasonable prospect of success.

Over those decades, the women have lived with the heavy burden on their conscience that the pregnancy test they took caused the problems faced by their children. As one woman said, 'I can honestly say that my heart is broken at the outcome of those two tablets given to me by my doctor.' Not only that, but the affected children have had to live with the physical and mental impact of the use of that drug.

When I talked to Marie Lyon, who has led the campaign to get to the truth about Primodos, she made the point that so many of the women who took the drug feel guilty about having done so. They should not feel guilty. They trusted their GPs and they trusted that the system would ensure the safety of anything they were prescribed. The government needs to tell them that they did nothing wrong.

So what exactly was Primodos? It might be helpful to explain the background to this drug and the way the system denied women their voices.

Strange as it may seem to us today, before the 1950s, women who might be pregnant and for whom it was decided a test was needed were given the Hogben or toad test. Yes, the toad test – so called because it involved injecting some of the woman's urine into a toad. If she was pregnant, then there would be a breeding response in the creature as a result of the hormones in the urine. This test had to be carried out in specialist facilities, was expensive and took time, so it was restricted to women who had a strong medical need to know whether or not they were pregnant.

Social Injustice

Between the 1950s and 1970s, Hormone Pregnancy Tests (HPTs) were introduced in the UK. One of the market leaders was Primodos, made by Schering. The other was Amenerone Forte made by Roussel. Together, Roussel and Schering made up over 90 per cent of the UK HPT market. Not all HPTs were used to test pregnancy as they were also prescribed for other conditions, such as secondary amenorrhoea.

On the face of it, the advantages of these pregnancy tests were plain to see. They were simple and reliable, and a much quicker way to test whether a woman was pregnant than the toad test. Moreover, they did not need professional or laboratory input, and the result would be seen by the woman herself: if she was not pregnant, after a few days of taking the HPT pills she would experience a bleed much like a period. No bleed meant she was pregnant.

The position changed again from the mid-1960s with the arrival of immunoassay tests, which tested blood or urine. While originally these tests were carried out by doctors or chemists, in the early 1970s home tests became available for women to buy and use themselves. The tests available today are refined versions of these. Although the immunoassay tests became available in the mid-1960s, HPTs including Primodos continued to be prescribed into the following decade.

When HPTs were being prescribed by doctors, the women who used them seem to have had no idea that there could be any adverse consequences. I use the word 'prescribed', but one of the factors here is that doctors sometimes had free samples of HPTs, which they just handed out without a formal prescription – and in some cases without even keeping a formal record.

There was no reason for the women to question the pills they were being given. They would have had absolute trust in their doctors. From the doctors' point of view, they presumably relied on the decision taken by the then-regulator that they could be used, and also on the advice of the drug company salesmen.

The truth, however, was somewhat different. There had been concerns raised since the late 1950s about HPTs and whether they could cause abnormalities in a developing baby, and there is no doubt that the issue remained contentious. Yet even when other options were available, HPTs continued to be given by doctors.

Back in 1958, a paper relating to evidence from Scotland proposed that non-genital malformations could arise from the use of HPTs, but gave no data to support the claim. In 1964, a paper by Dr Richard Smithells, who was at the time a well-respected expert in the field, suggested that on the basis of unpublished data, HPTs were probably not harmful to babies. The CSD/AR (the Committee on the Safety of Drugs sub-committee on Adverse Reactions) had this paper shared with them before it was published.

In 1966, the Senior Medical Officer at the then-Ministry of Health (Dr J. G. Thomson) wrote to several experts asking for their views on the use of HPTs as tests, focusing on both their accuracy and the desirability of using them. At least two of the independent experts consulted indicated that they would not recommend using them as tests. One of these was Dr A. J. N. Warrack, the pathologist in charge of the Group Pathology Laboratory at the City General Hospital in Sheffield, who wrote that having consulted with two obstetric colleagues, the general opinion was that the test 'is unreliable' and that 'it may well be dangerous in that it could possibly precipitate abortion in a not well established pregnancy'. These concerns reflected the views of practitioners rather than proof offered by clinical studies. Nevertheless, it is notable that despite the warnings, the Ministry did not recommend that HPTs should no longer be used as pregnancy tests. It did, however, recommend that immunoassays should be used to test pregnancy.

These moves may seem contradictory. Why, given that they recommended using other tests, did they not ban HPTs? Some might say that the promotion of one test and the failure to recommend another should have given a clear indication of what they expected doctors to do, but it is this failure to ban HPTs that was identified by the Independent Review as a clear mistake. Had the opposite decision been taken and HPTs been withdrawn as pregnancy tests at that time, there can be no doubt that fewer unborn babies would have been exposed to them with the risks that exposure presented.

Let's remember that the risks were high. The list of conditions that have been attributed to the use of Primodos and other HPTs is horrifying and worryingly long. The variety of outcomes reported includes miscarriages, stillbirths and babies born with deafness, blindness, congenital heart defects, spina bifida, shortening of limbs, speech learning disabilities, digestive system problems and shortened spines. That is just a small subset of the total.

You might reasonably assume that the continued use of HPTs occurred because no one carried on questioning their impact. But that is not the case. They continued to be used in the face of medical research, which raised further questions about the link between HPTs and birth defects.

There was one doctor in particular who championed the cause of those who wanted to see HPTs banned. The response to her work shows that the resolution of this issue seems to have suffered from attitudes towards women at the time. The doctor concerned was Dr Isabel Gal. She undertook research with others that, in 1967, showed a link between Primodos and severe birth defects, thus supporting the women's case. This work was the first statistically significant link between the use of HPTs and malformations in babies.

The work was not completely dismissed. Thus, the Medical Research Council was encouraged in a letter from Dr Derek Richter to fund further investigations. Dr Richter said that he had suggested to Dr Brian Kirman, who had worked on the study with Dr Gal, that the findings needed to be shared with the CSD as the possible link looks 'as if it could be another thalidomide story'.

The reference to the thalidomide story is significant, because thalidomide was another case where a drug prescribed for pregnant women had led to birth defects. The drug was developed in the 1950s by a West German pharmaceutical company. It was produced from 1958 in the UK and marketed under various brand names. One of these – Distaval – was advertised as safe to be given to pregnant women and nursing mothers without adverse effects. Thalidomide was prescribed for a number of conditions, but above all was used to help women in the early stages of pregnancy relieve the symptoms of nausea. It took time to identify a connection between the use of the drug and the impact on children for a number of reasons, among them the fact that the effects were wide ranging. Not only limbs and internal organs, including the brain, but also eyesight and hearing could be affected. The first time a link was made public was in 1961 and the UK government issued a warning about its use in 1962.

So it can be seen that the reference to the use of HPTs such as Primodos carrying the risk of being another thalidomide story should have raised real concerns. But this argument did not hold sway. With hindsight, we could well ask why the lessons of thalidomide had not been learnt.

Again, Dr Gal's paper was shared with the CSD/AR before publication, and in this case further expert advice was sought. While it was acknowledged that the evidence produced by Dr Gal and her colleagues at Queen Mary's Hospital for Children in Carshalton, Surrey, showed that indeed the foetal abnormalities concerned could have been induced by drugs, they decided that there were flaws in the methodology used to produce these results. Hence, Dr Bill Inman, Senior Medical Officer of the CSD/AR, dismissed the results, saying, 'The Carshalton workers drew their affected children and controls from different catchment areas, and this to my mind invalidates their work.'

This was the same Dr Inman who later wrote in his autobiography: 'Had we been convinced by Dr Gal's study, the Committee would have banned HPTs immediately in 1967.' If only they had done so. How many mothers and babies would have been spared the anguish and pain of the adverse impact of HPTs?

Indeed, it is clear that there were later real concerns about the implications of Dr Gal's work. On 4 August 1975, Dr Gal herself sent a critique of the Committee on Safety of Medicines (CSM, which the CSD had become in 1968) to Sir Eric Scowen, the CSM Chair:

By downplaying the significance of the original observation (as attempted in yours and in Dr. Inman's
letters, and as stated in the official press communique
and in the article in the 'Sunday Times' on 8th June)
the Committee's responsibility is not averted from
allowing the 8 years use of an unnecessary diagnostic
test table, whose serious irreversible adverse effects
were well known to them. It is also of interest that
the warning on the hormonal pregnancy test was
introduced earlier in the United States, Australia and
Ireland than here, despite the fact that the concept
originated in this country, and the Committee was in
the favourable position of having first-hand knowledge
of it in 1967. Although the Committee's own study
confirmed my observation (BMJ 28 Apr 1975) active
steps were only taken on 5th June, due to pressure
of the public press ('Sunday Times' 25 May).

Internally, Dr Inman acknowledged the CSD/CSM
shortcomings, writing in relation to Dr Gal and the eight
years between her original report and a preliminary position
paper (published by the Committee and based on work
which had started in 1969) that: 'It may not have escaped
her notice that, if the relative risk suggested by our publication turned out to be true, a large number of congenitally
abnormal babies have been born as a result of hormonal
pregnancy tests carried out after publication of her paper.'
Dr Inman subsequently met Dr Gal, who, and I can
quite understand this, reportedly felt that the Committee
had only acted because of the latest critique of the risks
involved in using HPTs. As a result, she would rightly
have been concerned that a significant number of abnormal

babies could have been born in the eight years between her report and the Committee's preliminary paper. Indeed, in an internal memo, Dr Inman said, 'we are defenceless in the matter of the eight year delay'.

That phrase is very telling. It is an admission that, had they acted earlier, fewer babies would have been born with abnormalities. Not just that, but fewer families would have had their lives turned upside down by having to cope with the outcome of births affected by the use of Primodos.

Hindsight is a wonderful thing, but looking back, one can't help but feel that the system let people down. Now it is, of course, the case that Dr Gal's work was just one study – although, as outlined above, it was not the first time that potential problems had been identified as arising from the use of HPTs.

The Independent Review concluded that, given there were other tests available at the time and that concerns had been raised about the use of HPTs, and against the background of the thalidomide case, the CSD should have operated with greater caution and withdrawn the official indication to doctors that HPTs could be used as pregnancy tests.

There was other adverse evidence, in addition to Dr Gal's paper and the studies I referred to earlier. Also in 1967, Schering UK had commissioned expert statistical analysis from Dr David Cooke, who looked at the increased sales of Primodos and the number of recorded deformities in newborns and found 'a rather alarming direct and strong correlation'. This work by Dr Cooke was independent of that undertaken by Dr Gal, yet still no action was taken to remove Primodos and other HPTs from the market, or to issue warnings about their use.

Certainly, the parent company for Primodos, Schering Germany, did not regard the evidence as requiring the withdrawal of Primodos from the market. Yet the Independent Review reported that in 1968, Schering UK wrote to Schering Germany: 'From an ethical point of view we are not satisfied with what has been done to remove the suspicion which has fallen upon us. Not enough has happened that we can confidently promote the fact that Primodos for pregnant women is available here.'

There were further studies that showed links between abnormalities and the use of Primodos and other HPTs – the report of the Independent Review gives a full timeline of the papers concerned. Yet it was not until 1975 that any warnings on their use were given, and not until January 1978 that Schering asked the UK government to end their HPT licences due to falling sales. The next month, they withdrew the pregnancy test indication on Primodos worldwide.

While the issue of Primodos and other HPTs related to its impact on babies, this is not an issue that is of only historical significance. Those babies have grown up with problems and difficulties in their lives resulting from the complications caused by Primodos and other HPTs. They still live with those consequences today. You only have to listen to campaigners on the issue or look at debates in the House of Commons over the years and hear MPs relating the issues their constituents have faced to start to understand not just the heartbreak of mothers whose babies were born with problems, but also the pain and suffering the mothers and their children have gone through over the years.

Take just one example, which I think amply shows the continued suffering of someone born to a woman who had taken Primodos. In a debate in the Commons in October 2014, Yasmin Qureshi, the MP for Bolton South East, quoted the case of her constituent Nichola Williams, who was born with life-threatening internal congenital deformities in her stomach, spine, heart and womb. Her first operation took place when she was seven days old. Her life since then had been full of visits to hospital as an inpatient and an outpatient. Nichola was quoted as saying: 'My stomach is on the wrong side. I have seven spleens. Throughout my life, I have had to have a number of operations to correct my stomach. I was born with a number of adhesions and obstructions. I have spinal defects.'* It seems extraordinary in the face of stories like this that the response of various governments over the years has been to say that the evidence did not justify a causal link between birth defects and Primodos or other HPTs.

In 2014, in response to campaigning by families, supported by MPs, the government commissioned a report from the Medicines and Healthcare products Regulatory Agency – the lead regulator – to review all the key evidence on this issue and produce a report. Based on studies published between 1960 and 2013, the MHRA's view was that the results were inconsistent, with some finding no association, some a weak association and some a strong association. Its conclusion was that the data did not provide conclusive evidence of an association between hormone pregnancy tests and birth defects.

The then-Minister George Freeman said in the House of Commons, 'As Hon. Members will appreciate, the Government have a duty to ensure that they are acting at

---

* Hansard, 23 October 2014, HC Deb., vol. 586, col. 1114.

all times on the best advice available from specialist agencies set up to advise them, which in this case is the MHRA. I believe that in commissioning the report, the Government have listened to and acted on the concerns that have been raised about this drug.'*

Nevertheless, the government did commission a further report from an expert working group of the Agency. This group reported in 2017. Its report came to be treated by the Department of Health as the scientific gospel that showed there was no reason for an inquiry into the use of Primodos. One can almost hear the sigh of relief in the Department when the result came through. This report was constantly quoted – and indeed is still quoted today – by ministers and others as the last word on the issue. After all, it was produced by an expert working group!

You might, therefore, be surprised to hear that it was this report that led to my decision to set up the Independent Medicines and Medical Devices Safety Review.

Politicians can't be experts on everything. One of the interesting aspects of the job is that it requires a willingness to get involved in many issues – anything that affects our constituents, in fact. As a backbench MP, you get to have some knowledge of a wide range of issues but in-depth knowledge of very few. As a minister, it is possible, indeed necessary, to acquire that deeper knowledge on the issues in your area of responsibility, but of course as Prime Minister, you need to cover everything.

That is why some of the critical faculties that a politician needs are inquisitiveness, a willingness to ask the damn-fool question and a readiness to challenge experts. I can be

* Hansard, 23 October 2014, HC Deb., vol. 586, col. 1141.

contrary at times, and when I'm told something is absolutely the last scientific word on an issue on which people have been campaigning for decades, I instinctively want to push back.

When the issue of Primodos was brought to me, I was told categorically by the Department of Health and by ministers in the Department that the expert working group had proved that there was no link between Primodos and birth defects. There could be no question of setting up an inquiry. The implication was that there had been no mistakes made by the health establishment. End of story.

Yet when I read the expert working group's report, I found the sentence: 'The totality of the available evidence from pharmacology, non-clinical, epidemiological and adverse reporting data was very limited and did not, on balance, support a causal association between the use of HPTs, such as Primodos, by the mother during early pregnancy and congenital anomalies in the child.'* To me 'on balance' meant that, while there was an argument that there was no association, it was far from conclusive. This shows, I believe, the importance of ministers taking the time to read the reports set before them rather than just relying on summaries by the civil service. This will have been particularly important during the Covid pandemic.

It was as a result of seeing that sentence that I asked the Department of Health to set up the Independent Review to look into Primodos and two other issues – the use of sodium valproate in pregnancy and vaginal mesh. These

---

* *Report of the Commission on Human Medicines Expert Working Group on Hormone Pregnancy Tests*, October 2017.

were also issues where women had been suffering over the years, had been raising concerns and had not been heard.

In presenting the report of the Review to the government, Baroness Cumberlege said:

> We have found that the healthcare system – in which I include the NHS, private providers, the regulators and professional bodies, pharmaceutical and device manufacturers, and policymakers – is disjointed, siloed, unresponsive and defensive. It does not adequately recognise that patients are its raison d'etre. It has failed to listen to their concerns and when, belatedly, it has decided to act it has too often moved glacially.

This was yet another example of a system more interested in protecting its own interests than those of patients, and of politicians too ready to believe the 'expert' advice they were given. In the early days of this scandal, there were also powerful commercial interests at stake. But the experts' job is to set such interests to one side and look calmly at where the evidence takes them; and the politicians' job is to be on the side of the public and to do what is right by them. This is an issue I will return to later.

While it is concerning enough that more attention was not paid to the results of Dr Gal's research, what is also of concern is the attitude adopted towards Dr Gal herself. It is perhaps worth spending a little time looking at Dr Gal and her experience. While her place in history will always be focused on her role as the first doctor to identify a potential link between the use of HPTs and serious birth defects, her life before this time had already been one of challenge and hardship. She was born in Hungary in 1925 and, the family being Jewish, she and her mother and two sisters were sent during the Second World War to Auschwitz concentration camp. She survived, and after the war studied medicine at the University of Budapest, qualifying as a paediatrician. She went to work at a children's hospital and married Endre Gal, and might have expected life to carry on without more dramatic shocks. In 1956, however, during the Hungarian revolution, she and her family fled to the UK via Austria. She then requalified as a doctor at Edinburgh University.

Isabel Gal went on to work at Queen Mary's Hospital for Children in Surrey, which is where she was when she first surfaced the issue of Primodos. She wrote about the link between Primodos and serious congenital birth defects in an article in the journal *Nature*. She also pointed out that the test used the same components as oral contraceptive pills.

As we have seen, there were others who had concerns about the use of HPTs as a pregnancy test, but Dr Gal's research was, to all intents and purposes, ignored. It is possible that one reason for this was a concern about the impact on women's use of contraceptives. Whatever the reason, it did not justify the years of suffering by women who continued to take Primodos, and their children who were born with defects as a result.

What was also not justified was the treatment of Dr Gal after her report on Primodos. It can be seen from her life story that this was not a woman who gave up in the face of adversity. Her position at Queen Mary's was terminated after her work on Primodos, and she was unsuccessful in securing another senior post. Eventually, she left the medical profession. What happened to her certainly suggests that the medical establishment saw her as a nuisance who had identified uncomfortable truths that they preferred to ignore, and that as a result her career suffered.

That this treatment of her was possible says a lot about the attitudes at the time. Her findings upset the relationship between the pharmaceutical companies and the medical profession. Remember: the Independent Review found that doctors were providing patients with Primodos not exactly by the back door, but out of their desk drawers. Certainly, the company provided some with free samples of Primodos.

Setting that issue to one side, the question is, what was the relationship between the 'regulators', whose task it was to ensure that medicines were safe, and the companies? Why did no one want to listen to the evidence produced by Isabel Gal? These issues are addressed by the Review and one of the report's recommendations – that doctors should declare any relationship with pharmaceutical companies so that there is transparency and accountability – reflects this.

In today's world, it may seem unthinkable that doctors should have been prescribing because of their links with companies or because of the better sales technique of certain company reps rather than according to the best research. And, as I have pointed out, in some instances these tests, including Primodos, were apparently just taken out of the doctor's drawer and handed over to the patient – and all this at a time when more than one doctor had identified potential harms from the use of these tests. I think this does show different forms of the abuse of power. While undoubtedly the pharmaceutical companies wanted to sell their products, doing so by providing drugs that could be offered to patients without prescription is, to me, an example of abusing the power they had over the doctors. In their turn, the doctors were arguably abusing their power over their patients, who they knew would trust them implicitly.

The position has changed since the 1960s, but it is not inconceivable that a doctor's judgement may be skewed by a company's offers. Today, some doctors disclose the payments made to them, but that is not the case for all and that is why the Cumberlege recommendation of transparency is so important. The Review's report was absolutely clear, as set out in Recommendation 8:

> Transparency of payments made to clinicians needs to improve. The register of the General Medical Council (GMC) should be expanded to include a list of financial and non-pecuniary interests for all doctors, as well as doctors' particular clinical interests and their recognised and accredited specialisms. In addition, there should be mandatory reporting for pharmaceutical and medical device industries of payments made to teaching hospitals, research institutions and individual clinicians.

Progress with this recommendation is ongoing. The government introduced a number of pilot systems for doctors to declare their interests in NHS and independent settings across the UK. The pilots will be reviewed and, if successful, a system will be fully implemented. Once a system is in place for doctors, the government will consider systems for other healthcare professionals. In addition, in the Health and Care Act 2022, power is granted to the Secretary of State for Health and Social Care to make regulations requiring companies to publish or report information about their payments to the healthcare sector.

Helping patients to know what is motivating their doctor, that there may be something other than best medical practice driving them, is important. But if nothing else, it would make it easier to identify the cause of some problems.

There is another question which underlies what happened with Primodos, and that is the attitude towards women. This was manifest in several ways. First, there was the assumption that when it came to women's issues generally, what they thought was a problem or pain was more in their heads than real. Secondly, there was a view that on women's issues, particularly involving pregnancy or gynaecological matters, women just had to put up with problems and grin and bear it. Pain relating to childbirth was something they had to go through, but it was for a greater good. As a result, genuine problems were not taken as seriously as they should have been, if they were even considered at all. Thirdly, there was still in some quarters the idea that women weren't as smart as men, and that their research work wasn't up to the same standards as that produced by men. To put it another way, if Isabel Gal had been a man, would her findings have been dismissed so easily?

It might be argued that all this was behaviour that reflected the attitudes of the day, but that doesn't make it right. Moreover, it doesn't mean that we should accept the same attitudes today.

Dr Isabel Gal was a professional who tried to make a difference, and in doing so effectively sacrificed her career. She saw her job as one of service to her patients, not as one purely for the exercise of power or for self-promotion.

She was in a position of power, as are all doctors who are making day-to-day decisions about people's futures, including decisions of life and death, but it was the exercise of power for the good of others, not for its own sake.

In the case of Primodos, as with other examples I cite in this book, these attitudes came together with the classic problems all too often associated with the public sector – a reluctance to admit mistakes, a desire to protect the institution rather than the public, and a casual abuse of power. I imagine nobody involved thought that what they were doing was an abuse of power, but at heart that was exactly what it was. They did not use the power at their disposal to search for the truth, and the way they used their power meant that the truth did not prevail.

To return to my theme at the beginning of the book, to be in a position of power is to be in a position of service. All too often, however, the fact of having that power entices the holder to exercise it in their own interests rather than in the interests of others. Power corrupts, it is said, and in the case of Primodos, that is exactly what it did. The result was that, just as at Hillsborough, the very body set up to protect the public – in this case the regulator – had failed to do that.

In one sense, the most concerning point about these examples is the way in which people whose job it was to put the public first consistently put their organisation first. I'm afraid this attitude continues to this day. As an MP, I have seen a good number of cases over the years where it is this attitude that has caused friction between organs of the state and my constituents.

The area of the public sector where this has been most sharply focused has been the NHS. When a treatment or an operation goes wrong, what the constituent wants in virtually every case is for the NHS to admit its mistake, say sorry and show they will learn from their mistake so that it will not happen again to somebody else. What they have been met with is a service that pulls up the drawbridge, refuses to admit its mistakes and may even try to portray the constituent as misguided and ill-informed. No wonder so many cases end in expensive litigation. In the five years between 2017 and 2022, the NHS paid out nearly £12 billion. As the individual gets increasingly frustrated with the response, the institution gets more entrenched in its position.

It shouldn't be like this, and it doesn't have to be like this. That much is clear from the example of the aviation sector. Here, pilots are encouraged to report problems and mistakes, near misses and so on. The expectation is that reporting will enable lessons to be learnt and problems to be addressed. This will be to the benefit of all, crew and passengers alike. The incentive for the airline industry is commercial, in that they don't want to lose customers as a result of safety concerns. That incentive does not exist in the NHS, although with the moves to greater freedom for patients to choose who provides their treatment, hospital trusts should start to think more carefully about their reputation as providers of quality care.

I hope that one outcome of the Cumberlege review will be that we see a greater willingness to embrace problems and mistakes as a means to improvement. Certainly, the introduction of a Patient Safety Commissioner should play a key role in ensuring that the voices of patients are heard. Dr Henrietta Hughes took up this post in September 2022.

In the case of Primodos, powerful consultants dismissed the pain and suffering of women and their children, powerful medical scientists dismissed the evidence presented by a woman, and powerful ministers were too willing to believe experts and did not ask enough questions. They all exercised their power in ways that were in the interests of the state and its institutions rather than in the interests of people and of finding the truth. They all abused their power – because they could.

7

Grenfell

The tragic fire at Grenfell Tower in the early hours of 14 June 2017 and the resulting loss of seventy-two lives shattered a community, devastated families and rocked the nation. Its aftermath continues to this day in the lives of the survivors and families and friends of those who died, and in government policy on building regulations and social housing. It has also been the subject of a lengthy public inquiry, which at the time of writing has still to publish its final report.

The recognition that the cladding used to refurbish the building was unsafe has led to the safety of other blocks of residential flats being called into question, with the resulting stress and costs for those living in them. The fire has also brought into question the way in which regulations intended to keep people safe were at best misunderstood or misinterpreted and at worst abused in the interests of commerce, or administrative or political convenience.

While the inquiry is ongoing, there is a limit to what can be said, but there is one aspect of this tragedy that I want to focus on, which has been clear to me from my very first meeting with survivors. That is the way in which the voices of tenants had been ignored, not just by the

Council, the Royal Borough of Kensington and Chelsea, but by the TMO – the Tenant Management Organisation – the very body that should have put tenants front and centre stage. This was an abuse of power, the belittling of a group of people because they happened to live in homes owned by part of the state.

Before I develop this theme, I perhaps should go through the days and weeks after the tragedy and explain why I felt strongly about this abuse of power.

I remember looking at the pictures on the television screen in the general office outside my room in Downing Street when I went down to start the day, and finding it difficult to believe what had taken place. Surely this could not be happening. Surely we had regulations that ensured this could not happen. But, of course, it *was* happening and with terrible and tragic consequences.

On Thursday, 15 June, I visited the site and met with the emergency services. The London Fire Brigade was still dealing with the smouldering building, which tells you how ravaging the fire had been. One thing was clear. No one in the emergency services had seen anything like this before. There had, of course, been fires in flats before, but the way most flats in tower blocks were constructed and the safety measures taken usually meant that the fires were restricted to the flat they originated in and could be dealt with by the Fire Brigade with relative ease. This was known as compartmentation, and led to the policy of advising residents of the other flats in blocks concerned to 'stay put'.

This 'stay put' strategy was also operated at Grenfell. On this occasion, it had tragic consequences, because compartmentation was clearly not functioning in Grenfell Tower. As was obvious from the TV pictures of the coverage of the fire, it took hold incredibly quickly, racing up the outside of the block and enveloping the tower in flames. Evidently something had gone very wrong indeed. This sort of fire was not supposed to happen.

On my way to the site, I spoke to the Secretary of State for Communities and Local Government, Sajid Javid. It had been suggested in radio reports that morning that the Council were not responding to the fire as comprehensively as they should have been. This was to become a key element of concerns raised with me later by survivors. Sajid assured me that the Council had been responding and were dealing with the needs of survivors. I assumed he had been briefed to this effect.

I was criticised for not going to meet the families on my first visit, something they know I regret, but my approach to the Grenfell tragedy was the same as to the terrorist incidents I had dealt with throughout my years as Home Secretary and Prime Minister. At such a time, I believe that the job of senior politicians is to ensure that whatever has happened is being properly dealt with, that the respondents – the emergency services – have all they need to do their job, and that there is the support needed for victims and survivors. We should also start asking the questions about how and why this has happened and what needs to change to prevent it happening again, all while recognising that the answers may be a long time coming. Much of this is not necessarily undertaken in the public eye. In this case, I was wrong. What lay behind the concerns of survivors and the community was the way they had previously been ignored by the authorities. By waiting to meet them, I compounded that concern. I should have met the survivors and people from the local community straight away.

On my return to Downing Street, I spoke to officials about what I had seen and I agreed that I would announce a public inquiry into the fire. My reason for doing so, as I said at the time, was that 'we need to know what happened'.

The next day, I visited some of the survivors in Chelsea and Westminster Hospital. The stories they told were truly harrowing. I remember particularly the young family who informed me that they had been told by firefighters to stay in their flat – the 'stay put' strategy. Indeed, others had been brought to their flat for shelter, but the point came when the father decided they had to get out. He, his wife and child left and survived – although, as his wife told me, she was wearing just her underwear and a t-shirt. Those left behind did not survive.

That same day, I chaired a meeting of key Cabinet ministers. That was the day when I first met a group from the local community, all of whom lived nearby and had been evacuated from their flats, as well as a survivor from the tower itself. They wished to discuss their experiences and explain what they felt had happened. We met in a local church as a neutral setting. Their pain was raw and overwhelming. The meeting was cut short because the police were concerned that an angry crowd was building up outside and they couldn't guarantee my safety or that of the other attendees. But I promised to resume the meeting the very next day at No. 10.

The following day – Saturday, 17 June – when I had been expected to attend the Trooping the Colour ceremony on Horse Guards Parade, I welcomed into No. 10 the group from the local community. We sat around the Cabinet table and they told me their harrowing stories of the night of the fire, and about the suffering they and their community were going through as a result. Their anger was obvious. They spoke clearly and movingly, and with much passion, not only about the fire and what their community now needed in terms of support from the government, but also about the years of what they felt was nothing less than neglect of their community by the Royal Borough of Kensington and Chelsea.

Another theme was their concern and anger about years of neglect in social housing more generally. They felt that they had been treated as second-class citizens because they lived in social housing. Yet here were hard-working people bringing up their children, striving for the best for their families, looking out for each other and building a tight-knit community.

It had been obvious from the first meeting in the church and from what I heard that day in Downing Street that all had not been right in the relationship between tenants, the TMO and the Council. It was also plain to see that this was a very close-knit community and that the impact of the fire and loss of life had not only shattered the lives of individuals and families but had been felt through the entire community. The strength and unity of local people were evident, not only in the volunteer support provided from just hours after the blaze, but also in the way the community came together to press their case with the government.

That Saturday in Downing Street, one of the tenants of a nearby block invited me for a cup of tea in her flat. I imagine she didn't expect me to take up her invitation, but I did. The following Wednesday, I visited her and her mother in their flat. From their small balcony, you could look on to the Tower itself and see the devastation the fire had caused. I spoke with them and some other residents who were looking for answers. One piece of advice I gave to them was that in order to get their message across to government, it would help if they could come together in some form of organised grouping.

Some of those who were there went on to form Grenfell United, which became a well-known and effective organisation – and is still working on behalf of the community today. We should never forget that these are people like any others. They have jobs and families but give up their time to work for their local community and to try to ensure that what happened to them can never happen to anyone else. They also long for justice and full accountability, and look to the police investigations and the public inquiry to provide them.

At the same time as I was meeting with residents, I was also chairing cross-Whitehall meetings to push forward the government's response to the disaster and support for the local community. This meant dealing with the Council and various parts of central government. In the first call I had with the Council, my sense was that this was a local authority which had been, if not neglecting, then certainly failing to listen to its tenants.

I must confess that my attitude towards the Council was partly coloured by the approach taken in that first call I had with it from an early COBR (Cabinet Office Briefing Room) meeting. The chief official at the Council introduced himself as the Town Clerk. In my experience – and I had been a London borough councillor – most councils had moved to appointing a chief executive. The use of the 'town clerk' label suggested to me that this was a council that was rather stuck in the mud. This attitude might help to explain its approach to tenants in Grenfell Tower and the surrounding community.

What was also striking about my early conversations with the local community was that tenants had been raising their concerns about the safety of the building time and time again over the years, but had been ignored. They told me that neither the TMO nor the Council had responded as they should have done. It is one thing to fail to respond to residents' concerns about matters like potholes, annoying though that still is for residents. It is quite another to dismiss concerns about safety issues relating to their homes.

To me, the authorities were clearly abusing their positions of power. The powers they held were there to be put to the service of tenants. Instead, they did the opposite. The authorities dismissed the voice of tenants because they could – with tragic results.

Alongside the meetings I was holding, the Department for Communities and Local Government was also taking the action needed to identify other buildings that might be at risk. Three days after the fire, the Department convened a group of technical experts who determined that aluminium composite material (ACM) cladding had been used on the building. This was thought to have been put in place when the outside of the tower block was refurbished. The Department then wrote to local authorities and housing associations asking them to send in samples of any ACM cladding on their tower blocks so that those samples could be tested. Housing associations, which are independent from local councils, manage social housing stock and are the main developers of new homes in the social housing sector.

Only a week later – eleven days after the fire – I learnt that sixty samples of cladding from twenty-five local authorities had failed tests. This was not sixty out of one hundred or more. It was sixty out of sixty. In other words, 100 per cent of the samples tested had failed – an alarming result which brought into sharp focus the extent of the problem. No wonder many saw it as a building-safety crisis. This point was driven home when the ACM cladding testing programme finished on 1 September, with only three combinations of ACM and insulation passing the tests as being safe to use. As a result, the government confirmed that all failed systems would need to be stripped from high-rise blocks. Further testing on non-ACM cladding materials was also promised.

Residents in the flats in the buildings now identified as having this cladding were, of course, very worried about what it meant for their safety. Many felt unable to sleep at night – or at least not with ease – and understandably so. It was imperative to ensure these buildings were safe, which is why the government then set up an Expert Advisory Panel to set out the immediate measures that needed to be taken. The Chairman of the panel was a respected former London Fire Commissioner who had also been Chief Fire and Rescue Adviser to the government, Sir Ken Knight.

In relation to Grenfell Tower itself, one of the key questions was how did cladding that failed safety tests come to be on the building in the first place? Was this the result of inadequate building regulations and safety standards, or was it the result of the incompetent application of those regulations – or, indeed, the deliberate misapplication of those regulations?

This is the fundamental question being considered by

the public inquiry chaired by Sir Martin Moore-Bick, who was appointed to the role on 15 August 2017, two months after the fire. The inquiry was formally opened on 14 September. In his interim report (relating to Phase 1 of the inquiry, which looked into what happened on the night of the fire), Sir Martin said:

> there was compelling evidence that the external walls of the building failed to comply with Requirement B4(1) of Schedule 1 to the Building Regulations 2010, in that they did not adequately resist the spread of fire having regard to the height, use and position of the building. On the contrary, they actively promoted it. It will be necessary in Phase 2 to examine why those who were responsible for the design of the refurbishment considered that the tower would meet that essential requirement.[*]

Sir Martin's interim report also raised serious questions for the London Fire Brigade and other emergency services. The 'stay put' policy was identified as an issue, as was the way the emergency services did or did not work together. This question of communications between emergency services had come to light when I was Home Secretary. A project was set up in 2012, initially under the Cabinet Office and then under the Home Office, to look at it. This was called JESIP – the Joint Emergency Services Interoperability Programme. This project, as its name suggests, was intended to ensure that there was better coordination and communication between the emergency services at times

---

[*] Grenfell Tower Inquiry, *Phase 1 Report*, October 2019, HC 49-I to HC 49-IV.

like this. Given that I had worked on JESIP as Home Secretary, this finding by Sir Martin's inquiry was particularly
disappointing and concerning.

Before the public inquiry got going, and in order to
ensure that the building regulations and fire safety measures required for high-rise residential buildings were fit for
purpose, on 28 July 2017, the government announced an
independent review of the regulations chaired by Dame
Judith Hackitt, who had previously chaired the Health and
Safety Executive (HSE).

Dame Judith's work led to an interim report on
18 December 2017,* which declared that the then-system
of building regulations was 'not fit for purpose'. This was
independent confirmation of what most people had assumed
– in other words, that despite the best of intentions in relation to building regulations, there was something wrong
with the system. The question, of course, was whether what
was wrong was the regulations themselves, their interpretation, the enforcement regime or indeed all of these.

Dame Judith's final report in May 2018† was comprehensive in its findings about the system and called for a
'radical rethink'. It identified that there had all too often
been a race to the bottom in the building sector, and that
there was ambiguity around the rules which allowed those
firms that so wished to 'game the system'.

This action by the government, important though it
was, was of little comfort to those who felt that the fire

---

* *Building a Safer Future: Independent Review of Building
Regulations and Fire Safety, Interim Report*, December 2017, Cm
9551.
† *Building a Safer Future: Independent Review of Building
Regulations and Fire Safety, Final Report*, May 2018, Cm 9607.

should have been prevented. In particular, it was argued that the government had not learnt lessons from previous fires in blocks of flats. The example that was consistently raised during debates about the Grenfell Tower fire was whether the government had fully implemented the recommendations of the coroner in the inquest into the deaths at Lakanal House.

In July 2009, a fire took place at the Lakanal House block of flats in Camberwell in south-east London. As at Grenfell, a fire which started in one flat spread to others, with external cladding burning through quickly. Six people died and twenty were injured. The policy of 'stay put' was also used by the Fire Brigade at Lakanal House. The inquest determined that substandard renovations had led to fire-stopping material between flats being removed, and that inspections by Southwark Council had failed to identify this.

The question raised by most people in relation to the coroner's recommendations was why the government had not retrofitted sprinkler systems in high-rise residential blocks. The impression has been consistently given that this was a recommendation made by the coroner. In fact, the coroner did not say that this should be done. What she did say was: 'It is recommended that your Department encourage providers of housing in high-rise residential buildings containing multiple domestic premises to consider the retro fitting of sprinkler systems.'* Many will consider this a petty point to make, but it is an example of how political debate on key issues can often get focused on an inaccurate

---

* Letter to Secretary of State for Communities and Local Government, 28 March 2013.

interpretation of events or findings. There is a genuine debate to be had about sprinkler systems, but it should be based on the facts.

Of more concern latterly in the debates around Grenfell has been the question of who pays for the removal of unsafe cladding on private residential blocks. In May 2018, I had announced that the government would fully fund the removal and replacement of dangerous cladding in relevant buildings owned by local authorities and housing associations. At the time, the estimated cost was £400 million. Many private leaseholders, however, found themselves facing significant bills for the removal of cladding on blocks when they had bought their flats with no knowledge that there was any problem or potential problem of this sort.

Six months later, it was announced by government that additional powers and financial support would be given, if necessary, to local authorities for them to take enforcement action to remove Grenfell-style cladding from private blocks. This was an effort to speed up the process, as we were now over a year on from the fire, yet there was precious little evidence of the owners of private blocks doing what was needed to ensure the removal of this unsafe cladding.

This was followed by the announcement by the government of the Private Sector ACM Cladding Remediation Fund in May 2019, set up to cover the cost of the replacement of unsafe ACM cladding on private residential buildings in England over eighteen metres in height, and in March 2020 the announcement of a £1 billion fund for the removal of dangerous cladding of all types in both the private and social housing sectors. Further announcements followed in February 2021, one of which related to an additional £3.5 billion of funding for residential buildings of eighteen metres and above, designed to ensure that lease-holders in these buildings did not have to pay the cost of removing and replacing unsafe cladding.

In addition to the provision of funding, the government introduced two new pieces of legislation. The first of these was the Fire Safety Act, which received Royal Assent in April 2021. The second, the Building Safety Act, got Royal Assent in 2022. This is the Act which implements the radical overhaul of the building regulations and fire safety provisions that were recommended by the Hackitt Review. It establishes a more stringent regulatory regime which will be implemented by a new role – the Building Safety Reg-ulator – within the Health and Safety Executive. Among other provisions in the legislation was one requiring every higher-risk building – defined in the Act as a building at least eighteen metres high, or with at least seven storeys, that contains at least two residential units – to have an identified accountable person with responsibility for safety matters, and for engaging with residents and setting up a formal complaints process.

The government also made provisions relating to the responsibilities of building developers for the remediation of unsafe cladding systems. These developed over time and culminated in 2023 in the legal contract that developers would be required to sign giving direct effect to the pledge made the previous year by major housebuilders to fix all the medium or high-rise buildings they had built or refurbished that were unsafe. This was accompanied by a promise to reimburse the taxpayer for work already undertaken at government expense.

The Secretary of State for Levelling Up, Housing and Communities, Michael Gove, made clear that any developers who did not sign the contract 'will be out of the house building business in England entirely unless and until they change their course'.[*]

Until the Moore-Bick inquiry has finally reported, it will not be clear where responsibility lies for the decisions that led to the Grenfell Tower fire. My own view is that it will not be a single decision but a number of decisions by companies and politicians that created the conditions that enabled the fire to take hold. Ensuring that building regulations and fire safety regimes are fit for purpose is essential. So too is getting companies, local authorities and government to adopt the right attitude. They all need to exercise their power for the public good. What seems to have happened is that a mixture of other interests has been prevalent. Some individuals might have been concerned about their career progression. Quite often in local government, as in national government, administrative convenience takes over as a motive, as can the desire for political gain. Finally, we have seen in other cases that inside companies, commercial opportunity can be the driving force rather than concern about the impact of a product or way of working.

If the end product is going to be of real benefit to the customer, it is critical to instil a sense that what matters is the outcome for the final user. I fear it is the interests of the providers that seem to have held sway until now. Alongside all of this, and an important part of ensuring that the end user is the focus, is the need to ensure that in future,

---

[*] Hansard, 14 March 2023, HC Deb., vol. 729, col. 727.

tenants' and residents' voices are heard, and critically that those in social housing are not dismissed as second-class citizens because they live in social housing.

While the government was dealing with issues around building regulations and fire safety, it also needed to address the simple human problem that a number of individuals and families who had lived in Grenfell Tower and the surrounding area no longer had homes to go to. They had to be rehoused.

On the face of it, this may not seem that hard. There were only so many people affected and surely the Council could find homes for them all. In reality, the issue was more complex. Some families had been living together in the Tower out of necessity. Given the option, they would prefer to split into two or possibly more family units, which meant the number of homes required was higher than the original number. Moreover, the trauma of the fire was so strong for some that, taken together with the distrust of the authorities which had already been prevalent but was exacerbated by the fire, they found it hard to accept the offers that were made. This meant that they remained in hotels. They simply needed more time to come to terms with what had happened before they could consider starting a new life in a new home.

Another issue was the question of whether to offer people a move from a hotel to temporary accommodation prior to a permanent move. The alternative was to leave people for longer in hotels but to make sure the offer made to them was for permanent accommodation so that they only had to move once. In the end, what was right for some people was not right for others. This meant that those working at the Council on finding suitable accommodation and making the offers needed to work very closely with the victims themselves.

The problem was that all too often, the victims felt they were kept at arm's length, were not listened to and were not treated like individuals. And of course, all of these issues were being dealt with primarily by a local authority which many people felt had previously failed to listen to their needs and concerns. Bringing in key people from other councils to oversee the response to the fire may have seemed harsh to some working at the Royal Borough of Kensington and Chelsea, but it was essential if there was to be any hope of finding a way to resolve the rehousing issue and to get some sense that the victims could trust what was being offered to them.

This did not just relate to the recent attitude of the Council. It was a far wider issue which went back many years. Social housing – initially just council houses and flats – was provided for those whose financial circumstances meant they could not afford to buy a place of their own or could not afford to rent in the private sector. The vast majority of people in council housing were hard-working, upright citizens, but their jobs paid too little for the luxury of home ownership or private-sector rental. There were of course some who were not hard working, as there are in private-sector homes, but most people were in council accommodation because they were in low-paid jobs.

What social housing in the shape of council homes did was to ensure that in any community, there were people from all walks of life. This was good for the economy in ensuring there were those who could undertake low-paid jobs and still live locally, but it was also beneficial for society as a whole to have people from different financial circumstances living in the same community. For some in politics, however, social housing became synonymous with the image of the ne'er-do-well.

Over time, more and more Conservatives came to see social housing as the generator of problems – problem families and problem individuals. Meanwhile, in my view, Labour did not want to encourage people in social housing into a better life, because, by and large, they thought social housing tenants voted Labour, but once they owned their own homes they would do so no longer. It was Margaret Thatcher and her government who saw the benefits of enabling those living in social housing to have the opportunity to own their homes, and so the policy of the sale of council houses was born.

The policy was very successful. It changed the lives of many and gave them something they thought they could never aspire to – not just a home of their own but a home they owned. It may also have encouraged the assumption by some Conservatives that those who had the get-up-and-go, those with aspirations, bought their homes, leaving the feckless in social housing.

The situation in London had also developed in a different way over the years. As the booms in the property market brought rising prices, they also made houses and flats less affordable, for those in better-paid jobs as well as for those in low-paid jobs. In addition to this, many immigrants had no opportunity to do anything but live in social housing when they came here. All this meant that the mixture of people living in social housing was far broader than it had been in the past, and included professionals as well as those in lower-income jobs. This was certainly true of Grenfell Tower. Yet the negative image remained, and it was this image that led to the attitude from some that social housing was in some sense second class.

When setting up the terms of reference of the public inquiry, we had decided not to include the wider issue of social housing, but it clearly had to be addressed. Hence in August 2018, a green paper on social housing was published – *A New Deal for Social Housing*. This green paper came out of the experience of the residents of Grenfell Tower and the surrounding community, but it also reflected consultations which ministers had had around the country with residents of social housing. There were fourteen events across the country, with nearly 1,000 tenants putting their views forward at the meetings. In addition, over 7,000 submitted their concerns online. Depressingly, the message that came back was the same – too often, complaints were ignored, repairs were botched or neglected, and problems were not dealt with. Put simply, the voices of social housing tenants were being ignored. The aim of the proposals in the green paper, therefore, was to rebalance the relationship between residents and landlords.

The green paper was followed in November 2020 by a social housing white paper – *The Charter for Social Housing Residents*. Among the proposals were moves to empower residents, ensure the effective resolution of complaints and strengthen the consumer standards social landlords must meet. It set out seven commitments that residents should expect from their landlords. These were:

1. to be safe in your home
2. to know how your landlord is performing, including on repairs, complaints and safety, and to know how money is being spent

3. to have your complaints dealt with promptly and fairly, with access to a strong Ombudsman
4. to be treated with respect, backed by a strong consumer regulator and improved consumer standards for tenants
5. to have your voice heard by your landlord
6. to have a good-quality home and neighbourhood to live in, with your landlord keeping your home in good repair
7. to be supported in taking your first step towards ownership

In addition to other measures, the roles of the Regulator of Social Housing and the Housing Ombudsman were to be strengthened with new reactive and proactive consumer regulation that works for tenants and not just landlords. The Regulator would inspect organisations with over 1,000 homes at least once every four years to review compliance with the consumer standards. The strengthened Ombudsman would allow tenants easier access to the Ombudsman's services and speed up complaint resolution, in addition to providing more information for tenants. These proposals would only cover England, as there are different arrangements for Scotland, Wales and Northern Ireland.

The proposals were welcomed, but disappointment was expressed about how long it would take to implement all the changes. As mentioned previously, some proposals required legislation and there was no timetable set for that. Crucially for many, the white paper was not mentioned in the Queen's Speech in May 2021. It was not at all clear why this was the case, and gave the impression that the government simply wasn't that interested. As Grenfell

United reflected in a letter to Boris Johnson, they had been waiting for almost four years for the commitment to act on social housing to be fulfilled. They felt that the exclusion of the *Social Housing* white paper from the Queen's Speech that year showed what they described as: 'the government's disinterest in our housing crisis. Their priorities are for landlords and developers, evidenced by the inclusion of the Planning Bill. This is a betrayal of the legacy we are so committed to achieve.'

It was clear that if social housing had not been addressed by the time the Moore-Bick inquiry completed its hearings, this would raise real concerns. As it was, the government introduced its Social Housing Regulation Bill into the House of Commons in June 2022. At a late stage, the government accepted a change requested by Grenfell United and Shelter, reflecting the deep concern about the management of social housing. As a result of their persistence, in future certain social housing managers will need to have professional qualifications. The Department for Levelling Up, Communities and Housing estimated that around 25,000 people would be required to have housing management qualifications regulated by Ofqual equivalent to Level 4 or 5 Certificate or Diploma in Housing, or a foundation degree from the Chartered Institute of Housing. I am pleased to have been able, with others, to promote the case put by Grenfell United to ministers. I did so because I was certain that the Grenfell tragedy reflected an attitude towards the management of social housing and towards social housing tenants that needs to change. This will be a real legacy of the Grenfell Tower fire.

Although there were many concerns expressed about the length of time it was taking to bring forward the legislation, the government did take steps to address the issues around social housing before it introduced the Bill by setting up, in August 2021, a group of experts from across the housing sector to provide scrutiny and advice to the government as it implemented the white paper.

Resolving the problems, however, is not just about legislation, regulation or administration. The white paper and ensuing legislation can enhance the rights of tenants in social housing, and put in place the means for ensuring that their voices are heard and their concerns registered and addressed. But it can only go so far. Legislation cannot deal with the fundamental problem of the stigma that is all too often attached to social housing.

This was something I had raised when I spoke to the conference of the National Housing Federation (the voice of England's housing associations) in 2018. As I put it then, 'Some residents feel marginalised and overlooked, and are ashamed to share the fact that their home belongs to a housing association or local authority. And on the outside, many people in society – including too many politicians – continue to look down on social housing and, by extension, the people who call it their home.'

Changing attitudes is the hardest thing to achieve and it can't be done simply by legislation or government decree. But there are steps that can be taken to help the process. A key issue I identified in 2018 was that of the buildings themselves. The problem is that all too often, the decisions taken about the appearance, location or quality of social housing sets it apart from the wider communities in which these buildings stand. In turn, this can reinforce prejudice and stigma among those who live in these communities and in wider society. This can then lead to lowered expectations and to restricted opportunities, which, of course, can then lead to greater reinforcement of prejudice and stigma.

It need not happen like this. In any mixed-tenure development, the social housing can be integrated rather than being tucked away behind the private homes, out of sight and out of mind. Rather, for anyone looking at the buildings, it should not be possible to say from their appearance which homes belong to social landlords. Similarly, you should not be able to identify which homes are affordable, which are fully owned by those living in them, or which are partially owned by the residents. Just because a home is to be managed by a housing association doesn't mean the quality of the design, aesthetic and build should be any lower than those built for private sale.

Social housing should never be seen as something that only has to be 'good enough', nor should anyone think that the people living in it should just be grateful and should not expect better. Social housing should be so good that people are proud to call it their home, regardless of whether it is managed by a local authority, a housing association or a TMO. People living in social housing are not second-class citizens, and they should not have to put up with second-rate homes.

The tragedy of the Grenfell Tower fire wrecked homes, destroyed lives and devastated a community. The government responded with new legislation, enhanced building regulations, and support for making high-rise residential buildings safer. The public inquiry should lead to an understanding of how it was possible for the circumstances to arise which led to the fire. It will then be possible for the government to take any further measures that are needed to ensure such a devastating tragedy cannot happen again.

I have no doubt that this was yet another example of power being abused and a failure to understand the importance of service to the residents. At multiple stages, it looks like other interests were prioritised over the interests of residents. The problem is that the various parties involved had the power to do that, and in so doing were abusing that power. If the people living in the flats had been a priority, different decisions might have been taken and the fire would never have happened.

It is so important, therefore, that what results from this is not just changed laws and regulations. That can only get us so far. If the residents are to be made a priority in the thinking of those taking key decisions, what is needed is a different attitude towards social housing and a renewed sense among social landlords that they have to recognise their responsibilities to residents. Above all, it means the abolition of the stigma attached to social housing for so many.

At the time of writing, the inquiry into the Grenfell Tower disaster still has some way to go. It has completed its evidence sessions for phase 2, but it is not expected to produce a final report until 2024. This does seem a long wait since the tragedy itself, but if it produces some clear recommendations and, more to the point, is able to put its finger on exactly what decisions and actions led to the flammable cladding being on the building, who was responsible and what action needs to be taken to prevent a tragedy like this ever happening again, then the length of time taken will certainly have been worth it.

Meanwhile, the victims and survivors of Grenfell have to live every day in the shadow of the tragedy, and without the family members and friends who lost their lives. For them, the memory of that night will live on. While they may be able to move on with their lives, they will never forget.

We owe it to them and to the seventy-two who died that night to ensure that out of this tragedy comes a better scheme for securing building safety, improved relations between the tenants of social housing and their landlords, and a societal change of attitude towards social housing.

Above all, there needs to be a willingness from those in authority to be serious about listening and responding to people living in social housing. What the Grenfell tragedy showed was that too often, those in authority responsible for social housing ignored the voices of tenants and hence abused their power.

8

Child Sexual Abuse

Of all the issues of injustice I have dealt with, in many ways the most harrowing and the most egregious example of the abuse of power is that of child sexual abuse. Listening to survivors, now long into their adulthood, was chilling. It was difficult to comprehend how any adult could treat a child like this. Every example was a blatant abuse of power: those with least power – children – suffering the most terrible abuse at the hands of those with power – adults. Very often, the power was heightened by the adult's position of authority – in the church, in children's homes, at sports clubs and so on. But all too often, the abuse took place in the home. In every case, this was adults satisfying their own desires and inflicting huge pain and trauma because they could.

These abuses of power were perpetrated by those whose responsibility, and in many cases job, was to protect the very children who were harmed. I say job because if you are a member of staff in a children's home, then you are there to look after the children and to protect them. If you are a teacher, you are *in loco parentis* and part of your role is a protective one. If you are a member of the clergy working with children in a church choir or serving at the altar, then not only do you have a role in teaching the children what to do, but you also have a responsibility to protect them. The children should have been able to trust these adults – teachers, clergy, parents, care-home staff – but that trust was cruelly abused.

This abuse of power was aggravated by the inactivity of those in positions of authority who refused to act when the abuse was referred to them, because they chose to defend the institution rather than the children. Some thought that what mattered was protecting the institution itself. Some didn't want to believe what they were told, maybe some even secretly connived in the abuse, and some were simply afraid to speak up. Whatever the reason, whatever justification they gave themselves, they failed to act. They failed to use their power to deal with the abuse, to protect the children in their care and to act to ensure the abuse could not continue. This failure to act was a further abuse of power.

That says a great deal about our society. People didn't want to rock the boat. Didn't want to investigate what went on behind closed doors. They had no thought for the victims. These were children whose lives would be changed for ever by their experiences. Hearing survivors talk about their abuse and their lives since then, it was all too obvious that this form of abuse never leaves you. It isn't possible to completely close the door on it and move on. It affects your attitude towards others, it makes your own relationships harder in adulthood, it means you find it hard ever to really trust anyone.

When, as Home Secretary, I set up the Independent Inquiry into Child Sexual Abuse in July 2014, I said that I thought the country would be shocked if they knew the extent to which such abuse had taken place. In March 2020, the Office for National Statistics estimated that 3.1 million adults in England and Wales had experienced some form of sexual abuse before they were sixteen. This gives some measure of the extent of the abuse that has occurred and that continues to take place to this day.

I also believed that people would be shocked by the nature of some of the organisations which allowed such abuse to continue unchallenged. The Church of England, the Roman Catholic Church, other faith groups, major sports organisations, local authority homes, public schools – the list goes on, and includes some of the most respected institutions in the country.

The history of setting up the inquiry was riddled with problems. In looking back, it is important to remember that this process was taking place against a background of heightened awareness of the issue of child abuse, and at a time when a number of people who had been very senior in government, in the public sector, including the military, and in the world of entertainment were being accused of abuse. Some of the most high-profile of these allegations were later shown to be false, but they meant that there was a growing interest in the problem in the media and mounting public concern about those who might have been involved.

Initially, I appointed Elizabeth Butler-Sloss, an eminent judge and former President of the High Court's Family Division, to head the inquiry, but she stood down after only a week because questions had been raised about her late brother Sir Michael Havers and the failure to examine allegations of abuse properly when he was Attorney General. In particular, Sir Michael had been criticised for trying to stop Geoffrey Dickens (an MP at the time) from naming a diplomat, Sir Peter Hayman, in Parliament as a paedophile.

I found this difficult because I believed Elizabeth to be a fair and honourable individual who would look at the evidence with the eyes of a senior member of the judiciary. But the court of public opinion was reluctant to accept that someone could look at issues independently if they were in any way related to, or knew, someone whose approach to the issue had been questioned.

Two months later, I appointed Fiona Woolf, another leading lawyer and at the time Lord Mayor of London, to chair the inquiry. It then transpired that she knew Sir Leon Brittan, who had been accused of overseeing an establishment cover-up of the issues of child abuse when he was Home Secretary. Her fitness to serve was taken up by the Home Affairs Select Committee and others in Parliament, and she quit nearly two months later. Again, this showed how difficult it was to be accepted as independent in the world of public opinion when just knowing, or indeed living in the same street as, someone whose behaviour had been questioned was seen as sufficient to disqualify an individual from leading an inquiry.

Following this, I disbanded the inquiry and set up a new statutory inquiry chaired by a New Zealand judge, Dame Lowell Goddard, who was endorsed in February 2015 by the Select Committee.

The inquiry was officially opened on 9 July 2015, and being a statutory inquiry, it had powers to compel witnesses. Its task was to determine whether state and non-state institutions had taken seriously their duty of care to protect children from sexual abuse in England and Wales. Four panel members were appointed: Drusilla Sharpling,

Professor Alexis Jay, Ivor Frank and Malcolm Evans. There was now to be no cut-off date for the work of the inquiry. We had originally set a cut-off date of 1970, meaning that offences committed before then would not be considered, but it became clear that the victims and survivors were concerned about this date because until that year, responsibility for children's homes and approved schools had lain with the Home Office. They assumed the date had been chosen to make sure the Home Office could not come under scrutiny.

As far as I was concerned, that was not the case – it seemed a suitable date, sufficiently far back but not too far back to make it difficult to establish the truth. But the cut-off date made it hard for people to trust the inquiry, so we made the inquiry open-ended.

When the inquiry began, the names of those on the Victims and Survivors Consultative Panel were also announced. From the start, I had wanted to ensure that the voices of victims and survivors would be heard, and that their experience could be available to the inquiry to guide its work. Often in setting up inquiries, it is important that victims and survivors are listened to, and they generally want to have a role in the inquiry to help it to do a proper job.

Too often, victims and survivors have been ignored, or officialdom has found ways to avoid looking into the core of their complaints. It is natural, therefore, for them to want to be able to guide the inquiry. The nature of a statutory inquiry is such, however, that it is not possible within the legislation to appoint victims and survivors as members of the inquiry itself because of the potential for conflicts of interest.

The 2005 Inquiries Act expressly states that the Minister who makes appointments to an inquiry panel:

> must not appoint a person as a member of the inquiry panel if it appears to the Minister that the person has –
>
> (a) a direct interest in the matters to which the inquiry relates, or
>
> (b) a close association with an interested party, unless, despite the person's interest or association, his appointment could not reasonably be regarded as affecting the impartiality of the inquiry panel.

While it might seem obvious to appoint a victim or survivor to the panel, it would be all too easy then for someone found responsible for abuse to claim that the result was flawed because that member of the panel was not impartial. This can be one of the most difficult aspects of setting up such an inquiry. Victims and survivors find it hard to understand why they cannot be members of the panel, but, if they were, their presence could lead to the determinations of the inquiry being at best rubbished and at worst set aside as being prejudiced.

While they cannot be appointed as members of an inquiry panel, however, it is possible to ensure that experience is available to the panel by setting up an advisory or consultative panel, which is what was done in the case of the inquiry into child sexual abuse.

The inquiry's first twelve investigations were announced in November 2015. They included allegations of child sexual abuse linked to Westminster, children in the care of Lambeth and Nottinghamshire councils, Cambridge House and Knowl View School in Rochdale and Rochdale Council, the Anglican Church and the Roman Catholic Church. The inquiry would also investigate child sexual abuse on the internet, custodial institutions, residential schools and child exploitation by organised networks.

It had previously been announced that the inquiry would investigate allegations of abuse which had been made against Greville Janner, who from 1970 to 1997 was a Labour Member of Parliament for a seat in Leicester. He then became a member of the House of Lords. He died in December 2015, suffering from dementia, shortly after a High Court judge had ruled that he was unfit to stand trial on charges relating to child abuse.

In August 2016, Justice Goddard tendered her resignation to the then-Home Secretary Amber Rudd, citing her career and family life as reasons for her decision. This came twenty-four hours after she had been publicly criticised for taking three months' holiday since being appointed. This was not the first media story about Justice Goddard, as there had been reports relating to her behaviour towards others involved in the inquiry, which she 'absolutely rejected'.

After Justice Goddard had resigned, Professor Alexis Jay was appointed as the inquiry's fourth Chairman. Professor Jay had been a panel member, but had also chaired the inquiry into the cases of abuse in Rotherham. She has chaired the Independent Panel since that point.

Arguably, she should have been appointed Chair of the panel from the start, given the excellent job she had done on the Rotherham inquiry. Indeed, we did discuss this in the Home Office. But there is a general perception among both politicians and commentators that an inquiry has more credibility if it is judge-led. I allowed myself to be swayed by those voices. For that, I apologise to Alexis Jay, who has done a first-class job and who nobly sat on the panel under a less experienced but legally qualified chair.

There are some inquiries for which a judge as chair is appropriate, but we must recognise that this is not always the case. There are issues where experience in the subject matter rather than legal training really does count.

The inquiry published a number of reports over the years, culminating in a final report in October 2022. All of them are deeply shocking. What is revealed over and over again is a horrific abuse of power by those who were in positions of trust and responsibility in relation to children.

During this time, I had a number of meetings with victims and survivors, some of whom represented thousands of other victims and survivors. My first such meeting was in November 2014 at the offices of the organisation NAPAC (National Association for People Abused in Childhood). When I went into the room, I honestly did not know what to expect, and I suspect that some of those present were wary of me because their trust in authority had been so cruelly shattered by their childhood experiences. NAPAC had brought together a group of people who had suffered abuse in a variety of circumstances. I was told about abuse by family members, and abuse at the hands of priests and others in religious settings. Each time, the message was the same. Not only had they suffered as children, but the memory and the impact of the abuse remained with them. Some had been able to come to terms with what had happened to them better than others, but the critical point that came through was that the memory of the abuse is with you every single day.

It is often easy to dismiss matters of the past by saying it happened a long time ago, people can move on. To say that about child sexual abuse would be to completely fail to understand the nature of the beast. The memory lives on, but more than that, the abuse affects people's relationships later in life. After all, they were abused by the very people they were supposed to be able to trust; and they were ignored by others who should have cared for them.

Not only does abuse in childhood affect their personal life, but it can have a knock-on effect on their working life, perhaps because of ongoing mental health problems, because their abuse meant their education was restricted, or because they are simply unable to work to their full potential.

How many people in the UK today have suffered over the years? How many people today have lives damaged because of their experience of abuse in childhood? How many people find it difficult to form trusting relationships because they were let down in the past? The answer is, as the numbers of people revealed by the inquiry as suffering abuse shows, far, far more than anyone would think. So this is not just an issue of the past, it is an issue for us today.

Another meeting I had was set up by the NSPCC with young people who had recently suffered abuse. Their abuse had been recognised and was being dealt with, and they were being supported, but again the impact the abuse had had on them was clear.

I also remember attending an event where I heard a young woman speaking about her experience of abuse at the hands of a teacher. She was bright and was expected to do well in her exams. She had tried to report the abuse, but the school took no notice. As a result of the abuse and the failure of those in charge to take her seriously, she acted up, her performance in school suffered and she experienced mental health problems. If the school had responded to her complaints, her story might have been so different. She was now doing well, but the school's failure to believe her had effectively led to the loss of several years of her life.

Government ministers receive many letters and emails from people relating to the issues they deal with. This is over and above our own constituency correspondence. As you might expect, given the volume received, most of this correspondence will be dealt with by officials. Sometimes they are clearly private, in that they relate to someone's personal story or circumstances. Many of these will still be dealt with by officials, but sometimes the particular nature of the correspondence means that the civil service escalate it as something to be shown to the minister. I remember one such letter that came to me as Home Secretary. It was from a woman who had been abused as a child. She told me that her partner had told her about a speech I had made in Parliament about dealing with child sexual abuse.

Until that point, she had not felt able to pursue the issue and see her perpetrator brought to justice. Having learnt that I had put the issue into the public domain, she bit the bullet and reported her abuse. Her perpetrator was charged, convicted and was, when she wrote, in prison. She told me that as a result, she felt a freedom that she had not felt before.

I also remember one day when I was door-knocking in my constituency, talking to voters about the issues they wished to raise with me. My team alerted me to the fact that there was a woman in the street who was keen to talk to me. She hadn't been able to respond when I knocked on her door, but she wanted to let me know that she had been a victim of abuse as a child and was grateful because the inquiry would give her the opportunity to talk about her experience as part of its work. She didn't want her testimony to be used in a criminal case. She just wanted to be able to tell someone about her experience; for her, that would take a great weight off her mind.

A lot of attention in politics is given to arguments about key issues of policy. Yet politics is about people. It is about serving the people. With that letter, and with that conversation in the street, I felt that I had done something to serve those who had suffered from the horrific crime of child abuse. That justified the action I had taken in arguing for, and setting up, the Independent Inquiry into Child Sexual Abuse.

The appalling nature of the abuse that has taken place in setting after setting over the years, and that sadly in too many instances continues today, has been brought home in the various reports published by the inquiry. The following are just some of the examples of what the inquiry has uncovered.

Take the report on Cambridge House and Knowl View, for example.* This related to children's homes in the Rochdale Council area. It also involved the late Liberal Member of Parliament for Rochdale, Cyril Smith. Cambridge House was run by a voluntary organisation of which Cyril Smith was Honorary Secretary, and provided a hostel for working boys. His position gave him easy access to the boys living in the hostel, which it is alleged facilitated his sexual abuse of them. Moreover, his prominence and standing in Rochdale were such that he was able to

---

* Independent Inquiry into Child Sexual Abuse, *Cambridge House, Knowl View and Rochdale Investigation Report*, April 2018.

exert influence locally, and in particular to put pressure on others to remain quiet about any allegations.

In 1988 he was awarded a knighthood for political services and, although it appears that there were discussions at the highest political levels about the rumours relating to him, the concerns expressed were more about the potential impact on the honours system and less about the alleged victims. The inquiry concluded that 'this demonstrated a considerable deference to power'.

Cyril Smith also had links to Knowl View School, which catered for children with complex needs, some of whom had already experienced abuse. The inquiry conducted a thorough investigation into that institution, hearing complaints of sexual abuse over a period of twenty-five years, starting in 1969. It concluded:

> far from taking additional steps to protect these children, the school and other institutions had come to regard their sexual abuse while at Knowl View as almost expected, or as something that could not be prevented . . . The institution failed in its basic function to keep children in its care safe from harm and, in particular, safe from sexual harm, both within and outwith the school.

The reference there to 'outwith the school' related to evidence that sexual exploitation of some boys took place in Rochdale town centre – in the public toilets and the bus station – by men paying for sex. The authorities had known about exploitation in the public toilets for some years, yet it seems that the records of the children showed no sense on the part of the authorities of needing to deal with the situation or to recognise the events for what they were – serious sexual assaults. It appears that the police were more willing to investigate, but no one was charged, although some of the boys did make disclosures to the police, who knew the names of the men involved.

The lack of action by Rochdale Council regarding an institution for which they were responsible seems completely incomprehensible. Leading councillors failed to accept any responsibility, often blaming officials. One Director of Education did commission reports into the school, but there was no sense of a need to take urgent action to prevent children from being abused. Officials had the power on the one hand to act to protect the children and on the other to ignore or soft-pedal on any action in response to allegations of abuse. They chose to put the interests of the institution first and the interests of the children they were there to serve second.

As regards those working in Knowl View School itself, the inquiry found that 'For most of the school's existence, staff were at best complacent but arguably complicit in the abuse they knew to be taking place,' and concluded that in relation to abuse by boys of other boys 'staff simply treated the sexual abuse between boys as normal'.

These findings reflect those seen elsewhere in cases of child sexual abuse. Authorities turning a blind eye. An assumption that this was what happened to children in these sorts of settings – nothing to write home about. A desire to protect the institution and the powerful against the interests of the powerless. This lack of interest in protecting the children came from the very people whose job it was to put the children's interests first and provide them with care and protection.

What I perhaps found most shocking in the Independent

Inquiry's work was the results of investigations into Churches. Surely these bodies, with their teachings of right and wrong, would do everything to ensure that allegations of child sexual abuse were properly investigated. Surely they would be the first to want to take action against any perpetrators in the Church, particularly the clergy and any others in positions of responsibility and trust. If you can trust anyone, surely you can trust a priest or someone with a position in your local church.

The inquiry found a rather different picture. I can do no better than quote directly from their findings, starting with the Anglican Church:

> The culture of the Church of England facilitated it becoming a place where abusers could hide. Deference to the authority of the Church and to individual priests, taboos surrounding discussion of sexuality, and an environment where alleged perpetrators were treated more supportively than victims presented barriers to disclosure that many victims could not overcome. Another aspect of the Church's culture was clericalism, which meant that the moral authority of clergy was widely perceived as beyond reproach . . . faith organisations are marked out by their explicit moral purpose, in teaching right from wrong. In the context of child sexual abuse, the Church's neglect of the physical, emotional and spiritual well-being of children and young people in favour of protecting its reputation was in conflict with its mission of love and care for the innocent and the vulnerable.[*]

---

[*] Independent Inquiry into Child Sexual Abuse, *The Anglican Church Investigation Report*, October 2020.

The inquiry also reported that:

> The Church has failed to respond consistently to vic-
> tims and survivors of child sexual abuse with sympathy
> and compassion, accompanied by practical and appro-
> priate support. This has often added to the trauma
> already suffered by those who were abused by individ-
> uals associated with the Church . . . Excessive attention
> was often paid to the circumstances of the alleged
> perpetrator in comparison to the attention given to
> those who disclosed they had been sexually abused or
> to the issue of the risk that alleged perpetrators posed.

Their findings in relation to the Roman Catholic
Church were similar. Having identified that faith organisations were differentiated by having a moral purpose, they
found that:

> In the context of the sexual abuse of children, that
> moral purpose was betrayed over decades by those in
> the [Catholic] Church who perpetrated this abuse and
> those who turned a blind eye to it. The Church's neglect
> of the physical, emotional and spiritual well-being of
> children and young people in favour of protecting its
> reputation was in conflict with its mission of love and
> care for the innocent and the vulnerable.*

(Note the use of the same language regarding its mission as for the Anglican Church.)

They went on to say, 'Throughout this investigation,
we heard appalling accounts of sexual abuse of children

---

* Independent Inquiry into Child Sexual Abuse, *The Roman
Catholic Church Investigation Report*, November 2020.

perpetrated by clergy and others associated with the Roman Catholic Church. The sexual offending . . . often involved deeply manipulative behaviour by those in positions of trust, who were respected by parents and children alike.'

These were not the only faith groups found seriously wanting in relation to the issue of child sexual abuse. In a report issued in September 2021 after an investigation into Child Protection in Religious Organisations and Settings, which looked at thirty-eight religious organisations with a presence in England and Wales, the inquiry found 'egregious failings by a number of religious organisations, and cases of child sexual abuse perpetrated by their adherents'.*

It also established that in some religious organisations and settings, which can include situations in which people come together for prayer, worship, education and leisure activities, there are real barriers to the reporting of allegations of child sexual abuse. They are similar to those identified above. In some cases, there is a culture of victim-blaming, shame and honour. Ideas of sexual purity and social and family standing can make it harder to report abuse. In some communities, sexual matters are not discussed openly, or children are not taught about sex or sexual relationships. There can be abuse of power by religious leaders, with children being taught to defer to religious figures who are considered by definition to be superior and therefore trustworthy. That trust can then be exploited in order to perpetrate abuse.

---

* Independent Inquiry into Child Sexual Abuse, *Child Protection in Religious Organisations and Settings Investigation Report*, September 2021.

Other issues that were relevant were the gender imbalance in some communities, where those acting as spiritual and religious leaders, as well as those in senior lay positions, were predominantly men. In some cases, there was a mistrust of external agencies. In addition, the idea of forgiveness could be misused to persuade victims not to report abuse and to justify the failure of leaders to act on allegations.

On top of all this, not all organisations had effective systems – understood and operated throughout the organisation in question – for responding to allegations of child sexual abuse and very few had formal arrangements in place to provide counselling or therapy for victims.

These are just some of the findings of the inquiry. Taken together, all their reports show an absolutely shocking degree of abuse and – just as worrying, if not more so – an incredible degree of failure by those in authority at various levels and in different organisations, both public and private, to take these allegations seriously and act on them.

Those making allegations were too often not believed. Over recent years, however, the opposite problem has also been seen in practice. When I was Home Secretary, one of the things that annoyed me, but that I was never able to change, was the way the police would often lurch from one position to the opposite. I saw this in 'stop and search', which I deal with in Chapter 10. When told they had to operate stop and search lawfully, some took it to mean that they couldn't do stop and search at all.

Just so with allegations of child abuse. They should have moved from their position of disbelief to one of accepting that any allegation merited investigation, and then going on to investigate. Instead, we saw them move to a position of immediately believing what someone making allegations said, and publicly accepting allegations before investigation. This was most vividly seen in the infamous case of 'Nick', who made allegations not just against senior politicians but also against senior members of the armed forces and others. The impact of this was to lead some to challenge further the efforts to identify child sexual abuse and to question whether the lengths the government were going to in order to identify the extent of the problem and give some sense of justice to past victims and survivors were really necessary.

A lot of politics is about balance, weighing different arguments and different interests against each other. But today's world has become more absolutist – a theme I will return to later. The term 'third way' may have come to be disparaged by his political opponents when it was used by former Prime Minister Tony Blair, but the reality of politics is that on many, if not most, issues politicians are searching for the centre ground between conflicting opinions. We should never forget Bismarck's observation in 1867 that 'Politics is the art of the possible.'

That sits uneasily with the growing assumption today that what is needed is tough absolutist positions promoted in a muscular way. Such absolutism requires little thought, gets headlines and appeals to a core of supporters. But on many issues, the really tough position is to seek a compromise.

What this means for the police is that when looking at allegations of child sexual abuse, it is important to retain an open mind, not to dismiss them out of hand simply because it is easier or more comfortable to do so, and not to automatically leap to accusing the alleged perpetrators.

Instead, they should do what police are expected to do and look for the evidence. I think we should acknowledge how easy it is in dealing with these painful issues for progress to be set back by a misstep.

As far as the abuse of power is concerned, the issue is more complex in these cases of child sexual abuse than in a number of other examples where the motivations often may well have been subconscious. Many of those who perpetrate the initial abuse will look for jobs and roles that bring them close to those they want to abuse. They are abusing their positions of power over children. It is not an unintended abuse. It is not a casual abuse arising as a by-product of other decisions or actions. Every act is intentional. They have carefully got themselves into the position where they have victims under their power. Others will have pursued a career for different reasons, but then, when in a position of power over children, fail to curb their desires and again abuse their power.

We should never forget, however, that many abusers have themselves suffered abuse as children. This shows the long-lasting effect that abuse has, staying with people throughout their lives and in some cases being reflected in their own behaviour at a later date.

Stopping those intending to abuse, or with a proclivity to abuse, depends heavily on the processes of checking applicants for these roles with children. Over the years, governments have enhanced these processes through what is now the Disclosure and Barring Service (DBS), which effectively certifies those able to work with children and vulnerable individuals. The government accepted that it needed to act on the inquiry's recommendations that it should strengthen certain aspects of the DBS. Organisations will rely on the DBS checks, but they have a responsibility over and above that to ensure they are confident that their employees meet the standards of behaviour expected and needed.

Looking beyond the perpetrators, what is striking is the abuse of power by those who choose to protect the institution or individuals within it. We need to worry about a society in which someone in a position of authority who hears an allegation of child sexual abuse thinks that it is of such little consequence that it is less important than the interests of the institution.

Surely, in this day and age, we have moved beyond the idea that this is the sort of thing that happens to children – to children from certain backgrounds or circumstances – and can be ignored. The value of every child should be recognised. Surely, also, we must have gone beyond the idea that these children simply can't be believed, and I hope that no one thinks that in today's world, people are enlightened and don't do this anymore. Looking at the reports of the inquiry should be enough to dispel that myth – as should looking at the cases the NSPCC deals with.

When the inquiry published its final report in October 2022,* it made over 100 recommendations, all designed to help protect children. It noted that current estimates were that one in six girls and one in twenty boys experience child sexual abuse before the age of sixteen. One of the recommendations which received most focus when the report was published was the proposal for a law of mandatory reporting. The formal recommendation was to make

---

* *The Report of the Independent Inquiry into Child Sexual Abuse,* October 2022, HC 720.

it a legal requirement for anybody working in regulated activity in relation to children (as defined in the Safeguarding Vulnerable Groups Act 2006), for anybody working in a position of trust (as defined by the Sexual Offences Act 2003) and for police officers to report child sexual abuse. This would cover, for example, those working in teaching or taking care of children. The idea had been mooted before, and undoubtedly such a law would have to be drawn up very carefully in order to avoid unintended consequences, but given the findings of the inquiry and the extent to which child sexual abuse had been ignored by those in authority, I urged the government to consider this very carefully. If those in positions of trust are shown to be ignoring cries of help from children, then surely action is needed. I am pleased to say that at the beginning of April 2023, the government announced its intention to accept this recommendation and introduce a legal requirement for those working with children to report abuse and concerns about child grooming.

As the inquiry's final report declared:

> The impact of past failures to protect children from sexual abuse and to support those who have been harmed is incalculable . . . The sexual abuse and exploitation of children is criminal and morally wrong. There is no excuse for those who perpetrate this crime. It has never been right or excusable whenever it occurred. To a significant extent, this also applies to those who knew about the abuse but did nothing, as well as to those who actively covered it up or contrived to assist a perpetrator in escaping justice or avoiding the scrutiny of the statutory authorities.

I can't promise there will ever be a day when there are no adults who have a desire or propensity to abuse children. But I do want to see a day when all in authority accept the need to put the interests of the children they serve first and to take allegations of abuse seriously and not simply ignore them. The extent to which child abuse has taken place is appalling. Equally appalling is the conspiracy of silence which allowed it to occur and to continue. All involved were abusing their power.

9

Rotherham

The Independent Inquiry into Child Sexual Abuse had a wide remit, looking at abuse in a variety of different settings. Even before it was established, however, there had been a number of reports of abuse in specific settings. The one with which I was most involved was the report into child sexual abuse in Rotherham.* The implications for the South Yorkshire Police meant that as Home Secretary, I had a particular interest in the inquiry's findings. It was this report on abuse in Rotherham that was a key factor that led to the wider inquiry.

The revelations in the early 2010s of the sexual exploitation and grooming of young girls and boys that had been taking place in Rotherham for around three decades were truly shocking. It was shocking that such criminality could continue for so long, seemingly without comment from the authorities. It was shocking that this could happen in our day and age in a town in the UK. What was perhaps most shocking was the way in which the police and the local authority, both of whom had responsibilities and

---

* *Independent Inquiry into Child Sexual Exploitation in Rotherham 1997–2013*, August 2014.

duties to protect and care for the public, had consistently failed to act.

The police and the local authority were the ones in positions of power. They were the ones with the means to act. They were the ones who could have protected the girls and boys and brought the perpetrators to justice. Instead, they failed to use their power in the interests of those they were there to protect. They abused their power – because they could.

It is worth reminding ourselves what happened in Rotherham. From the late 1980s to the 2010s, organised child sexual abuse was taking place in the town. When Professor Alexis Jay reported in 2014 on what had been happening between 1997 and 2013, she estimated that around 1,400 children had been abused over that period by men predominantly of Pakistani origin or heritage. That figure was only an estimate. Even after every effort had been made to find out the true figure, it was not possible to say absolutely how many children had been affected over time.

It was in the early 1990s that evidence appears to have first come to light about what was happening in the town, when some care-home managers reported that children from their homes were being picked up by taxi drivers. There were numerous reports from 2001 from families and others identifying perpetrators, which were passed to the Council and to South Yorkshire Police. In 2002, a draft report of a Home Office research project severely criticised the agencies in Rotherham that were involved in dealing with child sexual exploitation. This was suppressed, however, as the police and Council were unhappy with the report and questioned the data used in it. Rotherham

Council then commissioned Dr Angie Heal, a Strategic Drugs Analyst, to look into the issue of drug use in the area. Based with South Yorkshire Police, she produced two main reports, 'Sexual Exploitation, Drug Use and Drug Dealing: Current Situation in South Yorkshire' in 2003 and 'Violence and Gun Crime: Links with Sexual Exploitation, Prostitution and Drug Markets in South Yorkshire' in 2006. She established that organised child sexual abuse was taking place and reported it to the Council, but nothing was done. She later described what happened in Rotherham as the biggest child-protection scandal in UK history. Yet there was no conviction until 2010. The issue was constantly being brushed under the carpet or dismissed with claims that those making the reports had exaggerated the problem.

Pressure continued in the media and Parliament, which led to the Council commissioning Professor Alexis Jay to conduct her inquiry. Alexis Jay had had a career in social work, and from 2005 until 2011 was Chief Social Work Inspector at the Social Work Inspection Agency (SWIA), which scrutinised the provision of social services by local authorities in Scotland. She remained in that role for the Scottish government, after the SWIA had been merged into the Care Inspectorate, until 2013.

Her report was devastating. The abuse included gang rape, forcing children to watch rape, threatening to rape or harm the victims' mothers and sisters, threatening to set victims on fire and trafficking them to other towns for sex. Some of the girls became pregnant, some had terminations, for others the babies were brought up by their mothers – all of this added to the traumatic impact of the abuse and exploitation.

In her report, Alexis Jay set out the nature of the abuse in no uncertain terms:

> It is hard to describe the appalling nature of the abuse that child victims suffered. They were raped by multiple perpetrators, trafficked to other towns and cities in the north of England, abducted, beaten, and intimidated. There were examples of children who had been doused in petrol and threatened with being set alight, threatened with guns, made to witness brutally violent rapes and threatened they would be next if they told anyone. Girls as young as 11 were raped by large numbers of male perpetrators.

Despite all the evidence that was given to them, the authorities – both the police and the local Council – in effect simply turned a blind eye to what was happening. Too often, shocking though it is, it seems that the police did not view the child abuse taking place as a crime. They had the power to act, yet they abused their power by failing to act and by not addressing the issue properly. All because they could. As Professor Jay said in her report, 'the collective failures of political and officer leadership were blatant'.

This is not to say that nobody tried to help. In 1997, an organisation was set up called Risky Business, which comprised a small number of youth workers who were involved in outreach to the community. They identified many incidents of abuse, but all too often their reports to the Council were at best not treated with the seriousness they deserved and at worst simply ignored. There was a general sense at the Council that reports of abuse were exaggerated. All too often, there was a view in some cases that children like this, children from certain sections of society, could not be trusted to tell the truth.

Yet it was not just the children who were being side-lined. There were cases where the children's parents complained and begged for action, but their voices were not heard. There were cases where the girls' fathers went to the houses where their daughters were being abused to rescue them and take them home, only to find themselves arrested by the police at the scene for offences such as breach of the peace or being drunk and disorderly.

There appear to have been several issues that lay behind the failure of the Council and the police. Given that most of the perpetrators were described as being of an 'Asian' background and in fact were from the Pakistani community in particular, it is thought that the authorities were concerned that they could be accused of racism if they investigated. It was likely that there was also a concern that raising the profile of the ethnic element in this issue – in other words, the predominance among the perpetrators of men of Pakistani heritage – could have damaged community cohesion. Added to this, there may well have been a party-political element to the thinking, with the ruling Labour Council worried that any action they might take could affect the willingness of people in certain communities to vote for them.

The Jay report found no evidence that the children's social care staff at the Council were concerned about ethnicity, but did find a general sense that senior people wanted the issue of ethnicity to be played down. My suspicion is that, for the politicians particularly, ethnicity was highly likely to have been a concern. Undoubtedly, they did not want to alienate a part of the local community. I do have to wonder, however, whether that part of the community would have reacted as those in authority thought would be the case. I suspect that there will have been people in that community who were concerned about what they knew, or thought, was going on.

It is also important to reflect that, while the majority of the victims were white, there may well have been abuse occurring within the Pakistani community – that is, within the same ethnic group. Almost certainly concerns about honour, and on the other hand the shame that would have been felt by victims' families if the issue was raised, would have led to this being hidden.

I like to think that concern within the community about what was happening may well have been felt particularly by those close to the perpetrators, such as their mothers and sisters. The victims were predominantly female. It is hard to think of other women knowing what was happening and keeping quiet on the subject. Having said that, in this case the community strictures about male pre-eminence almost certainly will have had an impact. In some families, women would be kept behind the scenes, prevented from mixing with people outside the community, expected to remain in the background and not to challenge the men.

Anyone who went against the view of the elders would certainly have known the impact of daring to challenge the accepted hierarchy and accepted views about the role of women. It was those very same elders who were used by the Council as their main point of contact with the community, with the unsurprising result that little attention was paid to the problem.

All these factors will have played a part in ensuring that any concerns within the community did not surface. It is not possible that there were no concerns felt by others outside the community, and I am sure there will have been some who knew exactly what was going on.

There were two themes underlying this, and some of the other abuses of power which I have written about, which led to clear social injustice. The first of these was a sense from those in authority that the children concerned were second-class citizens. They didn't act because in their minds, this was what happened to children like them. Some will have been children in care, others working-class children, and some will have had difficult family backgrounds. As Professor Jay said in her report, the police regarded 'many child victims with contempt'.

Of course, this is inexcusable. That anyone should look on fellow citizens and particularly children as second-class citizens is appalling in itself. That this was the approach taken by both those elected to serve the interests of everyone living in the Council area, and by those whose job it was to prevent crime and protect people from crime, makes it so much worse.

Yet this attitude was also seen elsewhere. At Hillsborough, the police viewed the trouble as typical of the Liverpool fans and failed to appreciate what was happening before their eyes. In the case of the Primodos drug scandal, the scientists thought this was what happened to women and they should just put up with it. This sense of the superiority in those with power is one feature that leads to abuse of that power.

The second theme was the need to defend the reputation of the town and the Council. The revelation of what was going on would have had an impact on people's views of the town – and, by implication, of the Council, particularly given that some children were in local authority homes. They failed to see that the damage to the town's reputation was far worse when it was revealed that abuse had been going on over many years and that the local authority at both official and political level had known about it and had failed to take the action necessary.

As a result, hundreds of young lives were damaged. Hundreds of children were subjected to horrific violence and violation. Hundreds of children became sex slaves. Hundreds of children lived their lives in fear. But the damage was not just done at that time. This was not just about what happened to them when the abuse was taking place. There were significant longer-term consequences for the victims in adulthood. The impact doesn't go away when the physical abuse stops. The scars that are left may be physical, but they will be psychological too.

Hence, in the case of the victims in Rotherham, the Jay report stated that among the lasting impacts were the higher likelihood of becoming a victim of domestic violence, the development of long-standing drug and alcohol addiction, and problems with parenting their own children in due course, which led to the need for interventions for child protection. Victims also suffered from post-traumatic stress, mental health problems and emotional and psychological problems which often went undiagnosed and untreated.

The question of the authorities' response in Rotherham came to the fore again in June 2022, when the result of a complaint against senior commanders at South Yorkshire Police for failing to protect children against sexual grooming by gangs in the town was announced. The complaint was upheld, although the full findings of the report as they related to senior officers were not published. Aspects of it were included in a broader review of the role of the police.

Even getting to this point had been a battle. The complaint had been made by Jayne Senior, who was a youth worker, and Angie Heal, the Strategic Drugs Analyst at South Yorkshire Police who had written the internal reports identifying child sexual abuse in drug gangs. But along the way, there were attempts to dissuade them from pursuing their complaint.

Jayne Senior, who was awarded an MBE in 2016, was told by the body which would investigate the police – the Independent Office for Police Conduct – that 'if I continued I would be seen as a vexatious complainant which means I would be stopped from making any more complaints'. Having continued to press her case, there was a further attempt to stop her. She says that she 'received a very angry telephone call from someone in the IOPC saying very clearly that if I continue down this path I need to be aware that there's actually legislation that if a vexatious complainant continues to complain they can be looking at two years' imprisonment'.

As Jayne explained, 'They see us as a pariah. Rather than thinking "how can we change things?" they are thinking "how can we silence this person and how can we make it as difficult as possible for them to come forward?"' Angie Heal likewise expressed her discontent about the treatment of senior officers, saying, 'The senior officers are still being left out and if you don't understand what is going on at the top, then how can you ever put things right?'* The clear implication is that senior officers were being protected.

The IOPC, however, did face a lack of cooperation. Apparently, they contacted several retired police officers who had worked in roles related to child protection and

---

* Quotes from Jayne Senior and Angie Heal from Sky News Report, 27 June 2022.

intelligence, but as the IOPC said, 'they would not engage with us and we could not force them to do so. This has been a barrier to obtaining certain evidence.' As Jayne Senior said, 'How can people just get away with not only ignoring child abuse but then refusing to give evidence? These are people that are paid out of the public purse.'

In Rotherham, the authorities had the power and the opportunity to act, but chose not to. That choice was made for a variety of reasons – indeed, some might not even have seen it as a choice. Whatever the rationale, their inaction, their failure to understand that they held power in order to serve others, damaged the lives of hundreds of young people and deeply shattered trust in the authorities. Even though some were acting as they did out of a fear of being branded racist or of alienating the Pakistani community, they still chose to put themselves and their institutions first and the people second, because they had the power to do so – because they could.

10

Stop and Search

One of the fundamental jobs of government is to keep people safe – the protection of citizens. As we have seen from previous chapters, there have been many instances where the bodies charged with the power and responsibility to protect the public have simply not done so.

At its most basic, perhaps the protection of citizens is seen in the defence of the realm, but on a day-to-day basis, it is particularly present across our communities in the work of the police in preventing crime and catching criminals.

As the Code of Ethics published by the College of Policing in 2014 declares, 'The policing profession has a duty to protect the public and prevent crime. The public expect every person within the profession to fulfil this duty by being fair and impartial and giving a *selfless service*' (my emphasis). It goes on to say, 'Every person working for the police service must work honestly and ethically. The public expect the police to do the right thing in the right way.'

As I write, the College is consulting on a revised code. This follows a number of appalling examples of unethical, indeed criminal, behaviour by individual serving police officers, perhaps the worst of which are Wayne Couzens, who murdered Sarah Everard, and David Carrick, found guilty of eighty-five serious offences over seventeen years, including forty-eight rapes, making him one of the worst sex offenders in modern history. Both used their position as police officers to commit their offences. In both cases, there were signs of their unsuitability to be serving as police officers, indeed possibly of their criminal natures, which were overlooked by their force, the Metropolitan Police.

We expect our police officers to act without fear or favour and to do so with honesty and integrity. We are fortunate in the British model of policing by consent. Unlike in many countries, our police are not routinely armed on the streets. So the police officer turning up to a reported incident will generally not be armed. Often, that police officer will not know what the level of danger is when they attend that incident. Yet they turn up, regardless of the possible danger to themselves. Day in and day out, our police put themselves in harm's way to keep us safe.

They work with and within their local communities. Their approach is often best appreciated at major events, where they will line the streets to protect the participants and the crowds, but also manage to combine that job with entering into the spirit of the event – dancing in the Mall with members of the public at a royal wedding comes to mind.

Achieving this isn't just about our police officers and their training. It relies on a bond of trust and confidence between the police and the public. Of course, not everyone has that degree of trust. I remember a family in my father's parish who were regularly in trouble with the police and whose members were in and out of prison. They had an Alsatian dog that used to sit at their gate, guarding the property against the two people the family didn't want to see – the police and the vicar! But, overall, honest citizens trust the police and need to be able to do so if the police are to be able to do their job.

The strength of that bond of trust can vary from community to community. We see too often that the bond is weakest with Black, Asian and Minority Ethnic (BAME) communities, nowhere more so than in the operation of stop and search – particularly in Black communities.

Stop and search is a very useful tool, but it is at its most useful when it operates with community support and acceptance. It is at its least useful when it leads to the breakdown of trust, an atmosphere of suspicion of the police and, as a result, an unwillingness to help the police with their work – for example, by not passing on valuable information relating to incidents and crimes.

When I was Home Secretary, my eyes were opened to the problem of mistrust of the police by the Black community as a result of stop and search when I met a group of young Black people in the Home Office who told me about their first-hand experiences. One particularly struck me. Alexander Paul spoke movingly of the number of times he had been stopped and searched, including when just popping out to the corner shop for his mum. He was law-abiding. He had no criminal record. Yet he was regularly stopped and searched when he was going about normal everyday chores. Alexander also spoke about the impact this experience had had on his view of the police and on the approach his community took to the police.

If you are regularly stopped and searched by the police for no reason other than the colour of your skin, then pretty soon that bond of trust with the police is weakened

– even to breaking point. That doesn't help anyone, least of all the police, who need that trust in order to access information, ask questions and get answers.

Some time later, in 2014, Alexander addressed the Conservative Party Conference at my request. He had a huge impact on those who heard him. He also spent some time in the Home Office on a brief internship and impressed all who worked with him. Sadly, in 2017 he died from a brain tumour, but his legacy lives on, not least in the poem he wrote to explain what it meant to be a young Black man who was regularly stopped and searched for no reason. He made it clear that being stopped so frequently had had a real impact on him, above all leaving him with no trust in those who were meant to be there to serve and protect him.

All of this was reason enough to act on stop and search, but what added further to the need for action were the results of a review by Her Majesty's Inspectorate of Constabulary, which I commissioned in 2013.* To set the background to the review, in order to act under the main stop and search power, the officer has to have reasonable grounds for doing so. It is reasonable grounds if the officer suspects that the person may be carrying an illegal drug, a weapon, stolen property or something which could be used to commit a crime, such as a crowbar.

The remit given to HMIC was to review the way the police were using their powers of stop and search. That review showed that 27 per cent of stop and searches in one year had been carried out without the officer recording

---

* HMIC, *Stop and Search Powers: Are the police using them effectively and fairly?*, 2013.

reasonable grounds for searching the individuals being stopped.

So what? you may ask. But that finding was significant. What it meant was that just over a quarter of stops were being carried out unlawfully. In numbers, it meant that around 270,000 of the stops carried out in the previous year under the Police and Criminal Evidence Act had been unlawful. That's right, over a quarter of a million unlawful stop and searches.

The job of the police is to uphold and enforce the law. Above all else, therefore, we expect them to abide by the law. Faced with the evidence that in the case of stop and search the police were not doing so, I decided that something had to change.

Undertaken properly, stop and search can be hugely effective. But it loses its effectiveness if it leads to mistrust in communities. With people from a Black or ethnic minority background seven times more likely to be stopped and searched than someone who was white, it was clear to me that action was needed. Moreover, stop and search was supposed to help the police in preventing crime and catching criminals, but at that time only about 10 per cent of stops led to an arrest. The impression was that too many people were being stopped because of the colour of their skin. There were quite a few in policing and in politics at the time who failed to understand these basic and important points, and indeed there still are today.

That desire for action led in April 2014 to a package of reforms to improve the use of stop and search, as well as a revision of the PACE (Police and Criminal Evidence Act 1984) Code of Practice A, in order to clarify what constituted 'reasonable grounds for suspicion' – the justification for any stop and search. It was also made clear that officers who failed to use their powers properly would face formal performance or disciplinary proceedings.

In addition, I wrote to all chief constables and police and crime commissioners (PCCs) asking them to abide by the requirement in the Code that they should enable communities to hold forces to account on stop and search by making arrangements for the public scrutiny of stop and search records.

The Home Office also commissioned the College of Policing to review the national training of stop and search for all officers, including unconscious bias awareness training to reduce the possibility of prejudice in the approach officers took, and to bring in an assessment of officers' fitness to use their powers of stop and search.

Data on stop and search was to be added to crime maps on the police website as a way of providing better transparency and accountability. The role of Her Majesty's Inspectorate of Constabulary (HMIC), subsequently Her Majesty's Inspectorate of Constabulary and Fire and Rescue Services (HMICFRS), was also enhanced, as it was asked to include the use of stop and search in the annual general inspections of forces which it had introduced. HMICFRS was also given a further commission to review all other police powers that were similar to stop and search. These included Section 163 of the Road Traffic Act (power to stop a motor vehicle), where there was some evidence of disproportionality in its use. The aim of the review was to make recommendations to ensure there was no unfair or inappropriate use of these powers.

Work also began with chief constables and PCCs to look at including information on the use of stop and search on the new Emergency Services Network set up to enhance connectivity.

These steps constituted a significant body of work to improve the use of stop and search. The aim was to ensure the power was used lawfully and not disproportionately, and in so doing to create the environment in which trust in the police could be restored, thereby encouraging communities that felt they had suffered from an unfair use of stop and search to work with the police.

Finally, a Best Use of Stop and Search scheme (BUSS) was launched with the College of Policing. This was designed to create greater transparency, accountability and community involvement. The scheme was initially backed by the Metropolitan Police and other forces were invited to join it.

There were various elements to BUSS, such as better recording of stop and search outcomes, improved engagement with local communities and reducing the use of Section 60 no-suspicion stop and searches. One of the ways this was done was by changing the authorisation rules so that no-suspicion stops could only by authorised by a senior officer – that is, above the level of chief superintendent. Section 60 of the Criminal Justice and Public Order Act 1994 allows police officers to stop and search people even if they don't have suspicions about them, but is limited to an agreed geographical area.

The figures showed that BUSS had an impact. One of the aims was to reduce the number of no-suspicion stops significantly, and the number indeed fell. Between 2013/14 and 2017/18, the use of such searches fell by 36 per cent from around 4,000 to 2,500.

In March 2019, however, the Home Secretary Sajid Javid argued that the authorisation requirements for Section 60 were too onerous, and we agreed that the police could run a pilot on relaxing these requirements. This was thought necessary because of the number of young people being killed as a result of knife crime. The pilot was based on returning the level of authorisation to inspectors and super-intendents, on lowering the degree of certainty required by the authorising officer so that rather than reasonably believing that an incident involving serious violence 'will' occur, they just had to believe that it 'may' occur in a particular area, and extending the initial period a Section 60 notice could be in place from fifteen to twenty-four hours, with a possible extension of a further twenty-four hours, meaning the authorisation could be in place for forty-eight hours rather than thirty-nine.

Seven forces accounting for 60 per cent of national knife crime took part in the pilot, which was due to run for a year, with a review after six months. In August 2019, after I had left office, the new Home Secretary Priti Patel extended the pilot to the whole of England and Wales, and in July 2021, it was announced that the authorisation conditions on Section 60 would be permanently lifted.

In February 2021, HMICFRS published a report which stated that in 2019/20, Black people were eighteen times more likely than white people to be searched under Section 60.[*] In the same year, in relation to the general stop and search powers, HMICFRS reported that Black people were almost nine times more likely to be searched than white people, and for all BAME people the ratio was four to one.

---

* HMICFRS, *Disproportionate use of police powers: A spotlight on stop and search and the use of force*, February 2021.

In her foreword to that report, Wendy Williams, one of the inspectors, explained:

> Now that we have some long-awaited data through our most recent inspection work, we know that forces still do not fully understand the impact on individuals and communities of the use of police powers, despite stop and search data being available since the mid-1980s . . . The damage caused by unexplained disproportionality can be far-reaching and long-lasting. It may lead to more Black, Asian and Minority Ethnic people being drawn into the criminal justice system, disrupting their education and family lives, and reducing their work opportunities. It feeds perceptions among the public and police about Black people and crime and may also influence how the police allocate and deploy resources. This in turn exacerbates the imbalances in the criminal justice system . . . Forces should reflect on the findings of this report. They should analyse their data and either explain, with evidence, the reasons for disproportionality, or take demonstrable action to address it.

These relatively recent findings are deeply disappointing. As HMICFRS made clear, it means that the police still had not taken on board the problems caused when they do not use their powers properly. The point of the changes introduced with the new Code and with BUSS was to encourage forces and their officers to act in accordance with the law when conducting stop and searches. It should not have been too much to ask for – after all, these officers are there to uphold and enforce the law.

By ensuring that stop and searches were being conducted

within the law, it should have reduced the disproportion-ality, bringing us closer to a position where people are not being stopped and searched solely because of the colour of their skin. But the approach was misunderstood by too many in the police force and by too many politicians interested in burnishing their credentials for supporting the police.

Unfortunately, one of the characteristics of our police which I discovered at an early stage as Home Secretary was a natural inclination to take absolutist positions rather than accept a middle way. You might say, surely they must be absolutist in dealing with criminality? Either a crime has been committed or it has not. Either someone is guilty or they are not. And yes, that is true, but what I mean about being absolutist is the way they swing from one position to the exact opposite without anything in between.

Their attitude towards my attempts to ensure they were acting lawfully in their stop and searches was characteristic. Having sent a clear message that they should act lawfully when conducting stop and searches – not that they should cease using them – this was at best misunderstood and at worst wilfully misinterpreted to support the continuation of this abuse of power.

This was brought home to me at the Police Federation conference in 2015, after the introduction of the Code of Conduct, when in the Q and A session after my speech, an officer from the Metropolitan Police asked me why I was telling them to stop doing stop and searches. I was not. But in their absolutist world, either you used this power or you did not. It didn't seem to enter their heads that they could carry on using the power; they just had to do so within the law.

Stop and Search

Speaking at the Police Federation conference was never something to look forward to with eager anticipation, and certainly not when, as Home Secretary, I had to give a difficult message to those attending. The Chairman of the Federation always spoke before the Home Secretary, and I had to learn how to keep an absolutely poker face during their speech, which was invariably an attack on the government and particularly on the actions of the Home Secretary.

I have no doubt that the way police were unlawfully operating stop and search was an abuse of power. It was alienating communities and, in so doing, was making the job of the police in some areas even harder. I am concerned that the governments that followed me have encouraged the use of stop and search without the specific caveat that it must be done lawfully.

Talking to ministers shows me that they understand the importance of working with communities and using stop and search wisely and properly, but the danger is that public statements designed to get a headline paint a different picture – one where the police feel free to misuse, if not abuse, their power.

The issue of stop and search raises another question which is difficult to address but which needs to be tackled. That is the attitude of the police to race. This was first brought sharply into focus in 1999 in the Macpherson report into the murder of Stephen Lawrence.* Stephen was killed in a racist attack on the evening of 22 April 1993. His murder was later reported by the press as 'one of the

---

* *The Stephen Lawrence Inquiry: Report of an Inquiry by Sir William Macpherson of Cluny*, February 1999, Cm. 4262–1.

highest-profile unsolved racially motivated murders'.* In his report on the murder and the response of the Metropolitan Police, Sir William Macpherson found that 'The investigation was marred by a combination of professional incompetence, institutional racism and a failure of leadership by senior officers.'

That description of the Met as institutionally racist has resounded down the three decades since Stephen's murder. I have met his mother Doreen, Baroness Lawrence, and his father Neville on numerous occasions. On the twenty-fifth anniversary of Stephen's death, I was pleased to announce the creation of Stephen Lawrence Day. This is marked each year on 22 April as an occasion to bring people and communities together to honour Stephen's life and legacy, stand up against discrimination and work for a better future for the next generation.

The description of institutional racism still has echoes today. After the murder of Sarah Everard by a Metropolitan Police officer in 2021, Louise Casey was asked by the Commissioner of the Met, Dame Cressida Dick, to look into the culture of the force. Her report stated: 'I make a finding of institutional racism, sexism and homophobia in the Met.'† She added, 'we have to be able to have faith in the police . . . we give the police exceptional powers and we trust them to use them responsibly . . . The police want to earn our trust. And we want to trust the police.'

In May 2023, the Chief Constable of Police Scotland, Sir Iain Livingstone, gave a statement to the Scottish

---

* Press Association, 9 July 2010.
† Baroness Casey of Blackstock DBE CB, *An independent review into the standards of behaviour and internal culture of the Metropolitan Police Service*, March 2023.

Police Authority Board in which he acknowledged that institutional racism, sexism, misogyny and discrimination exist within his force, and went on to declare that 'Police Scotland is institutionally racist and discriminatory.' He also made the point that saying this did not mean that the police officers and police staff were racist and sexist, but that publicly acknowledging these institutional issues was essential to becoming an anti-racist service committed to equality.

The need to trust the police underpins the issue of stop and search – an important power that can be a significant tool in policing communities and apprehending criminals, but which depends on trust in the police. It is a power that must not be abused.

No one should be stopped and searched on the streets of the UK simply because of the colour of their skin. That they have been is clearly an abuse of power, exercised by the police because they could.

11

Daniel Morgan

The murder of Daniel Morgan in March 1987 was disturbing. His body was found in a pub car park in south-east London with an axe 'embedded in the right of his neck'. Equally disturbing was the inability of the police to identify the culprit or culprits and bring them to justice. Surely someone must have seen something. This was a pub car park, after all. Was there no one around who could help? It seemed incomprehensible that the police were finding it so difficult to investigate this murder. Morgan was a private investigator, a detail that added spice to the story. I'm sure many people constructed their own theory about who had done it. Indeed, from an early stage there were suggestions of police involvement, but to this day no one has been convicted of his murder.

I have a vague recollection of hearing the news of Daniel Morgan's murder and seeing the picture of the pub car park on television. To be honest, I didn't give it much thought until I became Home Secretary and was made aware that the family wanted an inquiry into what had gone wrong. At first, there was still a court case in progress following charges against five people – four for the murder and one for perverting the course of justice. When that case collapsed, it raised further questions about why the police had failed to find the killer or killers. After all, between 1987 and 2011, the Met and other forces had arrested sixty-eight people, eight of them police officers, in connection with the murder, yet no one had been convicted. To give some context, according to the Office for National Statistics, in the three years ending in March 2022, no fewer than 80 per cent of the suspects indicted for homicide (where there was information about court outcomes) were found guilty.

When I first met the Morgan family, it would be true to say that there was some scepticism in the Home Office about their case. That came partly from a natural disinclination to respond positively to calls for another public inquiry. But the family, particularly Daniel's brother Alastair, put their case with fervour and I began to recognise the years of struggle they had been through. They just wanted to know the truth and see someone brought to justice. They had been badly let down and every attempt to get somewhere had got nowhere. The question was why? They were severe in their condemnation of the police. In their view, only an independent inquiry could hope to get anywhere near the truth.

Following the collapse of the case, a number of reviews had been initiated by the Metropolitan Police and others and, given the various internal reviews taking place, there was an unwillingness at the Home Office to move to an inquiry. Truth be told, departments have a natural reluctance to set up inquiries because of the impact on budgets. If I'm honest, at first I shared some of that hesitancy. It was also becoming increasingly common for people to call for an inquiry as a first resort. This did not apply to the

Morgan family, who had been waiting for the police to do their job for many years.

I was to discover, however, that in this particular case, the reluctance in the Home Office had other causes too. I remember the meeting in my office with a senior civil servant and a senior police officer who wanted to talk to me about the question of an inquiry. They unravelled a lengthy sheet of paper which almost fitted the whole length of the long table in my room. It showed a timeline of investigations into the murder. What soon became clear was their argument that there was a danger that any inquiry would reveal a history of police corruption. The implication was unmistakable. If you launch one, it will open up a can of worms. Once again, the desire to protect the image of the institution was taking precedence.

They obviously didn't know me. I had thought carefully about whether to set up an inquiry, but it was this meeting that determined my decision. My view was simple. The inquiry should go ahead precisely because it might reveal police corruption. So in 2013, once the various internal reviews were over, I commissioned the Independent Panel to examine the case.

The purpose and remit of the inquiry Panel, which was chaired by Baroness O'Loan, was:

> to shine a light on the circumstances of Daniel Morgan's murder, its background and the handling of the case over the whole period since March 1987. In doing so the Panel will seek to address the questions arising, including those relating to:
> — police involvement in the murder;
> — the role played by police corruption in protecting

those responsible for the murder from being brought to justice and the failure to confront that corruption; and

— the incidence of connections between private investigators, police officers and journalists at the *News of the World* and other parts of the media and alleged corruption involved in the exchanges between them.

When I set up the Panel, I had the naive hope that it would be close to an answer within a year. It took them eight years, but once again their report shows the importance of their work. They made a large number of recommendations, some of which the government has taken forward. It is up to the Home Office to ensure that all of the recommendations are properly addressed.*

The Panel found serious failures of investigation. Unbelievably, the scene of the murder was never searched. Anyone who watches any TV cop show will know the detailed and forensic searches which take place these days. Granted, this murder took place over thirty years ago and not all of today's techniques were available to the police, but it still seems pretty obvious that a crime scene should be searched. In fact, the Panel noted that: 'In many respects that investigation was not compliant with the policies and procedures in force at the time.'

Perhaps what was most shocking about this case was the corruption that at best made it harder for the police to find the killer or killers, and at worst led to them deliberately hampering that search for justice. That trail

---

* *The Report of the Daniel Morgan Independent Panel*, June 2021, 3 vols, HC11-I to HC11-III.

of obfuscation, half-truths and failure has been laid bare in considerable detail by the Panel.

They recorded that the Metropolitan Police had concealed from Daniel Morgan's family and from the public the failings in the first murder investigation and the role of corrupt officers. As they put it, 'That lack of candour, over so many years, has been a barrier to proper accountability.'

The Panel set out their belief that 'concealing or denying failings, for the sake of an organisation's public image, is dishonesty on the part of the organisation for reputational benefit and constitutes a form of institutional corruption'. The use of this term 'institutional corruption' is disquieting, but I think it is important to understand what it means. There are those who will assume that it means that police officers are on the take, probably receiving bribes from organised crime groups. It does not, and they are not. The vast majority of police officers do their job properly.

What the panel specifically referred to was the culture of institutional defensiveness which they found. Notably, it was this desire to defend the institution by rejecting or hiding failings that they said is a form of institutional corruption. This desire to shield the institution at all costs corrupts the thinking inside the institution, its purpose and hence its actions. As I have identified elsewhere in this book, that corruption of purpose can be seen in too many other cases in the public sector.

The finding by the Daniel Morgan panel should be of deep concern to us all. Yet again, it reflects a part of the public sector putting its own interests before those of the people it was there to serve.

There may well have been more venal reasons for the failure of the police investigations. It may be that there were police officers involved with organised crime. Certainly the relationships between some of the players – police and others – raise questions about what lay behind the murder. Others could have seen the need to investigate these aspects and lay bare the truth; surely in their quest for justice, that should have been foremost in the Met's thinking. Did no one ever think that the reputational damage of failing to identify the killer or killers was of more concern than the reputational damage of identifying corruption?

It seems obvious that had they identified that corruption and rooted it out, and brought the killer or killers to justice, then their reputation would have been considerably enhanced. But that was not the thinking at the time. Indeed, the report shows that there was an environment where anyone who chose to blow the whistle or get things changed would soon find themselves moved to another area of work and their career would suffer. The whole approach was to cover up failings and corruption, because they could.

Yet again the desire to protect the institution came first. But this was not just defence of the institution. It was defence of the institution as it was at that time. In other words, in this approach there was no room for change or improvement. The system was working very well thank you, so don't change it.

At the heart of this story is the family of Daniel Morgan. Not only did they have to come to terms with their grief over his loss, but they also had to fight the criminal justice system for decades to get anywhere near the truth. In that sense, their story is very similar to that of the Hillsborough families. Both found themselves battling against the very organs of the state which should have been protecting and supporting them.

Their experience alone should make us think deeply about the approach taken by the police and the rest of the criminal justice system. The issue goes wider than that. One of the points which the family of Daniel Morgan consistently made, and on which the Panel commented, is that the behaviour of the police reduced the family's trust in them. The failure of the police to identify the killer or killers naturally sapped the family's confidence in them. But there was also a failure to keep the family informed as matters progressed. As the cover-ups and the inability to admit corruption emerged, the family developed an increasing distrust of the police.

Our democracy, the freedoms we enjoy, all depend on an acceptance of the need for law and order and a willingness to see the police and the rest of the criminal justice system protecting and enforcing that law and order. This works only if people have trust in the police. The more examples the public see of the police acting unlawfully, corruptly or in their view unfairly, the less they will trust them. This eventually will strike at the heart of the very democracy we enjoy.

In general, police officers will understand this need for trust. For example, in the recent pandemic, my local chief constable in Thames Valley was determined that in enforcing the government's regulations, his officers should never forget that after the pandemic, they still wanted the public to have confidence in them and trust them, and they should behave accordingly.

In the actions taken over the years in the examples I have set out here, it seems that all too often that understanding has been lacking and has been overridden by the desire to defend the institution or individuals within the institution.

Daniel Morgan

In politics, support for law and order, and to a great extent for the police, has always been seen as a key pillar of Conservatism. Indeed, law and order, the number of police officers and putting police on the streets have often been key electoral pledges and slogans. It would be wrong, however, to assume that this means that the police must be supported absolutely, all the time and whatever they do. As Home Secretary, I always made it clear to the police that I would support them as long as they were operating within the law.

It seems strange to even think of police officers operating outside the rule of law, but it happens. Hillsborough, stop and search and Daniel Morgan are examples of how this can happen, albeit in different ways. The politician who turns a blind eye to this and merely chants unwavering support for the police is doing them no favours. Allowing such actions to continue or to pass unnoticed encourages a sense that they can do whatever they like.

When I was Home Secretary, at one of the dinners for the annual police bravery awards – awards which recognise heroic acts by individual officers in the line of duty, and sometimes outside their duty – I remember being told that in a previous year, one of the people handing out the awards was the actor Philip Glenister, who played DCI Gene Hunt in *Life on Mars*. His character was known for bending the rules, fitting up criminals and generally putting up two fingers to authority. He had been greeted by the officers in the room with huge applause and, I believe, a standing ovation!

The vast majority of police officers operate with integrity and within the rule of law. As the bravery awards show, they are willing to put their lives on the line for us, and for that we should be eternally grateful. One of the best ways we can show our support for them is to identify, show up and root out those who act unlawfully or corruptly, those who put their own interests or those of the institution before those of the public they serve – because they can.

12

Windrush

In the previous chapters, I have looked at a number of examples of abuse of power exercised in different ways by parts of the public sector. The examples are ones that came across my desk as Home Secretary or as Prime Minister. It is now time to look specifically at the Department of which I was Secretary of State: the Home Office.

Put simply, I could not write a book about the abuse of power without including an account of Windrush. In this chapter, I aim to explain how the issue transpired. At its heart was the failure of successive governments over decades to use the power they had to ensure that people coming legally to this country possessed evidence of their right to be in the UK. That failure by government was an abuse of power which ultimately led to the pain and distress felt by too many of the Windrush generation. It was set out clearly in the 2020 report of the independent review commissioned by the government and conducted by Wendy Williams.

Let me set out the background. After the Second World War, the UK was in need of reconstruction but was also facing a shortage of workers. Moreover, key policies of Clement Attlee's government, notably the establishment of the NHS, had also created a need for staff. The answer to this shortage of labour was to encourage people to come into the UK from elsewhere. Among the countries to which the UK government appealed were those of the Commonwealth, and within that particularly the nations of the Caribbean.

There had been small movements of people into the UK before 1948, but the key movement was the arrival of 1,027 official passengers on the transport ship HMT *Empire Windrush* at Tilbury on 22 June 1948. Of these, 802 listed their last country of residence as in the Caribbean. Half of the arrivals had served with the British forces during the war – as 10,000 Caribbean servicemen had done. It is this ship that gave its name to the Windrush generation. Numbers varied from year to year, but by 1973, some 600,000 people from the Commonwealth had come to the UK, the majority of them from countries in the Caribbean.

We should be clear that the UK invited them here. They all left their homes to start a new life, but in doing so felt they were responding to a cry for help from what many of them saw as the mother country. They felt a sense of duty. They made their lives here, and they live on in their children, grandchildren and great-grandchildren, for whom the UK has been their only home.

They also came with hope. As the writer George Lamming from Trinidad, quoted in the Williams review of Windrush, said, 'England lay before us, not as a place or a people, but as a promise and an expectation.'* It is this sense that the Windrush generation came to the aid of Britain and arrived with optimism and hope for their future that makes

* *Windrush Lessons Learned Review*, March 2020, HC 93.

the treatment some of them received in later years all the more shocking. For this, I am profoundly sorry.

At the heart of the problems later faced by the Windrush generation lay the decision by the then-government, led by Clement Attlee, not to give them papers to show their settled status in the UK. Looking back now, we find this surprising, but at the time, immigration was not seen as the issue it is today – and, of course, these people were migrating to the UK because Britain had asked them to. Presumably, because they had been welcomed here by the government, no one thought their status would ever be in any doubt.

This problem was compounded over the years by successive governments as they proceeded with various changes in immigration law while continuously failing to understand the need to provide the Windrush generation with evidence that they were here lawfully. Indeed, as the years rolled on and second, third and now fourth generations were born to parents who were British and part of British life, the idea of doing anything about regularising the status of the original Windrush generation will have seemed more and more remote – if it even entered anybody's head.

Their status in the UK also owed a lot to the attitude of empire. Indeed, the provisions of the 1948 British Nationality Act amounted to a written contract that reflected what had been the assumed or implied contract of empire – of togetherness and of all being one under the aegis of the mother country. Following the Act, many Commonwealth citizens now had the right to live in Britain as citizens of the UK and colonies. The Windrush generation were not subject to immigration policy. They weren't 'aliens'. This term sounds harsh, but it is the term used to describe foreign-born individuals who are not British citizens by virtue of parentage or naturalisation. The Windrush generation had a right to be here and a right to carry on living here. This position continued until further changes in immigration law in 1962.

So the Windrush generation didn't just feel part of the country they had come to call home, but their legal status confirmed that. They were British citizens. The fact that no one had given them any papers to confirm this became more and more of a problem as the immigration laws changed and grew more onerous. I think it is important to give a sense of the increasing complexity of immigration law over the years.

What follows cannot be an absolutely comprehensive description of the twists and turns of immigration law, given the number of pieces of legislation enacted, but I hope it gives a sense of its ever-greater intricacy. It should also give an idea of the number of opportunities successive governments had while changing the law to recognise the problem that could befall the Windrush generation. These were opportunities to rectify the position, opportunities that governments continued to miss over the years.

The 1948 British Nationality Act established that those who came to the UK from the time of the Act and through the 1950s, and who had been born in or had a connection to one of the remaining colonies, were defined as citizens of the UK and Colonies (CUKC). The Act meant that by virtue of their citizenship of any of the colonies, they became British subjects. They also acquired this status if their father was a CUKC at the time of their birth. This enabled them to arrive and settle in the UK on their own or their parents' CUKC passports, with the same rights to come and go as the resident population.

Of course, over the years, not only were UK immigration laws changing but so was the position of many Commonwealth countries, which were steadily becoming independent. Those individuals who had a UK-born father were not affected by this, but for others the change in status of their country of origin led to a change in their own status. As countries became independent, individuals became Commonwealth citizens who could register for UK and Colonies citizenship after living in the UK for twelve months. They still had the legal right to come to the UK through their CUKC status, so no one was given legal documents and indeed no one needed them. They were here, they lived and worked here, they were part of us and many had no official immigration record.

As the years passed, the issue of immigration became more significant for both the public and politicians. As a result, governments started to introduce more restrictive arrangements. The 1962 Commonwealth Immigrants Act effectively ended the free movement from the Commonwealth that had served the country so well in its time of need. As a result of this Act, Commonwealth citizens would have to live in the UK for five years before registering in the category of citizens of the UK and Colonies. The Act also brought in a system for controlling the numbers coming to the UK by restricting entry to those with a job offer or with skills that were in short supply. That latter concept lives on today in the shortage occupations list.

Subsequent Acts – the 1968 Commonwealth Immigrants Act and the 1971 Immigration Act – tightened the rules still further. Under the latter, a Commonwealth citizen who was not a CUKC would only have a 'right of abode' here if they were born to or legally adopted by a parent who was a CUKC born in the UK. What this meant was that most of the original Windrush generation did not qualify to pass on their right of abode to their children and grandchildren.

The 1971 Act also introduced a concept that was to make life more difficult for the Windrush generation in later years. It established that the onus for proving an individual's status lay with them and not with the government. Fast-forward to recent times, and this is what led to the Home Office requiring members of the Windrush generation to prove their status, which of course many of them could not do because they had no official papers. They were caught in a Catch-22 situation not of their making.

The harsh reality is that many of the ways of proving that they were in the UK lawfully, in the sense of showing continuous residence here, lay in the hands of the government, such as registration with a GP, payment of taxes, children being at school, not to mention employment records for those who had worked in the public sector. The burden of proof, however, lay with the individual. Yet, while individuals might have some records of their own, they were highly unlikely to have access to the official records required to prove their case.

Under the 1971 Act, Commonwealth citizens who were already in the UK before January 1973 were either entitled to right of abode or had deemed leave to remain. Again, they were not given proof of their status.

The next major piece of legislation was the 1981 British Nationality Act, which aligned nationality and immigration law. Under this Act, CUKC status was abolished. In its stead, there were three categories of citizenship – British citizenship, British Dependent Territories citizenship and British Overseas citizenship. The Act also reformulated British citizenship, tightening up the definition.

This was followed by the 1988 Immigration Act, which among other things repealed an existing legislative protection for Commonwealth citizens and was criticised in Parliament as going back on a promise to safeguard certain rights in the 1971 Act.

While governments were dealing with the growing public concern about immigration and introducing progressively tighter restrictions on the number of people who could migrate to the UK and on the ability of migrants to qualify for citizenship, the impact on the Windrush generation and their descendants was little understood. Indeed, many of the Windrush generation would not have had any idea that the changes in law impacted them. What is also obvious is that, as far as the Home Office in its dealings with immigration was concerned, this was a forgotten generation. This meant that government wasn't looking at the impact of changes on this group.

At one point in the 1980s, someone in government did work out that there was a need to consider those who had come to the UK without being given proof of their immigration status – that is, the Windrush generation. There was an attempt to alert them to the changes in the law and what it meant for them. The 1981 Nationality Act had established a time-limited scheme to register those Commonwealth citizens who had arrived before 1973. The scheme expired at the end of 1987, and in the late 1980s the Home Office ran a publicity campaign to encourage people to sign up under the scheme. There were 130,000 applications to register between 1985 and 1987, but the Windrush review found evidence that the Home Office had been cautious about encouraging too many to register for fear of overwhelming the system.

Moreover, if you were a member of the Windrush generation who had lived in the UK for many years, worked here, had brought up your children here and had always believed you had a right to be here – which indeed you had – then you may well have thought, why on earth did you need to register? Why pay £60 to register when you were British anyway?

This view was also encouraged by the Home Office. In a 1987 leaflet quoted in the Windrush review, the Home Office said:

> If you have the right to register but you don't want to, you do not have to. Your other rights in the United Kingdom will not change in any way. You will not lose your entitlement to social benefits, such as health services, housing, welfare and pension rights, by not registering. Your position under immigration law is not changed.

So the Home Office was reassuring people that they did not need to worry about their status, while continuing to ignore the fact that so many of the Windrush generation did not have written confirmation of that status.

I have set out these legislative changes to show how complex the issue of immigration law was becoming over the years, as government after government of both mainstream parties changed the rules. It was becoming harder and harder to understand those rules and know what you were required to do – assuming that you even thought the rules applied to you. The Windrush generation didn't think they needed to understand the various legislative changes, because they had been told they had a right to be here. If it is hard to come to terms with legislative change when you know you are subject to its ramifications, it is impossible if you don't engage with the government bureaucracy because you don't think you need to.

The legislative changes set out so far all relate to the rules for entering the UK legally or for gaining British citizenship. In addition, in later years governments tried to enhance their ability to deal with illegal immigrants. This was an approach taken by both Labour and Conservative administrations. Much has been made of the use of the term 'hostile environment' when I was Home Secretary. In retrospect, it was not a good term to use. It was suggested at a time when it was clear that it related to people who were here illegally, but of course it became a term that was used in relation to a generation who had every right to be here. Whatever was thought of the term, this was not the first time it had been used. For example, in May 2007, under the then-Labour government, the immigration minister Liam Byrne announced a policy of fining firms for employing people who did not have the right to work in the UK, saying, 'We are trying to create a much more hostile environment in this country if you are here illegally.' The term was repeated in a Home Office strategy document published under Labour in February 2010. Successive governments were introducing policies to make it harder for illegal immigrants to live in the UK.

Over the period from 1948 to 2017, there were twenty-seven different Home Secretaries. But the rules introduced by different governments were all reacting to the concerns of the public. This was reflected first in attempts to clarify who had a right to reside in the UK, and secondly in the responses to the public's concern about illegal immigration. The public generally objected to the fact that people could come to the UK illegally and yet carry on living here with jobs, homes and bank accounts. They could not understand how this was possible.

So measures to deal with this were introduced over the years. As an example, in 1977, legislation was brought in which permitted those who were not ordinarily resident in the UK to be charged for NHS services. This concept was developed further in 1982, when regulations imposing a charging regime relating to hospital treatment for overseas visitors were first introduced. The 1996 Asylum and Immigration Act not only introduced fines for those who employed workers who were in the UK illegally but also made it a criminal offence to do so. The same Act established that anyone subject to immigration control – that is, anyone who required leave to enter or remain in the UK – could not claim housing or child benefit.

In March 2007, the then-Labour administration published a strategy, a cross-government approach, entitled 'Enforcing the Rules'. This set out 'to block the benefits of Britain to those in the country illegally'. This laid the foundations for the 'hostile environment'. The idea was to deny them access to work, benefits and services. Critical in this was the legislation in 2006, which reinforced the fact that it was a criminal offence to knowingly employ illegal workers and brought in a system of civil penalties for 'careless employers'.

In the 2014 and 2016 Immigration Acts, further measures were introduced in relation to access to housing, bank accounts and driving licences. I was Home Secretary at the time and was responsible for the new measures.

So through all this, we see on the one hand a group of people who had made their lives here, contributed to our economy and society, brought up their families here, who were British and saw no reason why anyone should question that; and on the other hand, successive governments of all parties introducing increasingly tight rules and not realising in doing this that their actions could have a devastating impact on those who were here legally but did not have anything from the government to prove it.

The impact was felt over a number of years. Under governments of both major parties and under the coalition government, there are examples of members of the Windrush generation whose lack of papers made it impossible to prove that they were here legally, and who found the authorities taking action against them. But the issue came to a head in 2017 as a result of increased public pressure following media coverage of certain individual cases.

Faced with this, it is entirely reasonable to ask why the government wasn't aware of the Windrush generation and the impact of these changes on them. Questions were raised about whether the new rules would lead to discrimination when the legislation was being debated. There was a particular focus on the proposal that landlords should be required to check the immigration status of prospective tenants. As a result, the new requirement for those renting accommodation to prove their legal status in the UK was brought in first as a pilot.

I am not aware, however, of any debate that pointed out there were people who had not been given evidence of their status here when they arrived and who would therefore be adversely affected.

Of course, the fact that there had been cases raised

under previous governments should have led those of us subsequently in government to recognise the potential problem. But for that to happen, the Home Office had to remember or identify those past cases and join up the dots. It did not do so. In her report, Wendy Williams shows that she detected a lack of concern among officials that had led to the injustice experienced by the Windrush generation. She described an 'institutional ignorance and thought-lessness towards the issue of race and the history of the Windrush generation'.

Dealing with immigration cases is never easy. My experience of Home Office officials was of people who wanted to do a good job and wanted to get the right result for individuals. Those same officials often found themselves dealing with cases where people were trying to abuse the system, were less than truthful and sometimes fabricated supporting documents. It is no good immigration officers believing everything they are told by every applicant. They need to be able to identify when someone is genuine and when they are not. One of the problems with the points-based system of immigration is that it does not allow for any discretion, which is why such systems have led to widespread abuse.

Unfortunately, it does seem that this approach of inbuilt cynicism led to what could, at best, be described as an overzealous interpretation of what an individual should require in order to prove their right to be here, and was in fact completely unrealistic. This impacted harshly on the Windrush generation. The fact that Home Office offi-cials were demanding documentary evidence for each year that someone had been in the UK – indeed, four pieces of documentary evidence for each year they had been in the

UK – was first brought home to me at a service commemorating the twenty-fifth anniversary of the death of Stephen Lawrence in 2018. In his remarks to the congregation, the actor Sir Lenny Henry made what was for me and others an uncomfortable reference to the Windrush issue and raised this very point. I found it hard to believe it at the time, and raised the issue with officials when I returned to No. 10. Not long after that, we announced the Williams review with the aim of getting to the bottom of what was happening. What Lenny Henry had said was later confirmed in the Williams report. I had continued to find it hard to believe that this was being required, as I doubted that anyone could produce four pieces of documentary evidence for each year they have been in the UK.

That report set out a number of recommendations for the Home Office. These were accepted in full at the time by the then-Home Secretary Priti Patel. Regrettably, more recently, Suella Braverman as Home Secretary announced that she was no longer going to accept three of the recommendations. These were: the creation of an Independent Migrants' Commissioner; the review and strengthening of the role of the Independent Chief Inspector of Borders and Immigration; and the organisation of reconciliation events between members of the Windrush generation and officials and ministers to strengthen the Home Office's understanding of the impact of what has happened and avoid potential problems in the future. The Home Office felt there were opportunities to fulfil the recommendation regarding a new commissioner through continued review of the department's external stakeholder management, and also that they had alternative ways of engaging with impacted communities other than reconciliation events. As regards reviewing the role of Independent Chief Inspector, the Home Office said they were considering other ways to fulfil the spirit of the recommendation. Given the impact on the Windrush generation of the actions taken by the Home Office, it was my view that the government should accept the recommendations in full.

In previous chapters, I have set out examples where people deliberately used their power to protect institutions and individuals within those institutions rather than the public they were there to serve. In this case, what happened was not being done to protect the institution but to apply and hence protect a policy. Is there a difference? Arguably there is, in the sense that in the former cases, there was a deliberate intent to use power in a way which could only damage others. I do not believe that was the case here. The fact remains, however, that decisions and actions by the powerful had a damaging effect on the powerless – and in this case, the Windrush generation were powerless to prove their point thanks to previous decisions by those in power.

What's more, this reflected an inability to see issues from other people's perspectives and an unwillingness to try to do so. I am also sorry to say that it reflected a view of a group of people being seen as in some sense second-class citizens, as Wendy Williams revealed. These are traits that are found in the other cases I have described.

There is no doubt the Windrush generation felt this was an abuse of power. There is also no doubt that power was used in a way which damaged others. In the terms I have identified in this book, there can be no doubt: this was an abuse of power.

13

Modern Slavery

I suppose most MPs appointed to a ministerial position assume they know the sorts of issues that will be raised in the relevant department – taxes, schools, health, crime and so on. Sometimes, however, an issue comes to the fore that is a revelation to many, including the majority of the public. So it was with modern slavery.

Slavery – surely that ended hundreds of years ago. After all, we've got a law against it, haven't we? That would probably have summed up the attitude of most people to the issue of slavery when I was Home Secretary. Indeed, it probably still applies to many people today.

Yet modern slavery is still here in our cities, towns and villages. The figure first identified in 2014 by the Home Office, after considerable work, for the number of victims here in the UK was between 10,000 and 13,000 in 2013 and it almost certainly underestimated the size of the problem. Around the world, it is estimated today that there are over 50 million people in slavery, including forced marriage. The latest estimate from the Global Slavery Index published by Walk Free is that there are 122,000 people living in modern slavery in the UK. This is why it is so important that the UK passed the Modern Slavery Act in 2015 and led the world in doing so. Of course, there is much more that needs to be done, but there is now much greater awareness of the problem worldwide, and a number of countries are actively involved in trying to identify and support victims and deal with perpetrators in an attempt to reduce and eventually eradicate slavery.

The previous attempts to deal with slavery occurred predominantly in the nineteenth century. The UK passed the Slavery Abolition Act in 1833, which came into effect in August 1834. But we were not the first. The institution of slavery was abolished in Mexico in 1829, and the Haitian revolution of 1791–1804 was a successful slave rebellion. Changes in the US led by Abraham Lincoln came somewhat later, in 1865.

I first became interested in the issue when in opposition, but at that stage saw it very much in terms of human trafficking and predominantly from the point of view of women being trafficked into sexual exploitation. At that time, with my women and equalities responsibilities, I worked with the Shadow Home Affairs team, notably David Davis and Damian Green, to put forward policy proposals to deal with human trafficking.

Trafficking is a very real problem. It affects men and women being moved across borders into sexual exploitation or labour exploitation. It has also affected children. For example, children have been trafficked into the UK from Vietnam to work in cannabis factories.

We should not, however, be lulled into thinking that slavery is purely about people being trafficked from abroad into the UK. Slavery is much more extensive. What highlighted this wider issue was a report from the Centre

for Social Justice – *It Happens Here* – published in 2013.*
It was this report that brought home to me and others that
people here in the UK – British citizens – were being taken
into slavery. It showed how slavery covered many areas of
labour exploitation and many sectors of economic activity,
including agriculture, construction and hospitality.

Shocking though it is, there will be people in slavery
in a town near you. Some of them will have been brought
into the UK by criminal gangs. Others will be vulnerable
people picked up from our streets and taken into slavery.
They will be made to work but will receive little or no pay.
They may be told their pay will be used to cover the costs
of their accommodation and food. In reality, they will be
made to live in squalid conditions and will be given little
to eat. In some cases, they will be forced to commit petty
crimes and their identities may be used for benefit fraud.
Many of them, if not most, won't really understand what
is happening to them. This is clearly an abuse of power by
the criminal gangs and slave drivers.

Those trafficked into sexual exploitation will have their
passports removed and will be threatened with exposure
as illegal immigrants if they try to escape. Often, the gangs
will threaten to harm their families back home if they don't
do what is required of them. They may be moved from
country to country. When I was Prime Minister, I visited
Nigeria in 2018 and met a young woman who had been
trafficked around several countries in Europe and who was
now being supported by the Salvation Army as part of

* The Centre for Social Justice, *It Happens Here: Equipping the
United Kingdom to fight modern slavery*, March 2013.

their work for the UK government on this issue. When the young woman returned to Nigeria – free once again – her family rejected her as having brought 'dishonour' on them.

Sometimes the families are, inadvertently or otherwise, complicit in the trafficking. For example, one of the victims I have met had been in domestic servitude in the UK and had also been forced into sex with friends of the family she lived with. She had been brought up in Uganda but with family finances being difficult, her mother had accepted an offer from someone who came into the village and promised to give her daughter a better life in the UK. Sometimes families will receive payment for handing over their child.

There are some people, indeed some governments, today who object to the use of the term 'slavery'. Certainly, many find it shocking to hear that there may be people in slavery in their town or city. I believe that we should have no qualms about calling slavery out for what it is. When men and women are being held in slavery, their liberty taken away from them, and are forced to work for their 'owners', there is no other term to describe it.

The perpetrators of these modern slavery crimes are mostly the criminal gangs who make their money out of illicitly trading commodities, be they guns, drugs or people. There are also cases where the slavery is imposed by an employer – for example, an individual may be brought to the UK to act as a domestic servant and then not given their freedom, while receiving little or no pay for their work. There are other cases where gangs identify vulnerable individuals and force them into slavery because it benefits the gang members financially, but for whom this is not big business.

The work to stop modern slavery, therefore, has different elements. Dealing with the perpetrators is vital. If we are to stop them, their business model needs to be broken. That means reducing the supply of potential slaves. This is a global problem. It involves ensuring there are better economic opportunities in countries of origin so that families don't feel the need to entrust their children to strangers who promise them a better life or, *in extremis*, the need to 'sell' some of their children so they can provide for the rest of the family. It means better education so that potential victims are given the life skills they need to earn an income and provide for their families, but also the skills to identify potential traffickers and slave drivers. It also means ensuring that vulnerable people are not able to slip through the net of societal support and become victims of slavery.

Looking ahead, it means recognising the interaction of other global issues with slavery. When Ukrainian women and children started to cross their country's border, mainly into Poland, in search of safety after the Russian invasion of their country on 24 February 2022, the traffickers were at the border looking for potential victims for exploitation into slavery. That was the result of a specific event. There are longer-term ongoing issues that are increasing vulnerability to slavery and trafficking around the world. The Covid-19 pandemic undoubtedly increased vulnerability to slavery by impacting on economic activity. Another key factor which will affect levels of slavery is climate change. For example, if changes in the climate make it harder to earn a living from agriculture in some parts of the world, then the temptation grows for individuals to entrust themselves to the traffickers who claim to offer a better life.

I should make it clear that I am not talking about individuals or families who pay people smugglers to get them into another country illegally. What I am talking about is the traffickers whose victims will, whatever they have been promised, ultimately be exploited as slaves.

In addition to dealing with factors that increase the vulnerability of the potential victim, breaking the business model of the criminal gangs means catching them, prosecuting them and putting them behind bars. While prosecutions across England and Wales have improved, the situation is still not good enough. Enhancing the power of the police and authorities to identify, catch and prosecute the slave drivers was one of the key aims of the Modern Slavery Act.

If the criminals are going to be successfully prosecuted, the police need the evidence. To obtain that evidence, it is important to ensure that the victims are willing to come forward to tell their stories. This is easier said than done because the victims are traumatised, sometimes don't know what has happened to them, are often far from home in a strange country, are worried that their families will be hurt, are anxious that their slave drivers may find them, take them back into servitude and wreak vengeance on them, and are concerned that they may not be able to support themselves when they have left their slave drivers – however appalling the conditions in which they have been living. Those who have been trafficked may be afraid that they will be punished for immigration crimes.

This is a challenging mix of issues to navigate through, and the one thing that is certain is that it cannot be done quickly. It takes time for victims to be willing to give their evidence. They need to be able to feel that they can trust those who are supporting them, and that they can trust the police. It may well be that some will have had bad experiences with the police in their home countries, or come from a place where there is deep mistrust of the police and/or a corrupt force.

The Modern Slavery Act aimed to increase the support available to victims as a means of helping those exploited human beings. But increasing support is also part of the work being done to encourage victims to give evidence against the criminals who brought them into slavery. This is why changes to legislation made by Boris Johnson's government through the Nationality and Borders Act 2022 are of concern. In April 2023, Greater Manchester Police reported a significant drop in the number of potential victims able to access support from the modern slavery and human trafficking victim care providers. Elements of the proposed Illegal Migration Act introduced by Rishi Sunak's government are likely to compound the problem. The harder government makes it for people to come forward to identify as being in slavery and to feel they can trust the state sufficiently to give evidence against their slave drivers, the fewer perpetrators who will get caught.

There was an added provision in the Modern Slavery Act. It is unarguable that those companies who exploit their employees and effectively hold them in slavery are abusing their power. Hence a new element of the Act was the requirement for businesses with an annual turnover of £35 million or more to prepare a slavery and human trafficking statement each financial year. The statement should show what has been done to ensure that slavery and human trafficking were not taking place in any of its supply chains or in any part of its business; if nothing has been done, the statement should show that too.

The aim was for companies to look down their supply chains and, if they identified slavery, to take action accordingly. That might mean working to get the supplier to change their practices, or it might mean not using that supplier any longer. I emphasise that companies were not required to examine their supply chains, only to report on whether or not they had done so.

Even getting this past others in government took a lot of work from the Home Office. In particular, there were advisers in Downing Street who were wary of imposing extra burdens on business. Without that reluctance, it might have been possible to have a tougher requirement in the Act. When it came to it, I accepted that it was better to have something in the Act on the supply-chain issue rather than nothing at all.

The legislation has led to some companies – mainly larger multinationals – taking this on board as part of their ESG (Environmental, Social and Governance) agendas. Identifying modern slavery in the supply chain is not always an easy task. The degree of difficulty varies according to the length of that supply chain and its circumstances. You would expect, for example, that looking into working conditions at suppliers here in the UK was easier than doing so for companies abroad. For smaller companies with lengthy supply chains overseas, it can be particularly difficult to identify what is happening, although there are now organisations that are able to provide this service.

I really believe that businesses have an absolutely critical role to play in the work to stop slavery. That is why the investigation of supply chains is so important. If businesses exploiting labour were not able to sell their products, they would have no business. But not every company around the world understands the significance of this issue.

This is not just about companies elsewhere in the world. It has been shocking to see reports of such exploitation of labour here in the UK. The most high-profile instance of this came with revelations in 2020 about exploitation in the supply chain of the fashion retailer Boohoo. In an independent report on Boohoo in 2020, Alison Levitt QC, who looked at just a small part of the business's UK supply chain, expressed serious concerns about the workers' human rights.* She found that workers were being expected to work in unacceptable and dangerous conditions, and in some cases received illegally low pay. This followed reports in *The Sunday Times* that workers employed by Boohoo's suppliers were being exploited. Following the Levitt report, the company significantly reduced the number of suppliers it used and placed extra requirements on them.

What is notable about this case is that the focus was on suppliers in the UK. This was not a question of long and difficult overseas supply chains. These were workers in factories here in Leicester.

In some parts of the world, the need for work to provide an income to feed a family and the lack of opportunities are so great that it is all too easy for companies to exploit their workers. But to do this, they need to be operating in a context where either this is not unlawful or, although it is unlawful, there is no enforcement of the law.

---

* Alison Levitt QC, *Independent Review into the boohoo Group PLC's Leicester supply chain*, 24 September 2020.

In these circumstances, governments that fail to act are arguably abusing their power, not through excess use of power over others, but from lack of proper use of their power. The company that fails to investigate its supply chain, when the law requires it to report on what it has done, is also abusing its power. The message should be clear. Businesses can make a real difference.

As I said earlier, dealing with modern slavery means addressing a variety of issues, including ensuring that the police have the tools they need to identify and catch the criminals involved. It also means ensuring that the police understand the issue and are ready and willing to look for it. It is only in recent years that the police have paid more attention to modern slavery as a crime in itself, and also as an indicator of other crimes. The gangs involved in slavery are often involved in other significant criminality, so identifying slavery can lead to identifying other crimes.

Looked at like this, it is clear that dealing with modern slavery is not just a benefit to those who are, or could be, victims of slavery; it has a wider benefit to society.

It can also work the other way round. I remember one force telling me they had a small number of individuals who were regular offenders carrying out petty crimes. When they started thinking about modern slavery, it led to them determining that these individuals were being forced to commit these crimes by their slave drivers. That, in turn, led to them identifying a number of victims, and bringing modern slavery charges against the slave drivers.

The first reported conviction of a UK-led business for a human trafficking offence came in January 2016. There have been other cases since then. For example, in 2017, eleven members of a Lincolnshire family were jailed for violently exploiting at least eighteen victims of modern slavery who had been kept in caravans without running water or toilet facilities. The group targeted homeless people and men with learning difficulties, and took them to live and work in squalid conditions, some for up to twenty-six years. Their offences were described in court as 'chilling in their mercilessness'.

Operation Fort, led by West Midlands Police, was reported in 2019 as the biggest case of modern slavery in the UK. It involved the exploitation of around 400 people, who worked for a pittance while their slave drivers were said to have made £2 million over a number of years.

As recently as June 2022, two people were convicted and sentenced to a total of twenty-five years in jail for trafficking at least twenty-nine vulnerable individuals from Slovakia and Hungary to the UK.

The greatest abuse of power, of course, is exercised by those who enslave others, whether a single employer or a criminal gang. These people are treating their slaves as commodities, not as human beings. They make their victims live and work in appalling conditions, and are merciless in using threats and violence to keep their victims in their power. They do it because it is to their own personal advantage financially. They do it because they can.

That is why breaking the business model is so important. If the criminal gangs could no longer make money out of trading individuals, then they would move away from this business. If the employer was required to pay decent wages and ensure that their domestic servants could enjoy all the rights that should be given to workers, this too would become a different story. If the vulnerable were not left to become the victims of slave drivers, this opportunity would not be there to be exploited.

As I mentioned earlier, breaking the business model is easier said than done. Often, the hardest to deal with are the gangs who act internationally as easily as they do nationally. Aided and abetted by technology, they ply their trade across the internet and across borders around the world. Their callous approach to human life is seen in the way they are quite happy to hold sales of individuals. In Thomas Hardy's novel *The Mayor of Casterbridge*, a drunken Michael Henchard is depicted auctioning off his wife with whom he had quarrelled. As we read that, we may be shocked at the idea, but it was much more shocking to hear the claim in recent years of a coffee shop at a UK airport being used as a base for the sale of slaves.

That slavery is all around us is a fact. That it is an international business for criminal gangs is a fact. That the lives of those taken into slavery will be full of unspeakable cruelty and misery, as they encounter appalling conditions and treatment not even fit for animals, is likewise a fact. But it is also true to say that around the world, there are NGOs and governments, individuals, companies and police working to stop it.

The UK led the way with the Modern Slavery Act. I was proud to have brought in the Act, and proud that we were able to shine a light on a forgotten injustice and show the way forward for other countries. It's sad to say there is now a debate about whether the system set up to support victims of slavery is being used by those who are here illegally to avoid being removed from the UK. If so, they would be adding to the pressures on the system, which can make it harder to address the needs of genuine victims. To my dismay, the government's approach to this issue has been driven by the desire to deal with illegal immigration rather than by the wish to stop slavery. Ensuring that the system of referrals of potential victims of slavery is genuinely operating in the interests of victims is important. On the other hand, the issue of modern slavery cannot and should not be addressed through the lens of illegal immigration. Doing so would mean consigning victims to yet more years of enslaved misery.

I am working with others internationally to set up a Global Commission to eradicate modern slavery and human trafficking, which should not only bring a greater degree of coordination of efforts around the world, but should also help us achieve consistency in legislation around the world and in businesses' approach to identifying slavery in their supply chains. The UK government under Rishi Sunak has committed its support to the Commission.

Modern slavery demonstrates abuses of power in many different ways. With the political will, the right tools and the beneficial use of power, it can be eliminated. It will take time, but we should all commit to working for its eradication and making sure there are no more victims of this appalling and inhuman crime – because we can.

Part Three

The International Scene

So far, I have concentrated on examples of the abuse of power within the UK. Yet arguably, nowhere can the abuse of power cause more damage to more people than in the world of international relations. The examples of social injustice I have set out in the previous section have affected the lives of individuals, families and communities, and in many cases have implications for our wider public life. Abuse of power on the world stage, however, may not just have economic and social consequences. It can lead to war, to inconceivable horror and loss of life.

The potentially devastating consequences for large numbers of people mean that international relations is the realm where political leaders need to be most sensitive, most aware of the interests of others and most thoughtful in their use of power.

But I suspect there are some, including a few in Parliament today, who think that this is the area where it is most important to wield power. That line of thought stems from the very macho attitude that you need to square up to others, show them who is boss, let them know you mean business. Of course, it is sometimes necessary to show such strength. There are players on the international stage, such as Vladimir Putin, who only respect strength and who will exploit any sign of weakness. The problem with a desire to show off power is that it can lead all too easily to missteps, with outcomes that were never intended.

Being driven by a sense of service does not mean manifesting a weak, lily-livered willingness always to give in to the other side's arguments. It is not synonymous with appeasement. It certainly doesn't mean pig-headedly, belligerently digging in your heels and asserting that only you are right. It does mean taking the trouble to develop an understanding of the full impact of decisions, and of the reasons why the other side are taking the position that they are adopting, and acting accordingly.

14

Power on the World Stage

In recent years, the trend in world politics has been away from the thoughtful and considered, and towards the belligerent and the absolutist. I have used the word absolutist before, but I want my usage to be clear. What do I mean by it? I mean the approach that says you are either 100 per cent with me or 100 per cent against me. With this comes the assumption, indeed the immutable conviction, that those who are 100 per cent against you are, by definition, not just wrong but close to being the devil incarnate. I exaggerate to make a point, but only slightly, because this absolutist approach is one that brooks no compromise, is not willing to give up anything for the greater good.

International relations are built on understanding when you can and should compromise and when you need to stand firm. In recent years, we have seen the development of international relations as strong men squaring up to each other – Presidents Putin, Trump and Xi, with President Erdoğan of Turkey on the edges of this group. This was exemplified by the unilateral approach taken by President Trump on many issues. Waking up in Downing Street to be told that American troops would be pulled out of the fight against Daesh in Iraq and Syria, without any reference to the UK and other nations whose troops were operating alongside them, and with no consideration for the impact on those troops, did not make for an easy day. That was just one example of the difficulties of dealing with someone whose only thought was for what *he* wanted to do and not for the greater good. From where I sat, this looked remarkably like an abuse of power.

Dealing with Donald Trump and his administration was like dealing with no other world leader. He was an American president like no other. His unpredictable decision-making, propensity for making major announcements via Twitter and apparent disregard for allies, together with the constant changes of key personnel in the White House and in his government, made life extremely difficult for those of us trying to forge a sensible Western approach to key issues.

I experienced this unpredictability when I visited him shortly after his inauguration in 2017. I went with a particular purpose, namely to encourage him to give wholehearted support to NATO. This was necessary because his previous statements about the organisation had suggested lukewarm support at best. Although my conversation with him in the Oval Office went well, I wanted him to affirm his support in the press conference. Usually in meetings like this with another leader, there would be agreement about what would be said at the press conference afterwards on the key issues that had been discussed. On this occasion, when we went into the press conference, I had no idea what he would say. I was prepared for him to say the opposite of what we had discussed. Fortunately, my fears were allayed and he gave his full support to NATO, but it made for some worrying moments.

Added to this was the way he saw certain issues in absolutist terms. At a dinner in my constituency, someone once said to me that I had to remember that Donald Trump was a real estate man, and in real estate there are two sides to the deal: one wins and the other loses. In international relations, this attitude was far too simplistic. From this arose his apparent lack of understanding of the depth of issues. For example, trade for him was just about goods. If America sold to a country one dollar's worth more than they bought from them, the trade deal was good. The other way round was bad. This completely failed to recognise that trade is complex and is about an awful lot more than goods – not least because while you might lose on goods, you could win on services.

To some extent this pattern has been broken by President Biden, who has over his political career shown more willingness to compromise and more understanding of the key role America plays as the leader of the Western world. As I outline in Chapter 16 on Afghanistan, however, the signs from President Biden were initially not as promising as many of us had hoped. It was as though America was still trying to find its new role in the world. Or at least trying to establish to what extent it needed to adapt its role in a new world with more players. That sense was to change with Russia's 2022 invasion of Ukraine and the firm stance taken alongside its NATO allies by the United States.

In a way, the international picture was much clearer in the Cold War when two great powers faced each other – America and Russia – and both sides knew how far they could push things before they would tip over into war. Today, the rise of China as a key power has made the global situation more complex. China exercises its power in a variety of ways. It is not afraid to square up to the West using methods that challenge the international rules-based order, as is seen in its development of sites in the South China Sea and in its reaction to Western navies sailing through what are international waters, but which China considers its own domain.

China has also been building up an increasing number of states which are in some way beholden to it. One example of this is in the Belt and Road Initiative, but we see it generally in the way China offers loans at cheap rates, as well as contracts to build needed infrastructure, and appears as the helpful friend to often small states whose economies limit their opportunities for development. We see these activities in the infrastructure support China has provided to countries in Africa, and in the support it has offered to small states in the Pacific Ocean, giving it, in due course, options for establishing military bases.

The trend towards absolutism is not over. It is linked to the growth of populism and nationalism that has beset so many countries. Populism and nationalism give rise to ideas that countries can retreat behind their borders, that some countries are exceptional just because of who they are, and that the job of those in government is to act as mouthpieces for the loudest popular view rather than to do what is right for the country.

The problem with judging popularity is that all too often it is based on opinion polling, the results of which depend on the question asked. To give an example from a different issue, if you ask people if they want to stop illegal immigrants, the answer will be yes, but if you ask them if the UK should help people fleeing persecution, the answer will also be yes.

The job of any government is to do what is right for the country. What is more, history shows that often, even if such actions do not appear popular at first, they gain support when people see the positive results of that action. What governments should look for from the public is respect, not popularity.

The initial coming together of the West in its response to the war in Ukraine was certainly positive, but the future of the Western alliance, and the willingness of countries to uphold and protect their values, is still under threat. What will happen when the next challenge to democracy and sovereignty occurs?

We should be worried about this because there is no doubt that democracy is under pressure across the world. It is natural to see that pressure in any one country as coming from external threats, but we should not ignore the pressures within our own countries. There is polling that shows a reduction in the percentage of young people in both the UK and the US who see democracy as the best form of government, while a growing percentage of people want to live in a society that provides greater security, not greater freedom.

We see this desire for security in a number of ways, but the implication for governments cannot be ignored. The danger is that politicians faced with this phenomenon see the answer in increasing power rather than service – indeed, that they are ever more willing to usurp the constitution and abuse their power. And the danger of that is that it leads to the erosion of existing freedoms. Perhaps it would be well to remember the words of Winston Churchill in the House of Commons in 1947: 'it has been said that democracy is the worst form of government except all those other forms that, have been tried from time to time'; in saying that he was insistent that 'public opinion, expressed by all constitutional means, should shape, guide, and control the actions of Ministers who are their servants not their masters'.

15

The Salisbury Poisonings

Even a Prime Minister experiences the unexpected – and I'm not just talking about having my hand held by the President of the United States of America in front of the world's press! On a more serious note, in the range of unexpected moments during my time in office, the moment when I was told of the Salisbury poisonings ranks above them all. As is so often the case, there is a limit to what I can say publicly about this, but there is a substantial amount of material in the public domain.

On 4 March 2018, a man and a woman were found slipping in and out of consciousness on a park bench in Salisbury and, while there were some theories about what the problem was, it wasn't clear what had happened. That was how the situation was first described to me by my private secretary in my office in 10 Downing Street. That there could be more to the story, however, became evident when he went on to explain that this was not just any couple. This was Sergei Skripal, a former Russian military intelligence officer who had become a British citizen, and his daughter, Yulia.

When the first descriptions of a terrorist or major criminal event come in, it is not unusual to have only sketchy information. It is important for ministers to interrogate the information being given to them, but they must not overreact and must be prepared to be patient. In this case, I was told that people hoped there was an innocent explanation for this mystery illness – indeed, that it might be related to drugs. Part of my mind was clinging to that hope. The other part of my brain recognised that Sergei Skripal's background immediately raised doubts and concerns. So I hoped that there was nothing to be overly concerned about, but feared that the truth would turn out to be more sinister.

I began to think through what the impact might be, what immediate action was required, what needed to be done to ensure the safety of others, what it meant for international relations, and what the fallout was likely to be. The civil service goes into preparation overdrive. If it is the worst-case scenario of foreign interference on British soil – above all, a foreign state attempting murder on British soil – how should Parliament be told and when? What are the options for action against the foreign state involved? And so forth. It is my experience that in times of crisis, the civil service, our security services and our police are second to none. They spring into action, working together in the national interest. While the civil servants and special advisers were going through the options, I was trying to sort out in my own mind what the UK's next steps should be.

The next morning, Salisbury NHS Foundation Trust, which covered Salisbury District Hospital, declared a major incident as medical staff were concerned about the symptoms they were seeing. This then became a multi-agency incident. As well as Sergei and Yulia Skripal, Detective Sergeant Nick Bailey, who had attended Sergei Skripal's house after the event, fell ill and was moved into intensive care at Salisbury Hospital.

The incident took place close to Porton Down, the UK's Defence Science and Technology Laboratory, and experts there proceeded to analyse results from the Skripals to identify what was causing their illness. It was at Porton Down that the source of the problem was identified as a Novichok nerve agent, later confirmed by the Organisation for the Prohibition of Chemical Weapons (OPCW).

It is always tempting for ministers in situations like this to want to go public early on. That is understandable, as the public are keen to know what has happened, and the media and other politicians on the government and opposition benches are pressing for answers. My experience of terrorist events while Home Secretary had shown me the importance of not simply responding to calls for information, however loud those calls were. I knew that it was particularly important in this case to speak with assurance. It would have been a significant mistake to have made claims which were then proved to be false, and which would have given other governments, specifically the Russians, the opportunity to paint the UK as irresponsible and untrustworthy.

By 12 March, just over a week after the Skripals had been taken ill, we had sufficient clarity and evidence for me to go to the House of Commons and make a statement:

I share the impatience of the House and the country at large to bring those responsible to justice and to take the full range of appropriate responses against those who would act against our country in this way. But as a nation that believes in justice and the rule of law, it is essential that we proceed in the right way, led not by speculation but by the evidence. That is why we have given the police the space and time to carry out their investigation properly. Hundreds of officers have been working around the clock, together with experts from our armed forces, to sift and assess all the available evidence, to identify crime scenes and decontamination sites and to follow every possible lead to find those responsible. That investigation continues and we must allow the police to continue with their work.

I went on to say:

. . . It is now clear that Mr Skripal and his daughter were poisoned with a military-grade nerve agent of a type developed by Russia. It is part of a group of nerve agents known as Novichok.

Based on the positive identification of this chemical agent by world-leading experts at the Defence Science and Technology Laboratory at Porton Down, our knowledge that Russia has previously produced this agent and would still be capable of doing so, Russia's record of conducting state-sponsored assassinations and our assessment that Russia views some defectors as legitimate targets for assassinations, the Government have concluded that it is highly likely that Russia was responsible for the act against Sergei and Yulia Skripal. There are, therefore, only two plausible explanations for what happened in Salisbury on 4 March: either this was a direct act by the Russian state against our country; or the Russian Government lost control of their potentially catastrophically damaging nerve agent and allowed it to get into the hands of others.*

As a result of this analysis, the Russian Ambassador was called into the Foreign Office and a clear message was given by the then-Foreign Secretary, Boris Johnson. In his diaries Alan Duncan, who was a Foreign Office minister at the time, said, 'Well done, Boris! I felt genuinely proud of him.' Russia had twenty-four hours to tell us which of the above explanations was correct. Was this a deliberate act against the UK or was it the result of Russia's dangerous incompetence?

I am sure there will be many who wonder why we didn't just go all out and identify this as a deliberate act by Russia straightaway. While that approach might have gained positive headlines for what would have been seen as decisive government, it was important for us to deal with this in a way that would give confidence to our allies and, critically, encourage them to support us in any action. It was also important for us as the UK to be seen to be dealing fairly with the issue. If we do not operate justly, why should we ask anyone else to do so? The longer-term aim was to send a clear message to Russia that its behaviour was unacceptable and that this view was shared around the world.

So this was a very good example of how pandering to the wishes of politicians or the media would deliver in the immediate term but might make it much harder, if not impossible, to deliver the longer-term aim. At times like this, leadership is about patience and restraint.

---

* Hansard, 12 March 2018, HC Deb., vol. 637, col. 620.

I did not make a further statement until Wednesday, 14 March after Prime Minister's Questions. By that time, the Russians had ignored our demand for an answer. More than that, they had made every effort to debunk our version of events. For example, on 9 March, responding to my statement that we would respond appropriately if the evidence showed that Russia was behind the attack on the Skripals, the Russian Foreign Minister Sergei Lavrov accused us of spreading propaganda. This was a good case of the pot calling the kettle black. At one stage, Russia even claimed that the UK itself, and indeed I myself, were responsible for what had happened to the Skripals.

As a result of Russia's failure to provide an answer to our request for an explanation, in my second statement to Parliament I was able to go much further:

> It was right to offer Russia the opportunity to provide an explanation, but its response has demonstrated complete disdain for the gravity of these events. The Russian Government have provided no credible explanation that could suggest that they lost control of their nerve agent, no explanation as to how this agent came to be used in the United Kingdom, and no explanation as to why Russia has an undeclared chemical weapons programme in contravention of international law. Instead it has treated the use of a military-grade nerve agent in Europe with sarcasm, contempt and defiance.

I had no doubt what all this meant:

> There is no alternative conclusion other than that the Russian state was culpable for the attempted murder

of Mr Skripal and his daughter, and for threatening the lives of other British citizens in Salisbury, including Detective Sergeant Nick Bailey. This represents an unlawful use of force by the Russian state against the United Kingdom. As I set out on Monday, it has taken place against the backdrop of a well-established pattern of Russian state aggression across Europe and beyond. It must therefore be met with a full and robust response beyond the actions we have already taken since the murder of Mr Litvinenko and to counter this pattern of Russian aggression elsewhere.[*]

This was a blatant abuse of power by the Russian state. But it was not the first time that Moscow had shown such a willingness to abuse its power, the murder of Alexander Litvinenko being a case in point.

It is worth looking back to what happened after the murder of Alexander Litvinenko. That killing had taken place in November 2006. The agent used was polonium-210, which induced acute radiation syndrome. On 1 December that year, there were reports that the Atomic Weapons Establishment had traced the source of the polonium to a nuclear power plant in Russia. It wasn't until late May 2007 that the government issued a formal request to their Russian counterpart for the extradition of a named individual believed to have been involved in the poisoning. As Russia has a policy of not agreeing to requests for the extradition of its citizens, that move did not achieve its aim, but it sent a clear message about who the UK authorities believed was responsible for the murder.

---

[*] Hansard, 14 March 2018, HC Deb., vol. 637, col. 855.

It wasn't until 21 January 2016, when the public inquiry headed by Sir Robert Owen reported,[*] that the involvement of the Russian state was given formal recognition. Sir Robert concluded that Andrei Lugovoy and Dmitry Kovtun were responsible for the murder: 'I am sure that Mr Lugovoy and Mr Kovtun placed the polonium-210 in the teapot at the Pine Bar on 1 November 2006. I am also sure that they did this with the intention of poisoning Mr Litvinenko.'

He added:

> When Mr Lugovoy poisoned Mr Litvinenko it is probable that he did so under the direction of the FSB [the Russian security service]. I would add that I regard that as a strong probability. I have found that Mr Kovtun also took part in the poisoning. I conclude therefore that he was also acting under FSB direction, possibly indirectly through Mr Lugovoy but probably to his knowledge.

But for many, the key finding was the very last conclusion drawn by Sir Robert: 'The FSB operation to kill Mr Litvinenko was probably approved by Mr Patrushev [head of the FSB at the time] and also by President Putin.'

Then, in September 2021, the overall conclusion of the inquiry was endorsed by the European Court of Human Rights, which in its judgment in the Carter v Russia case brought by Litvinenko's widow, ruled that Russia was responsible for the killing of Litvinenko and so liable for damages.[†]

---

[*] The Litvinenko Inquiry, *Report into the death of Alexander Litvinenko*, January 2016, HC 695.
[†] European Court of Human Rights Application 20914/07.

It found it beyond reasonable doubt that Lugovoy and Kovtun were responsible for the assassination, and that there was prima facie evidence of state involvement.

The same Andrei Lugovoy, who by the time of the attack on the Skripals was a deputy in Russia's state Duma, was reported as saying in an interview in *Echo of Moscow* on 6 March 2018: 'Something constantly happens to Russian citizens who either run away from Russian justice, or for some reason choose for themselves a way of life they call a change of their Motherland. So the more Britain accepts on its territory every good-for-nothing, every scum from all over the world, the more problems they will have.'

Following the attack on Litvinenko, the UK halted normal relations with Russia. That policy was still in place by the time of the attempt on the Skripals. In the intervening years there had been those who had suggested that we should ease back on our position, particularly given the possibility of greater economic interaction with Russia. I had always been one of the hawks on this. I saw no reason why we should soften our stance. Russia, and certainly President Putin, values strength. Backing down merely encourages their bad behaviour.

Even so, our continued stance of no business as usual did not deter the Russian state from venturing to attempt to commit murder on British soil once again with their attack on Sergei Skripal.

At the same time as I had been preparing for and making statements in the Commons on the source of the Novichok attack, across Whitehall the civil service machinery had kicked into action with the Foreign Office, the security services and our defence officials, working with others to keep key allies updated on our findings. An early decision was taken that we should share as much information as possible, as this was more likely to encourage support from others. It was our job to show the evidence on which our findings and crucially our attribution to the Russian state were based, and through that convince our allies of our analysis. This outreach was critical in bringing the Western world together to act against Russia.

Another key prong to our response was our work through the OPCW, the multilateral institution that works to prevent the use of chemical weapons. As ever with such organisations, votes on issues depend not just on the facts of the case but on the overall standing of the countries concerned and on the multiplicity of individual relationships between countries. This was one reason why it was so important for us not to have jumped to conclusions and for us to have given Russia the opportunity to explain that this all might have been the result of a terrible mistake.

At this point, the UK's general standing and the appreciation of the expertise and professionalism of Porton Down stood us in good stead. Nevertheless, our diplomats and officials still had to work hard to explain what had happened and how we had reached our conclusion about the involvement of the Russian state. To further show our bona fides and support our position, we asked the OPCW to conduct its own investigation into the agent used to poison the Skripals. This was entirely independent of the UK's own investigations and involved four different national laboratories. The result was clear. The analysis by Porton Down that the agent used was Novichok was endorsed by the OPCW.

Later, in June, we put forward a motion at the OPCW which condemned the use of chemical weapons since 2012 in Iraq, Malaysia, the Syrian Arab Republic and the UK. This was passed by 82 to 24. It was in this vote, and in an earlier vote instigated by Russia to make the UK's investigation a joint one with Russia, that the work to explain our position was shown to be valuable. We won both votes, despite the almost certain expectation by the Russians that they would be able to sway a majority against us.

More dramatically, it was the collective international response to expel Russian diplomats that was the clearest sign to Moscow that they had been found out by the international community. Following the UK's announcement of the expulsion of twenty-three Russian so-called diplomats, who were in fact intelligence officers, some twenty-seven other countries and NATO also took action, leading to the expulsion of 153 Russian intelligence officers in total. This was the largest collective expulsion of Russian intelligence officers in history.

I spoke to a number of world leaders following the events in Salisbury to encourage them to follow us and expel Russian intelligence officers. Key, of course, was the American reaction. Certainly, our understanding was that the American system was with us and ready to act. President Trump wasn't against acting but, as on so many issues, he did not show a proper appreciation of the role America played as the leader of the Western world. His main concern was that the United States was expelling far more than any other country – which was true, but reflected the fact that there were more Russian personnel in the US than in other countries. Surely anyone could work out that this simple fact would lead to the number of their expulsions being greater.

I remember the debate around the European Council table. This was an occasion when the EU countries rallied behind the UK, recognising the threat that Russia posed and the message its action gave: that it believed it could act with impunity anywhere it wished. But EU debates on Russia were never absolutely straightforward, given the histories of the countries sitting around the table and their different attitudes towards relationships with Russia. Eighteen EU member states expelled Russian intelligence officers. Six states and the EU itself recalled their ambassadors from Russia. The three countries that did neither were Austria, Cyprus and Greece.

Sadly, the story of Salisbury did not end with the expulsions or the vote at the OPCW. Weeks after the attempt on the lives of the Skripals, a local man, Charlie Rowley, found a perfume bottle and took it back to his partner, Dawn Sturgess. She used what was in the bottle, not realising that this was no perfume phial but that it contained Novichok. She died days later. So Russia achieved its aim of killing a British citizen – just not the one they had planned to kill.

This showed the reckless approach of the Russian agents. By discarding the bottle, they were leaving evidence of their crime. But it also showed the complete disregard the Russian state had for the consequences of its actions. The bottle could have been found by children. It could have been passed between more people. The number of deaths of innocent civilians could have been much higher than it was. That was irrelevant to the Russians. This was a very good example of the casual, callous approach of the Russian state to the lives of innocent men, women and children.

In September 2018, the Crown Prosecution Service authorised charges against two men, known as Alexander Petrov and Ruslan Boshirov – aliases for Alexander Mishkin and Anatoly Chepiga respectively. Evidence showed that both were members of the GRU – the Russian military intelligence service to which Skripal had also belonged. Later that month, charges were authorised against a third man known as Sergei Fedotov, an alias for Denis Sergeev, who evidence showed was also a member of the GRU. Arrest warrants and Interpol notices are in place.

The casual approach taken by the Russian agents suggests a lack of professionalism in those who were carrying out the initial attack. This was not a well-trained, finely honed set of agents able to enter unseen, carry out their attack successfully and leave the country without leaving any trace behind them. Either this was nonchalance on a significant scale, or the Russians just aren't as good as everyone thinks they are. Later events, such as the Russians' attempt to hack into the OPCW – and, indeed, their army's failures in Ukraine – suggest that the latter is more likely. They simply aren't as good as the image they have built up.

Salisbury was an example of the West coming together once again to defend its values. This was notable at a time when there had been a growing sense that the West was no longer the coherent whole that it once had been, and that the ties between us were increasingly weak. This was, of course, exacerbated by the attitude of the US, led as it was by a President whose mantra was 'America First', and who showed himself strangely reluctant to play the role required of the leader of the Western world.

Against that background, the reaction to Salisbury was a beacon of hope. It showed a West that was willing to unite in defending its values. That light was to be shattered the following year by the disastrous withdrawal from Afghanistan, only to be reignited in the response to Russia's invasion of Ukraine. But stop–start simply won't do. Russia under Putin has conducted many acts of aggression and consistently ignores the international rules-based order to which we adhere.

This behaviour is not confined to Russia. China, North Korea and others have also demonstrated a flagrant disregard for international norms. If we in the West are to defend our values and stand up to dictators and anti-democratic aggressors, then we must stay firm, remain united and call out the blatant abuse of power when we see it – and we certainly saw it in Russia's action in Salisbury.

16

Afghanistan

In looking at specific international events, it is always difficult to assess them objectively, and the decision by President Trump to sign a deal with the Taliban in Afghanistan – which led to the withdrawal of NATO troops in 2021 – is no exception. By this time, I had stepped down as Prime Minister, but the issue of Afghanistan was one with which I had been closely involved during my time as both Home Secretary and Prime Minister. I was also able to contribute to the debate from the backbenches of the House of Commons, as I did when Parliament was recalled to debate the withdrawal in August 2021.

Notice of that recall came to me when I was about to have lunch with my husband in a mountain restaurant looking out over Zermatt and the Matterhorn in Switzerland. Needless to say, a good bit of the conversation over that lunch was about making arrangements for an early return to the UK.

Throughout my nine years in government, I had sat in both the Cabinet and the National Security Council – the very bodies where decisions on the deployment of our troops were taken. More than that, I was involved in decisions regarding the security stance we had to take at home as a result of what was happening in Afghanistan. Against that background, it was harder to look at the withdrawal objectively, but it was important to do so.

I say this because it is difficult for me to comment on the stance that was taken by the United States without feeling a deep sense of concern about the aftermath of that decision, but also one of frustration that the UK found itself in the position where it seemed to have no option but to withdraw alongside the US and others. In that sense, it is arguable that the US was abusing its power.

I was on the opposition front bench when the initial decision was taken by Tony Blair's government in 2001 to go into Afghanistan, a decision which I supported – as, indeed, did the Conservative Party. Over subsequent years, I sat in the House when the names of those of our troops who had died in that country were read out at PMQs. One of them, Daniel Hume, was a constituent of mine who died in 2006 and whose funeral in Maidenhead I attended. As Home Secretary, I visited Afghanistan twice, mainly staying in Kabul. On my first visit, I was due to go to Camp Bastion – the principal area of British troop involvement – but the weather closed in and I was told that while I might be able to fly down there, it couldn't be guaranteed that the RAF could get me back. I did go to Camp Bastion on my second visit when the numbers there were being drawn down. What I saw from the troops I met on both these trips to Afghanistan was nothing but dedication to their task and to service.

It is easy to say that this was what they were trained for, and of course that is true. That does not take away what must have been all too often a feeling of deep dread, indeed fear, when going out on patrol and not knowing what they would encounter. Over the twenty years we were part of the NATO force in the country, 457 British service personnel died. For many more who returned, their service was life-changing through physical injury or the impact on their mental health. We will never forget the service given, both by the fallen and by those who returned.

Every one of the servicemen and women who served in Afghanistan should be immensely proud of what they achieved. Over the two decades the UK and others were there, the people of Afghanistan saw a significant change in their society. A government was established, although politics continued to be affected by tribal loyalties and there was too much corruption in the system. The criminal justice system was enhanced in key aspects, notably the ability to deal with drug dealers.

To my mind, the most visible and significant societal change was the freedom given to women. No one who has read Khaled Hosseini's novel A Thousand Splendid Suns can be in any doubt about the impact that the Taliban had on the lives of women in the country. They were second-class citizens, to be treated as the possessions of men and forced to subjugate their interests and lives to those of men. Now that changed. Girls could be educated and women were able to work.

Crucially, the country ceased to be the open hub for terrorist groups that it had been previously. Over the following years, we have still had to deal with terrorists who were inspired by or trained in Afghanistan. For example, the murderers of Lee Rigby in 2013 claimed they were responding to the actions of British servicemen in Iraq and

Afghanistan. Nevertheless, I have no hesitation in saying that NATO's action in Afghanistan directly improved the security of the UK.

This may sound strange, but in some ways it is easier to decide to take action and to go into a country with a clear purpose and mandate than it is to decide to withdraw. It will be said that you always have to withdraw at some stage. Since the Taliban retook control of the country in August 2021, we have seen a humanitarian crisis. The dire situation for so many in Afghanistan following NATO's withdrawal very much prompts the question whether it was really necessary to withdraw and at that time. What's more, was it right to do so?

It isn't possible to look at the decision to withdraw without considering the recent history of our presence there. The decision to send NATO forces into Afghanistan in 2001 came in the aftermath of the terrible terrorist attack on the United States on 11 September that year which horrified the world. On that morning, nineteen militants of the Islamist extremist group al-Qa'ida hijacked four planes in the US. They were all passenger flights, and were all to turn into death traps. Two of the planes were flown into the Twin Towers of the World Trade Center in New York. A third plane flew into the Pentagon, and the fourth crashed in Pennsylvania. Nearly 3,000 people from seventy-eight different countries died in the attacks, including emergency services workers. Of those who died, sixty-seven were British.

The attacks shook the Western world. I suspect most people alive at the time remember where they were when they first heard the news. I was working at home and, like so many, found it difficult to believe what was happening as the news reports came in. No one could be anything other than sickened by this appalling crime. No one could be anything other than deeply affected by the stories of heroism that emerged in the following days, and no one could be anything other than moved by the recordings of phone calls to their loved ones made by people on the plane which crashed in Pennsylvania, or by those trying to flee the Twin Towers.

An attack like this was never going to be allowed to pass without reaction, and certainly the United States was not going to let it happen on its soil without a swift and significant response. Operation Enduring Freedom was launched on 7 October 2001 by the United States with support from the UK. Its aim was to oust the Taliban in Afghanistan and destroy the al-Qa'ida terrorist network led by Osama bin Laden, which had planned the attacks. It was clearly an anti-terrorist campaign, reflecting what President George W. Bush had called a War on Terror.

Within months, the Taliban had been removed from effective power, but what ensued was an insurgency, and in December 2001, the international response changed in line with the Bonn Agreement. This agreement was enshrined in United Nations Security Council Resolution 1386 and led to the establishment of the International Security Assistance Force – ISAF – which was present in Afghanistan from December 2001 to December 2014. The British contribution to ISAF peaked in 2011/12 at 9,500 personnel, making the UK the second largest contributor to ISAF after the United States.

The role of ISAF was to help establish a permanent Afghan government, to train Afghan National Security Forces and to assist in the rebuilding of key government institutions. Its initial mandate covered Kabul and the surrounding area, and the provision of support for the Afghan Transitional Administration. In 2003, NATO took command of the mission and it was expanded across the country more widely, assuming responsibility for the whole of Afghanistan in 2006. All thirty of the member countries of NATO committed troops over the period of the mission, and in total forty-two countries contributed.

There was a further change in the mission at the beginning of 2015. On 1 January of that year, the Afghan National Security Force (ANSF) assumed security responsibility for Afghanistan. At the same time, following a request from the Afghan government, and in accordance with United Nations Security Council resolution 2189 of 2014, NATO's Resolute Support Mission replaced ISAF. The core mission of Resolute Support was to support the ANSF, so it was focused on providing training, advice and assistance to the Afghan security forces and the government institutions. Approximately 1,100 British personnel were deployed in Afghanistan purely as part of that non-combat mission. In May 2011, American forces located and killed Osama bin Laden in Abbottabad in Pakistan. The next month, President Obama announced large-scale US troop withdrawals. Final withdrawal was not to come until 2021, and the end was controversial. The last die was cast by President Trump in February 2020 when the US signed a deal with the Taliban in Doha.*

That agreement set a timeline for the withdrawal of all US troops, conditional on the Taliban preventing all terrorist groups from using Afghan territory to threaten the US. What is immediately interesting in this is that the

---

* Agreement for Bringing Peace to Afghanistan, February 2020.

mission was a NATO one. As is clear from the chronology set out above, the initial action was taken by the Americans – but not by them alone. They were supported even in those first days by the UK. The mission then expanded into a truly international one and from 2003 onwards was NATO-controlled.

As a NATO mission, it should not have been in the gift of the US simply to negotiate withdrawal on its own. Yet as we saw in 2021, the decision by the US effectively bound all its NATO partners. NATO is supposed to act as one. As its Secretary General said in October 2020, 'We went into Afghanistan together, we will adjust together, and when the time is right, when the conditions are met, we will leave together in a coordinated and orderly way.' In the event, the conditions were not met. The only condition that was relevant for other NATO forces was that the US was leaving – and with what appeared to those of us who were outside the government to be little meaningful discussion with allies.

Apart from establishing the fourteen-month withdrawal timetable, the 2020 agreement with the Taliban committed the US to withdrawing troops down to a level of 8,600 within 135 days of the agreement being signed. This enabled President Trump to say, in advance of the presidential election in November that year, that he had brought troops home. It is true that it also committed the Taliban to stopping other individuals or groups from using Afghanistan to threaten the security of the US and its allies, but these commitments on counter-terrorism only applied to 'areas under their control'.

The sharp-eyed will have seen an immediate get-out clause in this wording. But the US government did not, or if it did, it chose to ignore it. The Taliban committed to negotiating with 'Afghan sides', not specifically the Afghan government, and to putting a permanent ceasefire on the agenda for negotiation. But they were not required to commit to a reduction in violence, and although the discussions that led to the agreement had been accompanied by a limited ceasefire, once it was signed, the Taliban resumed attacks on government positions.

Alongside this agreement, the US and the Afghanistan government signed a joint declaration 'for bringing peace to Afghanistan'.* This mirrored many of the elements of the Taliban agreement, including support for the phased withdrawal of US and allied troops, and a commitment to preventing 'any international terrorist groups or individuals, including al-Qa'ida and ISIS-K' from using Afghan soil to threaten the security of the US, its allies and other countries. This was set out in more specific detail in the declaration. ISIS-K refers to Islamic State Khorasan Province, an affiliate of ISIS (also known as Daesh) based in the eastern Afghanistan province of Nangarhar.

The US committed to reducing its forces in the country over the ensuing 135-day period and to 'work[ing] with its allies and the Coalition to reduce proportionally the number of Coalition forces in Afghanistan over an equivalent period'. (The term 'Coalition' was used to describe the group of countries acting together with the US in Afghanistan.) There was a further commitment that the US and its allies would withdraw all troops by the end of fourteen

---

* Joint Declaration between the Islamic Republic of Afghanistan and the United States of America for Bringing Peace to Afghanistan, February 2020.

months from the declaration. It is worth noting that these commitments were 'subject to the Taliban's fulfilment of its commitments under the US–Taliban agreement'.

When the withdrawal came, President Biden was in the White House. Given that the Taliban arguably had not fulfilled all their commitments under the Doha agreement, this could have given him grounds to change course. The political situation in America made that more difficult, however, as the expectation that all of the troops would be returning home and that America's lengthy war would at last come to an end had become firmly established. Almost certainly the US would have been challenged for reneging on its agreement, but I suggest it would have had good reasons for doing so. In the end, President Biden went along with the decision taken by his predecessor.

Thus it was these deals that paved the way for the final and complete withdrawal of NATO forces from Afghanistan in summer 2021, and it was not a pretty sight. Whatever the UK government may say about the immense effort of all those involved in Operation Pitting (the evacuation from Afghanistan) – and they displayed not just enormous hard work but absolute commitment – the television scenes showed chaos. It is hard to forget the TV pictures of people chasing planes down the runway or handing babies over the airport fences in a desperate attempt to get them away from the country to a better future.

As an MP, I dealt with constituency cases relating to Afghans who were trying to get out of the country, particularly those who had worked with the British forces. Too many who were entitled to support from the outgoing countries were left behind. Schemes for those who had worked with the UK forces were maintained, but we have continued to see Afghans arriving in the UK illegally as they search for life in a free country.

As I write, Afghanistan has descended into a humanitarian disaster, with people starving all over the country. The economy has collapsed. Girls no longer have the freedom to be educated. Women no longer have the freedom to work. International aid agencies have been forced to stop employing women and, as a result, a number have pulled out of the country or have suspended operations. This has exacerbated the daily struggles on the ground for the Afghan people.

This fall backwards into the unenlightened society that the Taliban had introduced when they first controlled the country was swifter than the allied governments seem to have expected, judging by their public statements. Yet, in my view, it was entirely predictable. From the moment that President Trump signed the deal in 2020, all the Taliban had to do was ensure that there were sufficient problems for the Afghan government not to achieve full control of the country, and then sit, wait and prepare to move.

In July 2021, both President Biden and the UK Prime Minister, Boris Johnson, had indicated that they did not think that the Taliban were ready or able to take over control of the country. That the West seemed to be caught by surprise at the speed of the takeover by the Taliban suggests either a high degree of naivety or a complete failure of intelligence. Maybe it was just more convenient not to think about what might happen; that way, no one would have second thoughts about withdrawing.

From a process point of view, of course, as soon as the US announced its withdrawal, others were required to follow, because NATO operates as one. Yet, as I said in the

House of Commons at the time, I cannot but feel that more should have been done to try to find a way to keep sufficient troops in the country to maintain the security of Kabul and hence support a government. That could have included seeking to bring together an alternative alliance of countries to continue to provide the support needed to sustain a government in Afghanistan. After all, the numbers required were not that high. Indeed my colleague Tobias Ellwood MP noted in the House of Commons that the US had more personnel based in its embassy in London than it had troops in Afghanistan before the retreat. But the fact is that there was a reliance on American resources. It wasn't just a question of numbers. The US air capability was necessary for the continuing mission.

It was a feature of the American administration led by President Trump that there was often little discussion with allies before key decisions were taken and announced. In that regard, he did not respect the special relationship – or, indeed, respect any relationship. 'America First' all too often meant 'America Only'. When you are the dominant power in the West with a role across the world, and when you are a member of a multilateral organisation like NATO, you are expected to be more willing to discuss issues with your allies.

In Afghanistan, we were dealing with the consequences of a Trump decision taken months before, but also with the result of a decision by the Biden administration to hold to that. The US could take this decision because of its size and power, and the standing of America globally. But to me, it did not suggest that America was back, as President Biden had claimed. It suggested quite the opposite. The US took the decision, but the consequences are still being felt:

consequences that go beyond Afghanistan, although the impact there has been horrible enough. The humanitarian crisis is dreadful, and so is the murder and ill-treatment of people who worked with the allied forces, and the denial of female rights. Moreover, the attack by ISIS-K on Kabul International Airport in August 2021, and their attacks on religious minorities since then, show that it is not true, as governments, including here in the UK, initially stated, that the Taliban are ensuring Afghanistan is free of terrorists.

It also has ramifications for NATO. Although it has always been accepted that NATO acts as one, the reality in this case was that it meant NATO responds to US interests. Afghanistan was the first time NATO had operated outside Europe. It is possible it will be called upon to do so again in the future. Even regarding operations in Europe, the question arises: can everyone else in NATO be satisfied with being able to act only if America agrees?

Finally, we do not yet know what the long-term impact of the decision to withdraw from Afghanistan will be in other areas of the world where American support has been assumed. The most obvious example is Taiwan. If I had been in government in Taiwan at the time of the Afghanistan withdrawal, I would have been asking some very serious questions about what the American reaction would be to any attempt by China to take over Taiwan. I would expect other parts of East Asia to be uncomfortable too. Governments will be asking themselves: what does America's support and protection actually mean, and to what extent can it be relied on?

Of course, the US would say that the mission in Afghanistan had to come to an end at some point – that the West could not prop up the government in Afghanistan for ever. Withdrawal from a situation like this was always going to be difficult and the timing hard. In addition, over the years, the NATO presence had changed and numbers had been reduced. This was all seen in the closing down of Camp Bastion.

Was there a different approach the international community might have taken? I have already suggested that some form of international support could have been arranged to help ensure the security of the country in the interests of the Afghan people. Failing that, why did the US not ensure that the withdrawal was dependent on conditions being met, for example in relation to the rights of women? It's easy to ask questions like this after the event, but it is always important to learn from experience.

Some six months after the withdrawal from Afghanistan, America and its allies were able to demonstrate solidarity in defence of democracy and freedom in their support for Ukraine following the Russian invasion on 24 February 2022. But there can be little doubt that the withdrawal and the manner of it led to President Putin smelling an opportunity which he then seized in invading Ukraine. The solidarity of the West over Ukraine changed the perception of American intent. But the question of the longer-term commitment of the West remains. The withdrawal from Afghanistan showed a decision being taken because it suited America. For the individuals making the final decision, it suited their political aims and narrative. But did it suit the rest of the world? Opinions will differ, but my view would be that it did not.

Only time will tell what the withdrawal's impact will be on the fragile geopolitics of the globe. And, of course, as events unfold, other decisions as yet unforeseen will have an impact too. But the Afghanistan decision raised real questions about America's perception of its role in the world. The US had the power to withdraw as it did. Just as individuals have to ask themselves whether the decisions they take are for the greater good, so do governments. America occupies a special position as the defender of the free world, and that brings with it the need to consider more than just the interests of America itself when it acts internationally. In this sense, by acting in its own interests, it was abusing its power.

17

Ukraine and Putin

When I first had the idea for this book, I had no idea that before I had finished it, war would have broken out on mainland Europe. That it did marked a departure from the previous decades of relative peace and stability on the continent after the Second World War. Peace which, to a great extent, had been enabled by the multilateral institutions developed after the war and by the rules-based international order which operated alongside. The Russian invasion of Ukraine was a blatant example of abuse of power.

It is one example of such abuse with which I have not been directly involved. As Prime Minister, I maintained the policy adopted previously of providing non-lethal support to Ukraine, but obviously the outbreak of the war came some years after I had stepped down from office. However, I continue to contribute to the debate on international matters in the House of Commons.

The peace achieved for decades after the end of the Second World War was relative, because we had seen conflict in Europe towards the end of the twentieth century in the western Balkans. The war in Bosnia–Herzegovina led to the intervention of UN forces. Moreover, at the start of the twenty-first century, we saw Russia move into parts of Georgia in 2008 and then in 2014 invade Crimea – part of Ukraine. During the Cold War, the West and Russia faced up to each other, but in that period both sides knew the lines in the sand beyond which they should not go.

This all changed with the break-up of the Soviet Union, which finally took place in December 1991. President Gorbachev's decision to loosen military control over the Warsaw Pact countries was a key issue in these circumstances, and led to the toppling of regimes in Czechoslovakia, Poland, Hungary, Romania and Bulgaria, followed by the fall of the Berlin Wall in 1989. At the same time, pressure was building up in the Baltic States. In March and May 1991, all three declared that they had re-established themselves as independent states, and in August 1991, they were admitted into the United Nations.

In September that year, the Russian Congress of People's Deputies voted for the dissolution of the Soviet Union. On 8 December, Russia, Ukraine and Belarus agreed the formation of the Commonwealth of Independent States, and on the 25th, President Gorbachev declared that the Soviet Union was no longer.

To many around the world, including me, this was a cause for celebration, as people who wanted to live in freedom and democracy had been given the opportunity to do just that. To Vladimir Putin, it was not an opportunity. In 2005, he described the collapse of the Soviet empire as 'the greatest geopolitical catastrophe of the twentieth century'. Forget two world wars and the Holocaust – to him, the biggest disaster was Soviet disintegration. Herein we see at least part of the motivation behind his invasion of Ukraine.

Ukraine and Putin

Putin's decision to launch a further invasion of Ukraine in 2022 was clearly an abuse of power. It brought war to mainland Europe, led to the killing of innocent men, women and children, the displacement of millions of Ukrainians and the destruction of major cities. It also brought the West closer together once again, and led to a major reassessment by some countries in Europe of their approach to the acquisition of energy. The sanctions imposed on Russia by the West in response had an impact on key people around Putin, and will have a more gradual negative effect on the Russian economy, and so on the lives of the Russian people.

In many ways, therefore, Putin achieved the opposite of what he wanted. He had hoped to divide the West – he united it. He had hoped to reduce the presence of NATO on Russia's border – NATO increased its presence. He had hoped to cause division in NATO – NATO agreed to significantly increase the size of its rapid reaction force. He had hoped to damage NATO – his action led to Finland and Sweden applying for membership, and Finland joining in April 2023. Far from damaging NATO, his action led to its expansion.

So why did he do it – and could the rest of the world, notably the West in the shape of the US, the UK and Europe, have prevented it?

I have already pointed out Putin's inability to accept the break-up of the Soviet Union, and I set out some of the historical background to that change. But I believe that there were other factors at play as well. One of these was his attitude towards Ukraine itself. In the summer of 2021, he published a lengthy essay attempting to show that Ukraine had never been independent and that, in fact, people in Ukraine were Russian. This, of course, amounted to a claim that it was acceptable to invade because it was a liberation of a people who did not really want to be in an independent state, but desired nothing more than to be back in the bosom of mother Russia.

The strength of resistance demonstrated by the Ukrainians since the invasion showed how wrong he was in that analysis. This was not a people who longed to be back in Russia; rather, they were a people proud of their independence and sovereignty, who had no intention of giving up their freedom. Far from welcoming the Russians with open arms, they greeted them with armed resistance. Putin had seriously misjudged the mood of the Ukrainians.

Another reason for that miscalculation was that President Putin did not understand that desire for democracy. Not only did he think people wanted to be back with mother Russia, he also couldn't understand how anyone would actively want to live in a true democracy. To him, the desire in others for personal freedom is inexplicable.

It is also important to remember his interest in Russian history, even if it came to the fore more and more the longer he served in office. Certainly, he seems to yearn to recreate a Russia of the past.

This wasn't just about his approach to Ukraine. It was also about his need to bolster his own position with the Russian people. He has consistently done that by tapping into their deep-seated and traditional conviction that the rest of the world is against them. By portraying himself as defending Russia against 'invaders', by creating the image of an external threat, he was able to persuade the Russian people that any action he took against another country was not only acceptable but vital. We saw something of this in the comments at a virtual news conference in March 2022 of his Foreign Minister Sergei Lavrov, who said America had Europe under its control, and compared this to the objectives of Napoleon and Hitler. Truth doesn't play much of a role in this Putin playbook.

There was, I am sure, another element in his thinking in relation to Ukraine. With the eyes of the West increasingly turned towards China, Putin, ever the opportunist, took his opportunity. My former colleague Lord Hague describes this in a different way. He tells the story of accompanying Putin to a judo match during the 2012 Olympic Games in London. He and Putin both love judo and William makes the point that in judo, you wait until your opponent is off balance and then strike. Putin saw the West off balance and struck.

Putin had also seen the way the West had withdrawn from Afghanistan – chaotically and with little regard for what was left behind. Indeed, the message he and some others almost certainly took from Afghanistan was that the West was no longer willing to defend its values. His assumption, therefore, must have been that he could invade Ukraine without the West responding.

As we have seen, the invasion of Ukraine in February 2022 was not the first Russian incursion into the sovereign territory of other countries. In August 2008, Russia began its invasion of Georgia. The conflict lasted for only a few days, but the international reaction was remarkably low key. EU leaders were among those calling for a ceasefire, which was negotiated by French President Nicolas Sarkozy. When it came, the ceasefire reflected the interests of Russia rather than those of Georgia. In the US, the Bush administration resisted Georgia's requests for anti-tank and air defence weapons, and a few months later the new Obama administration called for a reset in relations with the government in the Kremlin. This approach meant that in reality, Russia suffered few negative consequences as a result of its invasion. It appeared to get away with it, so little wonder that there were those in Moscow who took this as a green light for further acts of aggression against their neighbours.

It is worth recalling that the invasion of Georgia came only a few months after a NATO summit at which it had been stated that both Georgia and Ukraine would be NATO members one day. Russia's action was a direct challenge to the right of those states to decide their future, a future that lay looking towards the EU and the US.

The message from Putin was clear. For those neighbours who he considered were in Russia's sphere of influence, he was prepared to use armed invasion – arguably war – to bring them to heel if they appeared to be pivoting away from Russia and towards the West. But while the United States and Europe were not able to prevent the conflict from taking place, they were able to stop Putin from destroying Georgian sovereignty. It is perhaps worth noting that the Bush administration organised a financial rescue package for Georgia with the help of a senator who was the vice-presidential candidate for the Democrats – one Joe Biden.

Following Russia's 2022 invasion of Ukraine, it is often said that history might have been different if there had been a stronger reaction by the West to Russia's 2014 invasion of Crimea. Perhaps the more pertinent question is whether things would have been different with a stronger Western reaction to Russia's invasion of Georgia in 2008.

The fact that Russia got away with its actions in Georgia was to play out six years later with Russia's invasion of Crimea. The US and Europe were unable to push back the Russians from their immediate gains, but were able to prevent Putin from destroying Ukrainian sovereignty.

The invasion of Crimea came after the overthrow of the Ukrainian President Viktor Yanukovych, who had been set to sign an Association Agreement with the EU in November 2013. Shortly before he was due to do so, however, he pulled out of the deal, sparking the public uprising which became known as the Maidan Revolution. This ended with the removal of President Yanukovych, who fled Kyiv and later turned up in Russia. The Ukrainian parliament, the Rada, appointed an acting president and prime minister to take charge. Following this, Ukraine continued to show its intention of drawing closer to Europe, and an Association Agreement with the European Union would eventually be signed in June 2014.

For Putin, the Maidan Revolution was clear evidence of Ukraine wanting to pivot from Russia to the EU: it was the signal to act. At first, in February of that year, armed men appeared, occupying certain key facilities on the Crimean peninsula. Dubbed 'little green men' by Ukrainians, they were Russian soldiers in all but name. This was at first denied by the Kremlin, but later admitted. At the time, the Ukrainian military presence in Crimea did not go into action. Kyiv did not want the first shots to be fired by Ukraine. They wanted it to be manifest that the first signs of aggression came from Russia.

But by early March, Russian troops had secured the whole Crimean peninsula and occupied the Crimean parliament building in Simferopol, and pro-Russian lawmakers had dismissed the sitting government and installed the leader of the Russian Unity Party as Crimea's Prime Minister. On the 6th, the Crimean Supreme Council, effectively the key authority in the area, voted to hold a referendum on Crimea's future relationship with Russia and Ukraine. This was to be about seceding from Ukraine and joining the Russian Federation. A referendum was set for 16 March, but it didn't offer people the choice of voting for what had been the status quo. Instead, there were two choices – to join Russia or return to the Crimean constitution of 1992, which provided significant autonomy for Crimea.

The referendum was not observed by any credible international group and the conduct of it was chaotic. In the event, the authorities declared that there had been a turnout of 83 per cent, with 96.7 per cent of those voting choosing to join Russia. Given that within the population of Crimea, ethnic Ukrainians and Crimean Tatars accounted for nearly 40 per cent, this result seems at best implausible. This appeared to be confirmed by a leaked report from the Russian President's Human Rights Council two months later, which put turnout as low as 30 per cent, with only about half of those voting choosing the option of joining Russia.[*]

The result of the referendum was rejected by the interim government in Kyiv, and the United States and the EU imposed asset freezes and travel bans on numerous Russian officials. Nevertheless, on 18 March, the Treaty of Accession of the Republic of Crimea to Russia was signed by Crimean and Russian officials. Three days later, the treaty

---

[*] Steve Pifer, 'Crimea: Six years after illegal annexation', Brookings Institution, 17 March 2020.

was ratified by the Russian parliament and Putin signed a law formally integrating Crimea into Russia.

I have a friend who, when asked who Putin's advisers are, says: 'Peter the Great and Catherine the Great.' Looking at Putin's whole approach to Ukraine, one might be tempted to agree. After all, it was during the reign of Catherine the Great that the Russians colonised Crimea and founded Sevastopol on the Crimean peninsula. This was later to become the home port for the Russian Black Sea Fleet. After the Soviet Union was established, Crimea was part of the Russian Soviet Federative Socialist Republic. In 1954, it was administratively transferred to the Ukrainian Soviet Socialist Republic, ostensibly because of the geographical proximity to Ukraine and the agricultural, cultural and economic ties between the two. There are those, however, who see it as a way of 'fortifying and perpetuating Soviet control over Ukraine'.[*]

The seizure of Crimea in 2014 came two years after Putin had returned to the Russian presidency, and against the background of a weak Russian economy. Putin had based much of his re-election appeal on Russian national-ism, and there is no doubt that the action in Crimea was popular with the Russian people – his approval rating climbed accordingly. But, as I noted at the start of this book, political leadership should not be about the exercise of power for personal advancement. It is about service, and that means it is about using power for the greater good.

The response of the West to this invasion of a sovereign state was sadly lacking, to say the least. The discussion

---

[*] Mark Kramer, 'Why Did Russia Give Away Crimea Sixty Years Ago?', The Wilson Center, 19 March 2014.

around the Cabinet table in London was led by Prime Minister David Cameron and Foreign Secretary William Hague, but there was a sense of the UK leaving others to take the lead. Sanctions were imposed, but they were by no means as rigorous as those used after the invasion of 2022. This lack of willingness to strike Russia hard persisted in later years, when I remember sitting around the EU Council table arguing that the sanctions should remain, only to find some others, such as Italy, being less willing to see a continuation of action against Russia. The argument for continuing sanctions won through. Thankfully, when the EU Council were asked to respond to the use of a chemical weapon on the streets of the UK – in Salisbury – they showed solidarity with the UK.

Alongside what happened in Crimea, there was the conflict in the Donbas in eastern Ukraine on the border with Russia. Efforts to resolve this took various forms. On the anniversary of D-Day in June 2014, discussions took place between the leaders of France, Germany, Russia and Ukraine. This process of negotiations became known as the Normandy Format. Initially, it led to discussions in the Trilateral Contact Group on Ukraine, composed of Russia, Ukraine and the Organisation for Security and Co-operation in Europe (OSCE). This work to facilitate dialogue between Russia and Ukraine led to the Minsk agreements – Minsk I in September 2014 and Minsk II in February 2015.

Minsk II was the framework for efforts to end the conflict, but contained significant deficiencies. It was hastily drafted and had an important element missing – it did not refer to Russia, although it was signed by the Russian Ambassador to Ukraine. This enabled Russia to claim that it was not responsible for the implementation of the agreement, and to stand to one side as an ostensibly disinterested party. Of the agreement's thirteen points, nine covered conflict management and four political issues. But the problem with the agreement was that it could be read in two different ways – either as supporting Ukraine as sovereign or not. Needless to say, the first interpretation is that of Ukraine and the second is Russia's view.[*]

Whatever the ins and outs of the details of the agreement, it did not work. The UK was not part of the Normandy Format. That process was driven by France and Germany. I sometimes wonder whether the agreement would have been any different if the UK had played a bigger role, as a party whose geographical position gave us a different interest in Russia.

This history, however, reinforces the picture of Vladimir Putin as someone who seizes opportunities and takes lack of Western action as a green light to go further. Just as in other examples of abuse of power, lack of action by authorities or interested parties at an early stage serves not only to enable the abuse to continue, but encourages it to become worse. We have seen that public authorities sometimes choose not to intervene when they see abuse, thereby protecting their own interests; nation states likewise sometimes choose to stand back in pursuit of their own interests.

Abuse of power needs to be identified and dealt with at an early stage. Failure to do so leads to damage to too many lives. The apparent lack of cohesion in the West and the view that Western politicians were not as willing to

---

[*] Duncan Allan, 'The Minsk Conundrum: Western Policy and Russia's War in Eastern Ukraine', Chatham House, 22 May 2020.

defend their values as they had been previously stemmed not just from the decisions of individuals in power at the time, but also from a complacency that had crept in to Western governments.

After all, we had won the Cold War, had we not? The Soviet Union had been broken up. West and East Germany were now united as one country. The nations of Eastern Europe and the Baltic States were now democracies and members of the European Union. And the Cold War had been expensive. Just think of the cost to the UK of keeping troops and bases in Germany. The British Army of the Rhine provided a training ground for the armed forces, but while personnel were performing a function in that area, they were less available for operations elsewhere.

There was this sense, perhaps mainly at the tail end of the twentieth century, that life had changed and that we could all relax in the knowledge that the West was dominant and our values and way of life were being increasingly accepted around the world.

The term 'the West' is frequently used, but it does not denote a geographical grouping. What it denotes is adherence to, and belief in, a set of values. So the countries of 'the West' share the values of personal liberty under the rule of law, respect for the right to hold dissenting views, freedom of thought and speech, and constitutional government. These principles underpin political life in all truly democratic states, and they underpin the rules-based international order that we have relied on since the end of the Second World War.

We read about them in the Charter of the United Nations, which talks of 'fundamental human rights . . . the dignity and worth of the human person . . . the equal rights of men and women and of nations large and small'. We also find them in the North Atlantic Treaty, the founding document of NATO, in which its members announce their determination to 'safeguard the freedom, common heritage and civilisation of their peoples, founded on the principles of democracy, individual liberty and the rule of law'.

Calling these values 'Western' does not mean they are the exclusive property of Americans or Europeans, but they are the values that have shaped the politics and economies of Western countries over the centuries. Sometimes we assume they are ancient and permanent, and it is easy to take them for granted – as I fear we all did during the latter years of the twentieth century. But you don't have to look too far into history, or search too hard in the present day, to realise that those values are still contested.

Free, liberal democracies are a relatively recent creation, and are by no means the norm. Long gone is the naive assumption popular after the fall of the Berlin Wall that liberal democracy was enjoying an unchallenged ascendancy. Today we are living through a time when our values, and the institutions built to promote and transmit them, are under pressure.

Whatever you think of these developments, they do suggest a background for politics which is different from the one that many of today's politicians have grown up with. If you add to this background a number of events that had a global impact and which challenged the West still further – notably the rise of Islamist terrorism seen clearly in the events of 9/11, the chaotic aftermath of the 2003 invasion of Iraq and the financial crisis of 2007–8 – and you see an instability which challenged the accepted thinking around the ascendancy of Western liberal democracy.

In these circumstances, however, it was easier for governments to focus on the issue of the day rather than wonder whether Western values were being eroded. One could say their electorates demanded this of them. After all, if you assume those values have been generally accepted and don't need to be protected, then it is all too easy to forget about them. And forgetting can all too soon turn into ignoring them; from there, it is a slippery slope to the erosion of those values. This doesn't happen in one fell swoop, but little by little, until you wake up one morning and realise those values are long gone.

I'm not suggesting we are anywhere near that end stage, but certainly we are at the beginning of the process. By forcing the Western countries to take a position, Russia's invasion of Ukraine jolted them into recognising the need to defend their values. The question is, how long will that joint recognition remain? Or will it just be so much easier to see the Ukraine war as a temporary aberration and return to the previous ways of reacting to events on a case-by-case basis without concern for fundamental and lasting values?

The invasion of Ukraine in 2022 was a clear example of the abuse of power. Russia under Putin believed it had the military power to invade and occupy Ukraine. Just as important was the fact that it felt it had the opportunity. It invaded Ukraine because it could. Russia has been weakened by its action in Ukraine, but that won't necessarily stop it from doing the same again elsewhere if it thought it was in its interests and the opportunity arose.

Part Four

Learning from the Past

When I started writing this book, setting out the clear examples of the abuse of power that I had come across, my only intention was to draw attention to the issue. But over time, I came to realise that to do that was not sufficient, and that as well as raising awareness of the issue, I also had to try to explain how we had come to be in this position.

Following on from that, it is not good enough to attempt such an explanation without offering some possible solutions. It's all very well saying we shouldn't have done this or that, but it is more helpful to say what we should have done. In this section, I try to do that.

18

How Did We Get Here?

I said at the beginning of this book that I would write about cases of abuse of power which had come across my desk in nine years in senior ministerial positions in government. By definition, therefore, they cover the public sector and national and international affairs. In case anyone gets the wrong idea, I want to stress that there will be plenty of examples of abuse of power in the private sector, albeit in some cases with different motivations. Some of the analysis I attempt in this chapter will also relate to the private sector, but as with the cases I have cited, I will focus on the public sector.

I also want to be very clear that in my time in government, I have met some outstanding individuals whose work ethic, commitment to public service and determination to do the right thing could not be faulted. The best of the civil service, the police and other parts of the public sector are among the best in the world. That is one reason why it is disappointing that so many are let down when the institutions become overly defensive or unwilling to acknowledge mistakes or problems.

In identifying examples of the abuse of power which show a lack of commitment to service and the overenthusiastic use of power, two aspects stand out. The first is the natural inclination of many in the public sector to put its own existence before the interests of the people it is intended to serve. Why is it that many in the public sector have for so long thought it more important to defend the institution than to champion the interests of individuals or the public? The second is the tendency for so many politicians to care more about their popularity or their career path than about the job they are there to do.

How did we get to this position? What is it about public service and about politics that leads to so many failing to prioritise the interests of those they are there to serve? Is this inevitable, or can we take steps to make sure it does not happen? After all, the Seven Principles of Public Life are clear that selflessness is one of the indispensable attributes expected of those in public office. The Nolan Principles, published in 1995, followed a six-month inquiry into standards in British public life which had been commissioned by Prime Minister John Major. Following such an in-depth review, surely the conclusions would be not just accepted but acted on. But not all the principles are as respected as they should be.

I have given examples of the issues that have crossed my desk during my time in Parliament which exemplify social injustices caused by the failure of the public sector in various forms. What stands out is that the tendency to defend the institution rather than the interests of individuals or the public collectively is not a new phenomenon. If it were a relatively recent trait, then it might be easier to address and easier to change. Over the years, this approach has become more and more entrenched, to the point where it is not questioned but has become the accepted way to do things. Because this is regarded as normal, anyone wanting to behave in a different way is seen as the odd one out or the troublemaker.

Apart from my first five years in work, which were spent at the Bank of England, I have not been an employee of a public sector body, nor have I ever been a civil servant. In that sense, it is hard for me to know exactly what the origin of the mindset within the sector is. I have not been imbued with the public sector approach. I can only observe from the cases I have cited and my experience of working with people in the organisations concerned.

My first observation is that the defensive approach of so many in the public sector has evolved over time and, I suspect, has grown out of an exaggerated view of the importance of the institution itself. I have long thought, as have others, that the civil service is a remarkable institution and a huge positive for the UK. You just have to look at the US, where they fill so many positions in government with supporters of the party that wins the presidency, to see the advantage of a civil service that works for the government regardless of the political party in charge. Yet we must ask if the belief in the value of the non-partisan civil service has led the institution to value itself too highly and to fail to recognise the importance of the people it is there to serve. By that I mean the public, not the politicians.

This reverence for the institution was satirised by Charles Dickens in a number of his novels. In *Little Dorrit*, we read of the Circumlocution Office, which 'was beforehand with all the public departments in the art of perceiving HOW NOT TO DO IT'. It was an establishment run purely for the benefit of its incompetent and obstructive officials. Reading this today may bring a smile to our lips, but it exemplifies what happens when the institution itself becomes more important to those working in it than the issues it was set up to resolve – and certainly more important than the people who are raising those questions.

In *Bleak House*, we read of Jarndyce and Jarndyce, a High Court case which had become so complicated that no man alive knew what it meant. This has become a byword for interminable legal proceedings, and a classic example of the way the process can become more important to those involved than finding a solution for the affected parties. Closer to home, it was well portrayed in the episode of *Yes, Minister* in 1981 entitled 'The Compassionate Society', in which the unsuspecting minister Jim Hacker is taken to view a new hospital. It is a fine building, with state-of-the-art facilities. But it has no patients. There wasn't enough money for doctors and nurses. What mattered was a building that could be shown off – caring about patients was only ever to be an afterthought. Fiction, but with a touch of real life.

Putting aside these literary examples, surely the only conclusion that can be drawn from the cases I have set out is that over time, in many areas of the public sector, the idea grew that the institution was so important that maintaining it became its main purpose. Against this background, the mindset of defence seemed perfectly natural. Mistakes made by or within the institution were seen not as a reason to learn or to adapt, but as weapons which could be used by others to challenge its very existence. Hence admitting to mistakes was seen as giving ammunition to those who wanted to attack the institution, and had to be resisted at all costs. I have spoken here of the civil service, but the same applies to other organs of the state, such as local authorities.

How Did We Get Here?

This all has real-world consequences, and too often it means that people get hurt. That hurt can come in the form of physical pain and damage. How many babies would have been born without defects or ill health if the initial warnings about Primodos had been accepted and the drug withdrawn then rather than years later? How many young boys or girls would have been saved the physical pain of sexual abuse if warnings raised by children or adults in Rotherham had been acted on when they were first raised rather than dismissed?

Hurt can also be experienced through psychological or emotional pain or damage. How many adults would have found it easier to form relationships throughout their lives if their reports of sexual abuse when they were children had been heeded and action taken to stop it?

Hurt has also been felt through broken relationships or families that have split up because not everyone can take the strain of the constant battle against the powers that be. Then there is the hurt of betrayal. The inability to trust authorities that have constantly let people down. The damage inflicted by a failure to see justice done. Campaigners involved in the cases I describe have told me that they were brought up to respect people in authority and to trust bodies like the police. Against that background, the impact when that trust is broken is even more devastating.

There is the sheer exhaustion of the weeks, months and years spent fighting authorities and challenging the system. I have seen this in the campaigners I have met, from Margaret Aspinall and Marie Lyon to Alastair Morgan. There is also the damage that constant battle can do to health, wellbeing and finances.

This institutional reaction of defensiveness can relate to issues raised within the institution concerned, but can also be a response to external threat. Here, politicians and the media should think carefully about their role in encouraging this approach. When either launches unreasonable attacks on public institutions, using them as the scapegoat for mistakes made by others, it exacerbates the desire in the institutions to move into defensive mode. On the other hand, both politicians and the media can also be the means of surfacing an injustice.

Nevertheless, just as we observe in the natural world that anything under threat becomes defensive, so if the public sector appears to be under attack from an external source, then its natural reaction is to go into defensive mode. But that is exactly the opposite of what is needed in those circumstances. Far better to admit mistakes and show a willingness to rectify them. As I have pointed out earlier, that is the approach taken by the airline industry, for example, where pilots are encouraged to report near misses or problems so that lessons can be learnt and any necessary changes to procedures introduced.

In the public sector, the relationship between politicians and officials is a complex one fraught with danger. Officials can try to sideline ministers or manipulate them to ensure that the decisions taken are the ones the officials want to see. I am sure many will be aware of the stories of officials hiding the most important paper which the minister needed to read in the middle of papers in the third red box. The hope was that, by the time they got to it, the minister would not read it but simply sign it off unread because they were too tired to do otherwise. The number of papers given to a minister was the key issue and the point at which I pushed back on this came as Home Secretary, the morning after I had had over fifty policy documents and letters to read, take a decision on or sign off in my red boxes overnight. Mind you, I don't recall my comment to my then-principal private secretary resulting in any reduction in the volume of work I was given.

Our civil service operates on the basis that it works all day to produce papers for the minister to read and sign off – or not – overnight. In concept, this works, but it does mean that both sides have to respect the limits of the process. Ministerial private offices have to show some discretion when filling red boxes, and ministers have to read their boxes and not simply postpone decisions night after night. On the other hand, ministers can be so focused on their chosen political view that they require officials to develop the ideas and arguments that suit that political position, rather than allowing officials to present, and advise on, the facts. I remember when I was first elected as a London borough councillor in Merton, the leader of our group and leader of the Council – Harry Cowd – told us that we had to be conscious of our role as councillors, not as employees of the local authority. As he said, there is a tendency for officials to try to behave like politicians and for politicians to try to behave like officials.

In my first major responsible elected role as Chairman of Education in that London Borough of Merton, I said to the Director and his deputies that what I wanted from them was not what they thought I wanted to hear, but their best information and their best judgement. What I did with that would be a political decision, but they should not try to second-guess my decision and provide the advice they thought would suit it.

In general, all too often what we see is officials at both local and national government level trying to shape their advice to what they believe is the view of the politician. Indeed, some politicians operate on the basis that this is exactly the approach they want from officials. Such a stance, I would suggest, betrays insecurity. The confident minister, like my good friend the late James Brokenshire, will have an initial view of the right way forward, what the right policy is, but will be willing to listen to the full facts as presented by the officials. If those facts challenge the initial view, they will be willing to debate the issue and, if necessary, adapt their thinking.

Another failing among ministers is to rely too heavily on the views of special advisers. These people – known as SpAds – are an important component of our system because they provide the political insight within a department. Ministers can be so busy – after all, the civil service fills their diaries day after day – that it can be hard to find the time to think in detail about issues or potential solutions. That's when good SpAds can come into their own, but ministers need to know their own mind too. The best relationship comes when the SpAds really know the minister's thinking, and hence the officials can have confidence that what the SpAds say is what the minister thinks. I was very fortunate in having excellent SpAds throughout my time as both Home Secretary and Prime Minister.

When I reached national government, in the Home Office, one of the early frustrations was finding that all too often mistakes or problems were hidden from ministers. Sometimes the assumption was that the staff could deal with the issue without bothering the minister. Sometimes they just hoped the problem would solve itself and disappear, and sometimes they were just too worried about what the minister's reaction would be. This was particularly true of the then UK Border Agency, which was often reluctant to escalate issues up to ministers at an early stage.

As a result, when the issues did reach ministers, they had often developed into much more significant practical and political problems, and as a consequence were much harder to deal with. Indeed, in the past problems had often been hidden from ministers until the point at which they became such a significant issue that they led to ministerial resignations. My message was clear: bring your problems to ministers at an early stage. That way, we were more likely to be able to find solutions and head off major problems. There was some change of approach as a result of my message, but it didn't always work out that way – the Passport Office problems of 2014 being just such an example.

When I responded to an urgent question from the opposition in Parliament in June 2014, the Passport Office had received 300,000 more applications than expected at that time. It meant significant delays for some people in getting their new passports or getting passports renewed, and problems overseas, particularly for British families wanting to get passports for children to travel back to the UK. Various steps were taken to deal with the situation, including changing the status of the Passport Office by bringing it back into the Home Office as a division of the department under the direct supervision of ministers, rather than being an executive agency and hence an arm's-length body.

This was not, however, something that had suddenly arisen. It had been evident that there was a problem building up for some time before ministers were alerted to the issue. But the issue wasn't raised until it had become a very big problem. Had it been shared with ministers at an earlier stage, it could have been dealt with sooner. That would have meant fewer anxieties and, in some cases, reduced costs for members of the public. That mattered for the people trying to use the service, and for their MPs. It should have mattered to the officials too. Of course, from the ministerial point of view, had there been earlier intervention, there would have been less political fallout for the government.

My experience of the civil servants I dealt with was that they were passionate about public service. I have worked with some outstanding individuals who could have had more lucrative careers in the private sector, but who wanted to serve the public. Being a civil servant can be a very intellectually challenging and rewarding career. You can see ideas that you have developed being put into practice for the good of the public and the country. What must be avoided is a sense that because you are in public service, every idea you have is the right one, and that nothing the public sector or your institution does can be wrong.

This sense of the importance of public service can be seen in other parts of the public sector, but – as we have noted in earlier chapters – when it turns into a belief in infallibility, it causes damage.

Apart from the natural inclination to protect something under threat, the mindset of defence when attacked is aggravated by groupthink. Efforts to build teams, to instil cultures and values, and to ensure consistent approaches are all necessary if people are to work well together, and, generally speaking, they lead to improved performance. But they cannot be absolutes. The system must allow for the different, for those who have an unusual approach to issues, for those who challenge the accepted view. I think that this was what underlay Dominic Cummings' well-reported attempts to change the civil service when he apparently was keen to recruit 'weirdos and misfits'. There was some truth in what he was trying to do, but – memo to Dominic – to achieve this, you don't need to employ weirdos and misfits, just the inquisitive and those who are ready to speak out of turn.

The challenge for any manager is to find a balance between the accepted and the different, and to be able to recognise when complaints or challenges are indicative of underlying problems that need to be addressed, and when they are unsubstantiated attacks. So often, this balance is not found, and the results, as we have seen in the cases I have described, are what I have termed the abuse of power, or what Bishop James Jones in his report to me in 2017 described as 'the patronising disposition of unaccountable power'.

It is worth dwelling on that phrase. The two words which jump out at me are 'patronising' and 'unaccountable'. They sum up the problem that lies at the heart of many of the examples I have cited in this book, including, of course, Hillsborough, with which the Bishop was closely involved. Patronising because of the notion that the public sector must be right. There could be no question of wrongdoing or mistakes. With this approach, the people raising questions or challenging the accepted view were seen as being troublesome individuals who couldn't hope to know what they were talking about, because the institution always got it right regardless.

In itself, such behaviour is problematic, but it can be dealt with if those adopting that approach are properly held to account so that when it is causing damage, it can be identified and dealt with. It is when it is linked to lack of accountability that most damage can be done, because the behaviour goes unchallenged.

The extent to which the defensive culture in the public sector had taken hold is perhaps seen in the way in which departments continued to hold fast to that approach, even when under both Margaret Thatcher and John Major, questions were being asked about the relationship between the public sector and the public. These focused on the extent to which certain bodies in the public sector were delivering for the public, and led to the privatisation of some parts of the public sector. In this way, both those Prime Ministers took action to assert a greater degree of choice and power for members of the public. Yet key government departments failed to recognise the need also related to them, and continued to set their face against complaints and against opportunities to learn and develop.

What led to this was surely an overabundance of confidence that the institution was always in the right, and too great a concern that change would lead to destruction rather than growth. I have always seen our civil service as a great jewel in the crown of our democracy. Officials' ability to operate under whoever is in government, whatever their views, is a strength which we should celebrate. Yet everyone in the public sector will be at their most effective if they acknowledge that the institutions they serve should not be preserved in aspic.

The examples I have set out in this book came to light because there were those who were either willing to blow the whistle from inside the public sector or who refused to believe the explanations being given. We should commend those who stood firm against the power of the state – the campaigners who kept the flame of the search for justice alight despite constant setbacks and rejection by the state. Their lives were changed for ever by what must have seemed like an unending battle against the powers that be.

That we know what we do today is thanks to them and their tireless campaigning. Above all, it is thanks to their willingness to put themselves second and the fight for justice first. What a contrast to the actions of the public sector in the examples I have described, actions which put the institution first and the fight for justice second. It is thanks to the campaigners that we have had chances to learn from mistakes of the past, although so often those lessons have not been identified – or, if they have been identified, have simply been at best forgotten or at worst ignored.

It would be nice to think that after all the cases I have written about in this book – and others that I have not recorded – there had been a change of approach across the institutions concerned. Of course, the introduction of the Freedom of Information Act under the Blair government and the improvements in transparency introduced by successive governments were all intended to shine a light inside the public sector. By doing this, one would hope that the pervasive attitude of defence would, albeit gradually, be changed. The reality is that, as we all know in our heart of hearts, you cannot change the culture of an organisation or institution through legislation. Culture is about people and leadership.

So, perhaps not surprisingly, the Freedom of Information Act did not change the public sector's defensive approach. There are campaigns, such as Primodos, where important information has been obtained through FOI requests. On the other hand, one of the problems with the Act is that it leads to too many general fishing expeditions which require responses that take up civil service time, and can lead to stories being created through simple misunderstanding of the facts or failure to see the whole picture. More problematic is the fact that, with so many fishing expeditions being launched to create stories rather than necessarily identifying real problems, responding to them once again becomes an act of defence. Thus, far from removing the inclination to defend the institution, the impact of the Act has been, in many ways, to reinforce the natural defensiveness of the civil service and ministers.

This has all taken place against the background of a change to our media, particularly the print media, which means there are fewer resources available for the sort of investigative journalism that has in the past helped to uncover abuses of power, such as the uncovering of the thalidomide scandal in the 1960s.

The identification of the abuse of power in the public sector hasn't really changed behaviour, either. The lack of change in attitude is perhaps best seen in the NHS and the amount it spends on defending itself against complaints, often through legal disputes. In the five years from 2017 to 2022, the NHS spent a total of nearly £12 billion on fighting or settling claims. There is now an approach by NHS Resolution, an arm's-length body of the Department of Health and Social Care, which focuses on early intervention and hence on avoiding unnecessary court action and other formal processes. It would be much better if the NHS didn't find itself faced with defending cases, but handled complaints rather better at an earlier stage by being willing to admit mistakes. It is a great strength of our parliamentary system that every minister in the Commons, including the Prime Minister, is also a constituency MP. This means we are able to see the impact of government action through our various conversations with constituents, as I have with my own constituents who are trying to get an apology from the NHS.

The problem doesn't just rest with defensive public sector institutions. Alongside this, we have too many politicians who have become increasingly careerist, focused more and more on what promotes them as an individual rather than on the overall good.

I don't know what triggered my early interest in being an MP, although in an environment where ideas of duty, public service, justice and equality were prevalent, combined with public speaking, perhaps it is of little wonder that politics beckoned. But the world of politics I grew up in, at least as I saw it, was very different from today.

There was a time when a large number of MPs were content to be elected and simply do a good job for their constituents and their country. Some saw themselves as becoming ministers, but many were happy to be good back-bench MPs. Today, it seems like everyone who comes into the House wants a career which involves ministerial office, and most probably see themselves as a future Prime Minister. That there aren't enough jobs to allow everyone to become a minister doesn't seem to restrict people's expectations.

This is one issue which makes Cabinet reshuffles so tricky. Everyone thinks they are capable of being a minister, and everyone thinks they are better than those currently in office. If they are not appointed, too often they resent being overlooked. Those who are sacked don't understand why and develop an intense dislike of the PM, and some then actively move to bring down that PM. Those who are promoted think it came far too late and aren't as grateful as the PM hopes they will be!

To be fair, when people were making a career out of being a backbencher, the demands of the job were less, constituents' expectations were lower and they were less likely to see the MP as the answer to their problems. This meant that MPs could more easily combine their work in Parliament with other interests. This also, of course, enabled them to supplement their parliamentary income. This flexibility was used by a good number of MPs, perhaps particularly those in my own party. They might be active lawyers or run a business, or work in other professions, perhaps as doctors and nurses, and the hours when Parliament sat made that easier by leaving the mornings clear. If votes weren't held until 10 p.m., you could do something else all day and still do what the whips wanted. As the hours of sitting changed – rightly, in my view – that became harder, although not impossible. There are still some MPs today who do other work as well, but for many Parliament is their only paid occupation.

This issue is brought into sharp focus when the Parliamentary Standards Commissioner is asked to investigate allegations of paid advocacy by an MP. The rules are clear – MPs should not get involved with paid advocacy. That is as it should be. MPs lobby on behalf of their constituents and their constituencies, not on behalf of an individual, company or group willing to pay them to do so. But discussion of this issue often leads to questions about whether MPs should be able to undertake any other duties, including paid jobs. Setting aside the fact that being a government minister is a second job and, therefore, at its most extreme, if second jobs were banned, no government could be formed, this is conflating two issues. The first is the rules against corruption and whether they are sufficient – this is a matter for Parliament. The second is whether an MP is serving their constituency, and that is a matter not for Parliament, but for the electorate.

The key change in relation to MPs and their roles has been the expectation of the public. Much more is demanded of politicians today. There is more of a sense from constituents that their MP is there to serve them – as indeed they are. That is hardly surprising, and is a change of attitude encouraged at least in part, I believe, by the approach of Margaret Thatcher's and John Major's governments to the public sector.

Between 1979 and 1997, and particularly under Margaret Thatcher, the government took the view that people should demand more of the public sector. That was absolutely the right approach. For example, it was no longer good enough for people to have to wait weeks or months to get a new telephone line installed in their home. The initial solution was to privatise the nationalised industries. This meant they had an incentive to put the customer first and a greater interest in listening to and providing for their customers. The customer – the public – would be more in control.

This change swept across key areas of public service. What those driving the change forgot, or maybe never considered, was that at some stage, the public who had been encouraged to have greater expectations of their public services would eventually apply the same approach to their politicians and demand more from them. They wanted MPs who were in the community and working for them on their local issues and interests. This was to be as much about responding to local issues as it was about running the country.

I remember being told the story of a newly elected MP in the north-west – albeit some years ago – who made his way down to Westminster. His office in the constituency took a call from a constituent. She wanted a meeting with him that Monday. It was explained that he was in Westminster that day. She could do the Tuesday, she said, but was told he would be in Westminster then as well. She then complained that she had just voted for him to work for people in the local area – what on earth was he doing gallivanting off to London?

For the Conservatives, this change coincided with the need to respond to the pavement politics of the Liberal Democrats, who were the first to tap into this new zeitgeist. Arguably, it has taken the Labour Party even longer to change, and the 2019 election result in the so-called Red Wall seats suggests that voters had finally felt that Labour wasn't working for them.

So, people came to demand more of their MPs. On top of that, the development of internet communications and social media means that people have more access to their Members of Parliament. One of my parliamentary colleagues once told me of the time he received an email from a constituent asking for his help on an issue. He was about to go into the House of Commons chamber to speak in a debate, so left the email until he returned. A couple of hours later, after he had spoken, he looked again at the email. By that time, the constituent had not only emailed a second time to ask why he hadn't yet answered, but had also sent a third email which said that as he hadn't replied, they were never going to vote for him again!

How Did We Get Here?

There was another strand of social change that affected public life at this time and, arguably, was also encouraged by the Thatcher government's push for people to take a more consumerist approach to their services. Far from merely accepting what the public sector provided, the public felt emboldened to challenge the public sector and the service it offered. It may be hard to say whether this developed into a willingness to challenge authority more widely, or whether it merely reflected or intensified cultural changes that were taking place generally. Whichever way round it was, the unintended consequence was that people came to have less respect for, and less trust in, authority. This was seen most starkly in those parts of the public sector that were privatised.

Organisations which, for years, had rested on their laurels and expected respect for what they were, rather than for what they did, found that respect falling away. While those parts of the public sector that went into the private sector experienced this most dramatically, it applied more generally across the board. No longer were public sector organisations to be revered and their work accepted without challenge.

There were two possible responses to this. Institutions could recognise the need to open up, increase transparency and accountability, and respond positively to this new approach from the public, or they could retreat further into themselves, defend the institution as it was and shut the door in the face of the public. Unhappily, much of the public sector, as is clear from the examples in this book, did the latter. They saw the challenges to them as attacks, and in response became even more defensive.

These trends had another consequence which can be seen in the accounts in this book. That is the increasing sense of what can be described by some as individualism but others would call selfishness. The sense that what really mattered was them and their position and not the public good. I am sure there are learned academics who have long debated theories about what led to this attitude – and doubtless they continue to do so.

Personally, I believe that an approach by government that encouraged people to be more demanding of the services they received in turn led to changing expectations and an increased sense of the importance and value of individuals. In some cases, this led to a sense of entitlement, which has continued to this day. By this, I don't mean that people should not expect to receive good services – of course they should – but that the service people expected to receive became more and more what suited them personally rather than what was objectively sensible or deliverable.

The development of the 'instant society', a world where people expect to receive what they want immediately, has led to a more selfish and, in many ways, an angrier society. All of these trends led to a greater willingness to challenge what was being offered to people by the authorities. We see this sometimes at a local level when individuals continue to argue for what suits them in the face of reasonable and practical reasons why it does not work for their community.

That sense of the importance of the individual has been encouraged by the cult of celebrity, which has, in many ways, degraded the value of achievement. You can be a celebrity today just by being in the media or by being followed widely on social media. What you have actually achieved is sometimes neither here nor there. This isn't true for everyone, but it is certainly true that celebrity has become a devalued status. So there is a sense in which everyone feels they can be a celebrity and that the world is eternally interested in what they do, say or think. Matters that previously would have been treated as private and considered not to be of interest to the outside world are now proclaimed across different platforms. This further increases a sense that the only thing that counts is the individual.

There are aspects of this that can be beneficial, for example in encouraging some to have a greater sense of their self-worth. But it can also be damaging when the value of 'me' totally eclipses the value of 'us' as a society, when individual good always replaces collective good. It isn't the case that life has to be all of one or the other. What is needed is a balance between the two: knowing when 'I' matters most and when 'my' interests should be sublimated to those of us all.

At the end of the day, MPs are doing a job. We are not special because we have been elected. We are not in a different category from other people. We are not exceptional human beings. We are elected to serve our constituents and constituencies. We have the power to change legislation, to create new rules that govern their lives. We exercise that power in their interests, not our own. We work in the service of others, not in order to exercise power over them. We should be accountable and we should not patronise.

The view that somehow MPs are different can lead to the expectation that the rules we make are for other people rather than for ourselves. Perhaps no better example of this can be given than the infamous 'lockdown parties' in

10 Downing Street. What the public saw from these events, apart from the fact that they contrasted so spectacularly with the image of Her late Majesty Queen Elizabeth II sitting alone in the chapel at her husband's funeral, was that there were those at the top of politics, including but not limited to Boris Johnson as Prime Minister, who did not think that the laws they made applied to them. Far from assuming that being an MP gives some special status, we should make every effort to be even more scrupulous in obeying the rules to set an example. If we don't follow them, why should anyone else?

Every MP has to know the point at which they would be willing to say no to their party, or their employer if in government, regardless of the impact it would have on their career. A very good example is the late MP Dame Cheryl Gillan, who rarely rebelled against her party in a vote, but did step down from the Cabinet on the issue of the building of the new high-speed train line HS2, which had a major impact on her constituency.

Today, we see two different trends among our elected politicians which could be described as contradictory. On the one hand, social media leads to an ever-greater move to form groups and to act together on individual issues or on big policy judgements. During Brexit, many was the occasion when I bemoaned the existence of WhatsApp groups where MPs could instantly send messages to their group on what to say or how to vote as events unfolded before their eyes.

On the other hand, there is also a trend for MPs to act more independently. When I first entered the House, unless it was on an issue of very particular concern to the constituency, most new MPs would not have dreamt of defying the whip. In late 2021, within two months of his coming into the House as the result of the by-election caused by the untimely death of James Brokenshire, Louie French rebelled against the government. How times change. Yet his rebellion is an interesting example of service. He had promised his electorate that he would not support Covid passports, so when the government proposed them, he voted against. He did what he had promised to do.

The willingness to rebel had, however, been a growing trend by then. Perhaps more than many Prime Ministers, I have felt the impact of rebellion among my own MPs. As I set out in the chapter on Brexit, there were occasions when MPs were abusing their power, because they were not putting the interests of the whole country at the heart of what they were doing. It is at best frustrating, and at worst reaches a point of no return where resignation from the post is the only answer.

It has been my view for some time that we are edging little by little to a situation more akin to the United States, where party starts to mean less and how an individual votes on particular issues matters more to their constituents. Not only do representatives and senators in the US vote more often in line with their constituency interests rather than those of their party, but there are organisations which actively ensure that voters know how their representatives vote on every individual issue before Congress.

That is quite different, however, from the situation we had with Brexit, where rebellion was being stoked up by those who had a personal career interest in using rebellion to oust a Prime Minister, and by those who believed that they were adhering to a theological interpretation of a policy.

Learning from the Past

This greater willingness to act independently should be good news for those campaigning on issues that relate to the behaviour of the public sector. It is not enough for MPs to be willing to take up causes or rebel. If action is going to be taken and lessons learnt, it is important for those who become ministers to understand the need to listen and to challenge. As leaders look to form their teams, they ought to consider not just who has supported them or shares their outlook or philosophy. They should promote those who will put the job before themselves – those who will understand that being a minister is a position not of power but of service.

19

The Answer is Service

It's all very well writing about examples of the abuse of power and identifying various trends – the defensiveness of the public sector, political selfishness, a belief in being above the rules, polarisation of politics and increasing absolutism. It is quite another to identify what can be done to resolve the problem. The theme throughout this book has been that the root of the problem lies in the attitude of individuals. This is about people who think that their power is there for them or for the organisation for which they work, to be exercised in their or its interests rather than for the people that body is intended to serve.

For many, this will not have been their view throughout their careers. Instead, they acquire this attitude as they progress. To some extent, this will be because that is how others around them behave. They simply adopt the accepted group behaviour. In other cases, there may be one instance where they put the institution first and if it works out for them, they assume that is the way to continue. Others adopt it because it gives them a real sense of having and using power over their fellow human beings.

To change, therefore, would imply changing attitudes or cultures inside institutions. Doing that is always the hardest thing to do, but there are ways in which changes can be made which help to deliver different cultures.

The first of these lies simply in the type of people being recruited to these organs of the state. If everyone working in an organisation comes from the same background, it is little wonder that they will, by and large, have the same attitudes and approach. This is one of the reasons why I believe it is so important for business and politics to have within them people from a diversity of backgrounds. By that, I mean both men and women, people from different ethnic communities, and people of different education and experience. Hence the civil service needs to ensure that in its recruitment, it does not look for clones of those who have gone before. What's more, the public sector both collectively and in its various individual manifestations needs to do much more to encourage challenge. While not everyone needs to be challenging and questioning, those who do should not be ruled out for fear they will rock the boat.

It may be argued that this already happens. I must confess to having taken the civil service exam when I was leaving Oxford, as I had been inspired by the now late Lord Carrington to apply for the diplomatic service. I failed. In retrospect, the civil service was right not to employ me – I would have found accepting different political masters too difficult. But I remember that one exercise in the exam was to analyse a set of statistics, which I duly did. Later on, someone I knew at Oxford who had passed the civil service exam told me that success depended on not just analysing the statistics, as requested, but explaining why they were deficient and what further statistics, presumably collected by yet more civil servants, were needed. Some might see that as challenging the system, but really it was just about expanding and justifying the system.

Identifying reasons for employing more civil servants is not what I mean. I mean having people who are constantly questioning accepted wisdom and not just delivering groupthink. In the example above, that would have meant explaining why fewer statistics were needed or indeed asking why anyone would want to analyse the figures at all. Again, when I was working in the Bank of England, I remember that one category on the appraisal form was the extent to which an individual slavishly followed precedent. It was not good to be seen as someone who did that. On the other hand, it wasn't good to be seen at the other extreme.

This is not about political correctness or wokeness. As businesses around the world have come to accept, the greater the diversity of people employed, the stronger the business. Indeed, the group that only admits those who are willing to adopt unquestioningly the view of the group and defend it to the bitter end will be the group that holds within it the seeds of its own destruction. My first two successors showed that this is a lesson that Prime Ministers don't always heed when forming their governments.

It is also the case that a group of people with the same background, education and experience will not make decisions as good as those made by a group of people with a diversity of backgrounds, education and experience. That is quite apart from the natural social justice of such a policy.

In recent years, the civil service has made efforts to expand its recruitment pool. If it is to be really successful, it must not just reach out to a wider variety of potential recruits. It needs to show actively that it is welcoming to those from diverse backgrounds. In addition, I believe it must reconsider the skill set it requires. The civil service values those who can develop policy – understandably, as this is a central part of its work. To progress in their careers, however, individuals are often required to show that they have operational skills as well. Some people are good at both. Many are not. Recognising specialist skills and enabling career progression to match that would be a good start.

All too often, civil servants are expected to change roles every two years or so. Longevity in a role is not encouraged, yet this means that people move on just when they are experienced and knowledgeable enough to make a real difference. I used to joke as Home Secretary – a role I held for six years – that I was the collective memory of the Home Office. This was shown once when there was a change of immigration minister in Belgium. I remarked that the individual concerned had been my opposite number early on in my time in office. I was told that I was wrong and must have been talking about his father. They checked. I was right. You see, I had been there long enough to remember!

This issue of recruitment has come most clearly to the fore recently in relation to the police. The incidents of criminality, particularly sexual violence and, of course, in the case of Wayne Couzens, murder, raised sharp questions about the vetting procedures used by the police. This was identified clearly by Dame Louise Casey in her scathing report on the Metropolitan Police. In that report, she tellingly wrote, 'Recruitment and vetting systems are poor and fail to guard against those who seek power in order to abuse it.'

The Answer is Service

It is all too obvious that the police need to overhaul their vetting systems. Senior officers will say, as they have done to me in the past, that everything is better than it used to be, but given the appalling examples of criminality by serving officers that have been revealed in recent times, that manifestly isn't enough.

There is also a need to ensure that officers approach their work with the right attitudes. It is probably only a decade or less ago that I saw a very good example of this at the Police Federation conference. I used to say the good news is you've been made Home Secretary, the bad news is you will have to speak to the Police Federation conference. On this particular occasion, the Fed chose to play a video before my speech which purported to show all the issues the police had to deal with that weren't to do with crime – in other words, that shouldn't be their job. On some issues, they had a point, given that they are so often seen as the body of last resort, for example when dealing with people in mental health crisis.

On this occasion, however, the video included an example of domestic violence. This showed that old attitude of 'it's only a domestic'. I had no difficulty in pointing out when I spoke that domestic violence is a crime and therefore absolutely something they should deal with. The point is that the incident demonstrated an old-fashioned approach not suitable at any time, but certainly not suitable today.

I also believe that the police need to reconsider their approach to management. I find it surprising that the rank of inspector counts as a federated rank – that is, they are members of the Police Federation. While the police are not able to strike, the Federation is effectively the police trade

319

union focused on the interests of its members. Inspectors are clearly middle-ranking managers who should have a greater focus on the overall issues their force is dealing with, and as such their rank should not be a federated one. The question of management goes further. One of the issues is the way that sergeants all too often consider their job to be looking after their people rather than the interests of the public. That is a sweeping statement to make, but I do believe that any change in attitudes needs to start at that level.

The police have worked to increase diversity in their ranks, and there are some good examples of forces that have made active efforts to increase the proportion of recruits from Black, Asian and Minority Ethnic groups. Yet the latest published figures show that 93.1 per cent of police officers are from the white ethnic group, and there are only three forces with over 10 per cent of police officers from BAME communities – the Met, West Midlands and British Transport Police. What is also of interest is that while there has been a steady increase in the (albeit small) percentage of Asian officers – between 2007 and 2019, it grew from 1.5 per cent to 2.9 per cent – the figure for Black officers stayed virtually the same: 1 per cent in 2007 and 1.2 per cent in 2019.

One of the issues that needs to be given greater attention is not just recruitment but retention. This point was brought home to me forcefully at a meeting in the Home Office which I held to discuss how to increase diversity in police forces. The representative of the National Black Police Association argued that it was all very well recruiting more BAME officers, but the problem was how they were treated when they joined. If they met racist behaviour and attitudes from other officers, they would not stay, and that in turn would discourage others from joining. Louise Casey's report identified significant problems in the Met relating to behaviour towards BAME officers. Changing vetting systems is one thing, but changing the culture is the real challenge.

Another area where the culture needs to change is Parliament. Politicians play an important role in setting a standard of behaviour that can drive expectations elsewhere. When in office, ministers need to be open to receiving advice that doesn't just accord with their preset view of the world. They also need to question and challenge the advice they are given in the search not for the answer they want, but for the truth, for the workable solution and for the answer that best serves the public. It is not good enough to demand a policy that will grab a headline. The policy needs to work, and they need to do the right thing.

This in turn means that political parties have to give rather more thought to who would make good ministers. It isn't just about showing oneself to be willing to parrot the party line or to express adoration for the leader at every opportunity, or even to be able to promote oneself and party thinking on every social media platform available. Ministers need to put in the time and effort to get to know their briefs and work with their civil service teams. It's not about them, it's about what they deliver for the public.

One of the everlasting questions is whether the public simply get the politicians they deserve; that is to say, do the politicians drive public attitudes and behaviour, or is the behaviour of politicians simply a reflection of society at large? In today's age, where politicians spend what in my view is too much time on social media, you could say it is the latter. But it is also undoubtedly true that the behaviour of politicians can drive behaviours elsewhere. Again, if the people who make the rules don't follow them, why should anyone else?

One way in which the attitudes of the age are driving political attitudes is seen in the expectation that decisions are instant and answers easy. The successful politician can too often be the one who appears to deliver the easy answer. We live in a world of instant expectation. The development of IT has meant that everyone can be connected virtually all of the time. Instant internet searches mean that we expect to have answers at the touch of a key. When the answer is not available straightaway, we get annoyed. This is something of a two-way street. Just as politicians often need to give more thought to the public, so the public need to think about their expectations of politicians and recognise that policy change cannot always be delivered instantly.

The story is told of Harold Macmillan as Prime Minister arriving back from a foreign trip with his Foreign Secretary and being met at the airport by a lone BBC reporter, who asked if he had anything to say. Macmillan turned to his Foreign Secretary and asked, 'Do we have anything to say to the BBC?' The answer came back – 'No' – and the Prime Minister turned back to the reporter and said, 'No, we have nothing to say to the BBC,' to which the reporter responded, 'Thank you, Prime Minister.' Those were the days!

Today, the politician who has nothing to say to the BBC – or ITV, or Sky or Twitter or any other outlet you care to mention – is the politician who is written off. Never mind that they might think an issue needs proper consideration, or that the matter is so complex that it cannot be dealt with in a soundbite. Being out there is what matters.

What this leads to is a greater sense of self-importance, and that in turn can harbour greater selfishness and less interest in service.

But this is not about the media. It is about the type of person who wants to become an MP, and here is part of the answer. Because I firmly believe that if we are to ensure that we employ politicians who are driven by the sense of service, parties must (as I said in Chapter 2) pay greater attention to their systems for selecting candidates. There is an important question here: does politics attract people who yearn for power rather than for the opportunity to serve, or do they become like that once in the political environment?

I referred earlier to there being too many careerist politicians in Parliament today. I was reminded of this in a conversation I had recently with a young woman who showed an interest in politics. I said we needed more good women in Parliament, and asked if she was interested in becoming an MP. She had indeed given it some thought and was not dismissing the possibility, but she wanted to know how to become a Cabinet minister. This misses the point. The core of an MP's job is providing service for their constituents. Anyone who doesn't see that as good enough in itself is failing to understand the essence of our democracy. We need to spend more time extolling the virtues of a political career rooted in the constituency and in Parliament.

It is also important that candidates are not selected because of their views on key issues. Of course they must support the party's philosophy, and at any election they need to support its policies, but leaders must not try to select candidates in their own image. The Conservative Party has shown just such a tendency in recent years, particularly in regard to the attitude towards Brexit, and it can be seen in the absolutist approach taken by MPs to issues like the treatment of refugees. The Labour Party went down this absolutist road under Jeremy Corbyn when Momentum were trying to build a more left-wing party.

No party should ever think that it has a selection system that will be good for all time. We must constantly be looking to ensure there is no unconscious bias in the system, so that we can have a diversity of candidates, but we should also create a system that is delivering people who want to serve and who are willing to put their constituents first. I am not suggesting that we go back to the days of *Private Eye*'s 'Sir Tufton Bufton', the backbencher who rarely came into the chamber of the House of Commons but was thought to be a jolly good chap by his electorate. However, we do need to have MPs who are in the House to be good MPs, not just in the House to become a minister and get driven around in a government car. Being an MP is a privilege in itself. Anything beyond that is icing on the cake.

So selection procedures should be constantly monitored to ensure they deliver the quality of candidates required. But once people have been elected, the party processes in the House need to be able to identify those who have the skill set required for front-bench roles. Promotion should not just be a question of whose 'gang' you are in or who you supported in the most recent leadership election. Neither should it rely on how many posts you have made on Instagram or other social media. This means that whips' offices should be making rigorous assessments of the capabilities of individuals.

The whips should also be more willing to give feedback to individuals and to provide advice on aspects of their work that need more development. Given that this, in turn, would require a degree of expertise in HR that is usually lacking among MPs, this is easier suggested than done. The whips' office is the HR department of any political party in Parliament. It is also the body charged with ensuring discipline and adherence to the party line. Doing both tasks at the same time is difficult, but political parties do need to give more thought to how they could provide a proper supportive HR function to MPs.

Giving greater thought and prominence to the skill set of individuals would be quite a change from the current position, where any Prime Minister forming a Cabinet and a junior ministerial team primarily takes account of balancing internal party factions and the different intakes, while satisfying both the need for diversity and the expectations of those who have supported them.

I referred earlier to ensuring that challenge is possible within the public sector. There is a wider issue to be considered here, which is how to ensure that the voice of people affected by the actions of the public sector are heard and acted on. This covers both those whose voices are raised to warn of problems and those who raise their voices to call for justice after the event.

This is why it is important to cultivate a culture inside institutions which allows for challenge but also welcomes individuals within those organisations reporting activity which they believe to be wrong. The balance to be struck here is between encouraging people to believe that they can report wrongdoing and will not suffer as a result, and at the same time making sure that the frivolous and malevolent are dissuaded from taking action. Far better to encourage people to report wrongdoing and see action taken to rectify it than to rely on revelations on social media.

This is about attitudes, but it can be enabled by the right structures. For example, after the Grenfell Tower tragedy, I initiated work by the government that has led to the strengthening of the system for regulation of social housing so that those providing such housing place a greater emphasis on putting the interests of their tenants first. This has been enshrined in legislation, as described in Chapter 7.

The other concern here relates to providing support for survivors and the families of victims to ensure, as far as possible, that they do not have to spend years or decades trying to break through the wall of bureaucracy and the unrelenting defence of institutions. In the Conservative Party's manifesto for the 2017 election, we included the setting up of an Independent Public Advocate. This advocate would act for bereaved families after a public disaster and support them at public inquests. In his report *The patronising disposition of unaccountable power*, Bishop James Jones backed this proposed role and added that he would expect one of the duties to be to ensure that the families were kept properly and fully informed at all times. I am pleased to say that the current government will be introducing such a role in legislation. I want to see the role set up in a way which would genuinely help victims and families. Being able to deliver the facts quickly and establish the truth at an earlier stage would be better for the victims and families, but also makes sense for the taxpayer as it would undoubtedly mean less cost to the government.

The Answer is Service

I referred earlier in this chapter to the need to review recruitment to the public sector and selection of those standing as candidates for political parties. Another important factor here is the expectations set for those individuals once they are in post. For the civil service, this is primarily in the Civil Service Code. It is very clear about the need to serve governments of all political persuasions, to act fairly and always to be non-partisan. There is little within it about serving the public. I suggest that the code needs some further revision to make it explicit that public service is about service to the public.

For ministers, the expectations of behaviour are set in the Ministerial Code. One way of strengthening the system to provide proper scrutiny of ministerial activity is to require every Prime Minister to appoint an ethics adviser, an independent adviser on ministerial interests, tasked in particular with assessing cases where it is believed that ministers have broken the Ministerial Code.

Having someone in such a role used to be a given. Indeed, I believe from my own experience that it is very helpful for a Prime Minister to be able to ask an independent adviser to assess such cases rather than expecting it to be done internally by other politicians or civil servants. Regrettably, following the resignation of Sir Christopher Geidt under Boris Johnson, the post lay vacant until Rishi Sunak entered No. 10 and appointed a replacement. But the appointment he made differed from those made previously. It had always been the case that the adviser was someone with extensive civil service experience who understood what was expected of ministers. Rishi Sunak's appointee, Sir Laurie Magnus, has no such experience.

Apart from a period chairing Historic England, which is a regulated public appointment, Sir Laurie's background was in financial services. He does have experience in audit and governance generally, which I hope will stand him in good stead in his new role.

Currently, it is up to each Prime Minister to decide whether to appoint an ethics adviser. I believe it should be a statutory requirement.

It has been recommended that in addition to their usual powers, the adviser should also have the power to launch investigations into ministerial behaviour – that is, the right to do things off their own bat and not have to wait to be asked by the Prime Minister. I have mixed feelings about this. The last thing that is needed is a busybody who jumps at the slightest suggestion of a problem in the media. On the other hand, this would increase not just the adviser's power but their independence. I suggest there is another approach, which would be for the adviser to have the right to identify areas of ministerial behaviour which they want to investigate, but to be required to refer that to the Prime Minister for approval. *And* they should make the fact of that referral public. If the Prime Minister then refused to allow the investigation to go ahead, they would have questions to answer.

The key for me is that the Prime Minister should still be able to decide who sits as a minister in their government. If they insist on continuing with a minister who has broken the code, of course it brings their own behaviour into question. More than that, it would not be forgotten by the opposition or the electorate. It is unfortunate that we have to look at changes like this, but the system was designed to be operated by people of good intent and integrity. If that comes into question, then change is the next step.

Overall behaviour by MPs is governed by the Seven Principles of Public Life, known also as the Nolan Principles, which I referred to earlier. These are selflessness, integrity, objectivity, accountability, openness, honesty and leadership. While these are generally known, I don't think enough is done to ensure that everyone who is elected understands the importance of abiding by them. One step would be for the political parties to do more in their selection procedures to make sure that potential candidates were not just aware of the principles, but also understood what they meant for their behaviour if elected.

There are changes that can be made by the civil service, government and political parties to encourage a greater sense of the importance of service rather than the exercise of power. Whatever changes are made to systems, however, any institution, public body, parliament or government is only as good as the people within it, and above all only as good as the leadership of the organisation. At the end of the day, this is all down to leadership. The message of service to others needs to come from the top of all these organisations.

If people see leaders who are more interested in their own positions, careers or personal interests, they will react accordingly. Why should they prioritise the interests of others if their leaders do not do so? Why should they sacrifice their time and effort to put others first if their leaders' interests lie only in themselves?

We are hugely fortunate in living in a parliamentary democracy governed by the rule of law. While I have set out examples of the abuse of power which I encountered over the years, I have also shown how the indomitable spirit of people determined to seek the truth and justice has so often won through.

So what should we look for from leaders? A belief in service rather than the exercise of power. Self-sacrifice rather than selfishness. Willingness to take decisions for the long term, not just for the media headline. A readiness to do what is unpopular if it is in the national interest. A desire always to do what is right, not just what is expedient. Above all, putting the common good above personal interest. Then we might consign the abuse of power to the past.

In 2022, the nation mourned the loss of Queen Elizabeth II. What came through all the tributes paid to her both domestically and internationally was that she was a woman whose whole life had been driven by service. Her absolute devotion to duty was clear for all to see. On her twenty-first birthday, she said in her speech from South Africa, 'I declare before you all that my whole life whether it be long or short shall be devoted to your service.'

What better legacy for her life than that those in public service, particularly politicians, should cast aside the mantle of selfishness and devote themselves unashamedly to duty and the service of others.

Acknowledgements

Sadly this book has been necessary because of the suffering of the victims of the abuses of power I have described. I pay tribute to them and to all those families and friends who campaigned long and hard for justice. In particular, I would like to acknowledge the work of Margaret Aspinall, Trevor Hicks, Jenni Hicks, Marie Lyon, Alastair Morgan, the National Association for People Abused in Childhood, Grenfell United and members of the Grenfell community. I would also like to acknowledge the work of Bishop James Jones, Alexis Jay, Julia Cumberlege, Wendy Williams, Louise Casey and the other authors of the various reports which have uncovered the truth of so many abuses of power.

My thanks go to Marilyn Warnick for guiding me in the very first stages of bringing this book to light, and to my agent Jonathan Lloyd at Curtis Brown for his patience and encouragement, and to Olivia Edwards. Thank you to Martin Redfern at Headline for his enthusiasm, to Holly Purdham who has helped me to understand the world of publishing and the other staff at Headline who have helped this book on its way. My editor Peter James was reassuringly thorough, and thanks also go to Kirsty Howarth.

Thanks also to Emma Willis and Liz Sanderson for their support and encouragement and for their ability to keep a confidence. Thank you to James Caldecourt for reading and commenting on the proof.

It is through my work as an MP and government minister that I came across these various abuses of power and my

Acknowledgements

thanks once again go to my Maidenhead constituents for the trust they continue to place in me.

Finally, a huge thank you to my long-suffering and supportive husband, Philip, who was and is always there for me even when dinner was delayed because I was just finishing a chapter!

Index

Index

Brokenshire, James 298, 313
Building a Safer Future reports 138
building regulations 129, 138, 141–2
Building Safety Bill, 2022 141
Building Safety Regulator 141
bullying, Parliamentary 25, 32–5
The Bullying and Harassment of House of Commons Staff: Independent Inquiry Report 26–31
Burke, Tarana 24, 25
Burnham, Andy 98–9
Bush, George W. 263, 277–8
Butler-Sloss, Elizabeth 155–6
Byrne, Liam 215

Cabinet 305
Cabinet ministers 32
Cambridge House, child sexual abuse 158, 163–5
Cameron, David 1–2, 43, 51, 59, 67, 89, 282
Camp Bastion 260
campaigning 303
careerism 305–7, 323, 329
careful speech, political importance 10
Carrick, David 185–6
Carter v Russia 252–3
Casey, Louise 196
Catherine the Great 281
celebrity, cult of 310–11
Centre for Social Justice 223
Centre of Expertise on Child Sexual Abuse 68
The Charter for Social Housing Residents white paper 146–8, 148
chemical weapons 254–5
Chepiga, Anatoly 257
Child Abuse Image Database 68
child sexual abuse 3, 75, 153–74
  allegations 155
  Cambridge House 158, 163–5
  churches and religious organisations 155, 159, 165–9
  conspiracy of silence 174
  cover-up 156
  DBS checks 171–2
  difficult to comprehend 153
  failure to act 154, 155, 161–2, 163–5, 176, 178, 179, 180–3, 184
  grooming 175
  handling of allegations 169–71

impact 160–1, 181, 295
Independent Inquiry into Child Sexual Abuse 154–60, 163–8, 172–4, 175, 177–8, 179–81
internet content 67–8, 77
Knowl View School 158, 163–5
location 153
mandatory reporting 173
organised 175–84
perpetrators 171, 172
police and policing 175–6, 177, 178, 179–80, 180, 182–4
recommendations 172–4
The Report of the Independent Inquiry into Child Sexual Abuse 172–4
Rochdale 158, 163–5
Rotherham 175–84
TM meets survivors 160–3
and trust 154, 168
victim numbers 155, 172, 181
victim-blaming 168
Victims and Survivors Consultative Panel 157–8
voice of victims ignored 161–2
China 241–2, 258, 270, 277
Christchurch Call to Action to Eliminate Terrorist and Violent Extremist Content Online 73–4
Christchurch terrorist attack, 2019 73
Church of England, and child sexual abuse 155, 159, 166–7
churches and religious organisations, child sexual abuse 155, 159, 165–9
Churchill, Winston 244
citizens, protection of 185
citizens of the UK and Colonies (CUKC) 210–11, 212
civil servants, passionate about public service 300
civil service 293, 297, 300–1, 329
  recruitment 316–18
Civil Service Code 327
climate change 225
COBR (Cabinet Office Briefing Room) 134–5
Cockerell, Michael 44
Cold War 274, 284
collective good 6
collective interests 5
College of Policing 185–6, 190, 191
commitment to service, lack of 291–2

Index

Index

Index

Hillsborough Independent Panel 85–6, 87–9, 90, 92, 93–4, 95, 97, 99, 104
Hillsborough Justice Campaign 104
Hillsborough Stadium disaster 19, 85–106, 126
  abuse of power 95–6, 98
  blame 90
  deaths 86, 91, 93
  emergency services reactions and coordination 93
  events 90–3
  first inquests 88–9
  government statements 101
  pain of loss 104–5
  Panel conclusion 96–7
  Panel investigation 87–9
  police failure 89, 91–2
  political narrative 98–104
  politicians failure 98–104
  public narrative 88
  second inquests 88, 89, 90
  sense of injustice 86
  stadium concerns 93–5
  Sun allegations 96–7
  suspicion of the authorities 86–7
  Taylor report 89, 101–2
  TM and 85–8
  twentieth anniversary 98–9
  unlawful killing verdict 89
  West Midlands Police review 99
  witness statements altered 95
The Hillsborough Stadium Disaster, 15 April 1989: Inquiry by the Rt Hon. Lord Justice Taylor, Interim Report 101–2
Hillsborough: The Report of the Hillsborough Independent Panel 88–9
hindsight 116
His Majesty's Inspectorate of Constabulary and Fire and Rescue Services 190, 192–3
Home Affairs Select Committee 156
Home Office 87, 190, 198–9, 200, 201, 212, 213, 213–14, 215, 218–20, 221, 228, 299, 318, 320
honesty 329
Hormone Pregnancy Tests (HPTs) 110–12, 116, 117. *see also* Primodos
hostile environment 215
House of Commons
  Behaviour Code 31

Bullying and Harassment Policy 31
  culture of 28–9
  Independent Complaints and Grievance Scheme 31
  Independent Panel of Experts 31, 33–5
  Parliamentary Commissioner for Standards 33–5
  Sexual Misconduct Policy 31
  staff 29–30
House of Commons Commission 25–30
House of Commons Home Affairs Select Committee 74
Housing Ombudsman 147
Hughes, Dr Henrietta 127–8
human life, approach to 232
human trafficking 222
  children 222
  convictions 230–1
  into sexual exploitation 223–4
  tackling 225–30
  Ukrainian women 225
  victims 225–7
  see also modern slavery
Humble Address, motions for 45–6
Hume, Daniel 260
Hurd, Douglas 89n, 100–1
hurt 295–6

illegal immigration 216, 233, 242–3
Illegal Migration Bill 227
immigration. *see* Windrush scandal
Immigration Act, 1971 211–12
Immigration Act, 1988 213
Immigration Act, 2014 216
Immigration Act, 2016 216
immigration law 209–17
immunoassay tests 110
independent action, willingness to take 312–14
Independent Chief Inspector of Borders and Immigration 219, 219–20
Independent Complaints and Grievance Scheme 31
Independent Inquiry into Child Sexual Abuse 154–60, 163–8, 172–3, 175, 177–8
Independent Medicines and Medical Devices Safety Review 107–8, 112, 116, 117, 119, 120–1, 124, 127
Independent Migrants' Commissioner 219

337

Index

Index

Index

Index

Index

Index

film industry 25
#MeToo campaign 24–5
Parliamentary 24–32
perpetrators 30
pervasiveness 27
Working Group 25–6
Shadow Home Affairs team 222
Sharpling, Drusilla 156
Shelter 148
Sinn Féin 53
Skripal, Sergei, poisoning 245–7, 251, 257
Skripal, Yulia, poisoning 245–7, 251
slavery, abolition 222
Slavery Abolition Act, 1833 222
Smith, Cyril 163–5
Smithells, Dr Richard 111
Snow, John 12
social care policy press conference 51
social housing policy 129, 133, 144–50, 151, 152, 326
Social Housing Regulation Bill 148–9
social injustice 6–7, 19, 83–4, 292
social media 62–79, 312, 321–2
abuse 64–5, 66
anonymity 64
and Brexit 65
as communication 63
duty of care 77
encryption 75
and extremism 69–75
and freedom 66, 75, 77–8
impact 64–5
increasing role of 62–3
and mental health problems 64
power of 63–6
providers 66–7
regulation 66–78
social responsibility 77
as weapon 64
social responsibility 77
Social Work Inspection Agency 177, 179–80
South China Sea 242
South Yorkshire Police 87, 90, 94, 95, 96, 98, 175, 176, 176–7, 179, 182–4
Southwark Council 139
sovereignty 6, 243
Speaker of the House of Commons, role of 44, 47
special advisers, reliance on 298

sprinkler systems 139–40
Standards in Public Life: First Report of the Committee on Standards in Public Life 23
Starmer, Keir 58
Stephen Lawrence Day 196
The Stephen Lawrence Inquiry: Report of an Inquiry by Sir William Macpherson of Cluny 195–6
stop and search 169, 185–97
BAME community 192–3
BUSS scheme 191
data 190, 192–3
HMIC review 188–9
impact 187–8
justification 189–90
numbers 189, 191
training 190
and trust 187–8
Stop and Search Powers: Are the police using them effectively and fairly? (HMIC) 188–9
Stormont brake, the 56–7
stress 37
Sturgess, Dawn, death of 256
Sun 96–7
Sunak, Rishi 56, 227, 233, 327–8
Sunday Times 229
Supreme Court 46
survivors, support provision 326
Sweden 275

Taiwan 270
Taliban, the 261, 263, 264–5, 268
Taylor report 89, 90, 99, 100–1, 101–2, 103
Tenant Management Organisation 130, 133, 135
tenants rights 146–9
terrorism 69–75, 261–3, 285–6
thalidomide 113–14, 116
Thatcher, Margaret 53, 99, 101, 103, 145, 302, 307, 309
third way, the 170
Thomson, Dr J. G. 112
trade unions 53
transparency 303, 309–10
Trilateral Contact Group on Ukraine 282
Trump, Donald 239–41, 255–6, 257–8, 264, 268, 269
Afghanistan decision 259–72

343

Index

trust 109, 154, 168, 186–7, 187–8, 204, 295

tweets 63

Uganda 224

UK Borders Agency 299–300

Ukraine, Russian invasion of 225, 241, 243, 258, 271, 273–86
  annexation of Crimea 274, 279–82
  the Donbas 282
  little green men 279
  Minsk agreements 282–3
  motivation 274–6
  Putin's attitude to 275–7, 281
  response of the West 281–2, 283–6
  strength of resistance 276

UN General Assembly 72

unaccountable power 301, 326

unconscious bias 190

United Nations Charter 284–5

United Nations Security Council Resolution 1386 263

United Nations Security Council resolution 2189 264

United States of America 313
  Afghanistan decision 259–72
  expulsion of Russian intelligence officers 255–6
  role in the world 241, 272
  Trump administration 239–41, 255–6, 257–8, 259–72, 264, 269
  withdrawal from Afghanistan 264–72

USSR, collapse of 274

US–Taliban agreement 266

victim support 37, 326

vocations 13

Waddington, David 102

Walk Free 221

Walker, Kent 72

Walters, Simon 4

war 237

Warrack, Dr A. J. N. 112

Washington, DC, storming of the Capitol 75

Weinstein, Harvey 25

#WePROTECT Children Online summit 68, 75

West, the 284

West Midlands Police 87, 99, 231

Western values 284–5

Westminster 158

Westminster Bridge terrorist attack, 2017 71

WhatsApp groups 312

whistle blowers 302

White, Gemma 30–1

Williams, Anne 104

Williams, Kevin 104

Williams, Nichola 118

Williams, Wendy 193, 207, 213–14, 218, 219–20

Wilson, Sammy 54

Windrush Lessons Learned Review 208, 218, 219

Windrush scandal 207–20
  applications to register 213–14
  background 207–10
  CUKC status 210–11
  discrimination 217
  documentary evidence demands 218–19
  failure by government 207
  impact 213, 217
  institutional ignorance and thoughtlessness 218
  legislative changes 209–17
  reconciliation events 219
  Williams review 207, 213–14, 218, 219–20

Windsor Framework 56–7, 61

Winsor, Sir Tom 104

wokeness 65–6, 317

women
  in Afghanistan 261, 268
  attitude to 125–6
  bias against 38–9
  patronising attitude to 108
  see also Primodos

Woolf, Fiona 156

world politics 239–44

Wright, Jeremy 76

Xi Jingping 239

Yanukovych, Viktor 279

Yes, Minister 294

Yip, Mrs Justice 109

YouTube 73